# GOLF IRELAND:
# A COMPREHENSIVE GUIDE

by

**Bob and Anne Jones**

Pen and Print
139 NW 6th Ave.
Canby, Oregon 97013, USA
www.penandprint.com

Int'l Standard Book Number: 978-0-9799555-9-9

# TABLE OF CONTENTS

# Introduction

The Ireland of the *Quiet Man* and *Ryan's Daughter* movies, with its quaint villages, pastoral lanes, and character-filled pubs is rapidly being replaced by freeways called motorways, older villages jammed with traffic, housing developments with look-alike box homes, and Super-pubs crowded with out-of-control stag and hen parties. If all this is happening to Ireland now, why produce another guide to Shamrockville? The answer is that while the traveler's fantasy Ireland may be disappearing, it's not yet completely gone. Just down the street from Langton's Super-pub in Kilkenny is Kyteler's Inn, with the look, feel, and mythology of 100 years ago. Just as the motorways stretch their arms out from Dublin, Sky Road near Clifden still entices visitors with winding twists and turns which expose glorious sea vistas. And even though the hundred new cracker box homes double the size of Collonsay Village near Sligo, locals still gather around the coal fires in the pub of the Mountain Inn to talk about sheep, the weather, and the best way to make a Hot Toddy.

In our several visits to Ireland since 2002, the Irish saying, "When God made time, He made lots of it," has had the most impact upon how we view Ireland. Be prepared to take your time to enjoy the sights and sounds of Ireland. Enjoy and join in on the pub *craic* (engaging conversation). Visit the castles and the stones of a long past Ireland. Soak in the beauty of places like the Cliffs of Moher and the Burren. Play the fantastic links and parkland golf courses north to south, east to west, and all across what really is an "Emerald Isle". Though time may remain to see the real Ireland, make haste if you want to enjoy the Ireland of yore.

# Chapter One:
# Things You Need To Know

Payne Stewart Statue at Waterville GC, Co. Kerry

The arrow-shaped sign on the main road pointed up the hill where we could see a large stone structure above the surrounding trees. "Abbey," is what the sign read. No other information or directions, just "Abbey." We took the first turn leading up the hill. The small lane wound around and in a short while led away from the abbey. Backtracking, we took another route and found another dead-end. On our third try we saw that we were getting nearer our quarry. Finally, after doubling back a couple more times, we arrived at the mud-covered road which led us past the "abbey," a much ruined structure about 100 yards into a mucked up field with a herd of muckers milling around and in the ruins.

This wasn't the first time, nor would it be the last, we'd engage in a fruitless quest in Ireland. In several months of touring, spring and fall of different years, we'd run into a fair number of blind alleys. Anne and I had also visited more than a hundred of Ireland's finest attractions; cultural, historical, and touristy alike. In that same time we played 87 diverse Ireland golf courses (links, parkland, famous, unknown, 9-hole and 18) and eaten at more than 90 of Ireland's interesting pubs, restaurants, and tearooms. Only a couple times did we have to turn around or go around the traffic circle to switch directions.

The fact that you will lose your way or get completely lost during your Ireland trip is but one of many things you need to know when taking a self-guided golf tour of the Emerald Isle. This opening chapter, and the complete book, is designed to help make the planning and execution of a trip a bit more enjoyable.

## GETTING AROUND

Though golf may be your main objective in traveling to Ireland, since you are eschewing the organized, expensive golf tour, you will have to get around the island by car. In Ireland that poses it's own challenges:

**1. Navigating.** The problem with navigating in Ireland is that the roads are small and poorly marked or not marked at all. It should be telling that even the most sophisticated GPS systems have trouble in Ireland. Having said that, we've found almost every golf course we've tried to find and most of the attractions we've sought. First, get a good map. We've had great success using *The Complete Road Atlas of Ireland* (Ordinance Survey Ireland) which can be found in most comprehensive bookstores, Amazon, or in shops at the Dublin and Shannon airports when you arrive. Second, ask for directions. Ask at the golf course, at the B&B, at the pub. Don't be surprised though, if the directions are difficult to follow. In Bandon we asked several times for directions to the local golf course, but the directions led us in circles. That was one course we never did find. Third, be prepared to have to turn around. Even with the best map reading navigator, or the best directions, you will miss a turn or turn on the wrong road. The solution is as simple as leaving extra time and trying not to be bothered by turning around—roundabouts or traffic circles are great aids to those directionally challenged times. It helps navigators to know that road signs often name only the largest or ultimate destination on a route. As we drove north from Dublin on our first trip we didn't see signs for our destination on a particular route, we only saw signs for Derry. It took us a while to discover Derry meant Londonderry (on our map) and that it was the direction we wanted to go. Our advice to you is to look further on the map than you'd think to find out if you're on the correct route. The overriding thought about navigating in Ireland is that if you leave enough time and keep your cool, you can get to where you want to go.

**2. Driving.** Remember to drive on the left. The steering wheel is on the right and the inside mirror will be to your left along with the shift stick in a manual transmission car. Cars will come at you from the right, so you need to stay on the left. With clues such as the steering wheel, gear shift, and sign in most rental front windows saying "Drive Left," it is often more important for the pedestrian to know to look right since that's where the traffic will come from. A little practice in the rental car parking lot to get familiar with your car is a good idea, and all that most people need. I have to warn you, though, that driving on the left can affect your driving when you get home.

A month after our last trip (five weeks in Scotland and Wales) I pulled into a circular driveway to turn around. Since I went around the driveway clockwise as I would have in the British Isles, I pulled out into the left hand lane of the road as I would have in Ireland. A hundred yards down the road I saw a car coming towards me on my side. "Oops!" I said as I pulled over into the proper lane. When driving in Ireland keep thinking all the time, and continue to think when you get home.

Car rental in Ireland comes with a special condition. In most cases, Visa and Master Card won't cover your collision insurance as it will in the UK or Europe. In Ireland it is important to have as complete coverage as you can get. Many roads are narrow and rutted with rock walls beside them. It is easy to accidentally hit a wall or a curb and damage tires or wheels. The rental companies will charge big for any and all damage, unless you have the full Collision Damage Waiver (CDW). It's costly, but it would be more costly to have even a small accident and not be covered. Be sure, too, to let the car rental company know if you plan to go into Northern Ireland (remember, it is another country) and there is a charge for that.

Learn to love traffic circles or roundabouts. We are starting to see this kind of traffic control system in America, but it is well in use in Ireland. Instead of approaching a corner with cross traffic, you'll come to a circular road, usually around a small island. Traffic enters the circle from the right and exists left onto roads coming off the circle. Three to five roads may spoke off the circle. Your jobs are to enter the roundabout without disturbing the flow of traffic, and exit left onto the proper road. Most of the time stop signs are not present where you enter, but you are expected to give way to traffic on the right. Remember, you're going left around the circle. After you've driven through a few roundabouts they make more and more sense. I find them very efficient. Traffic circles or rotaries (as some call them) may be scary at first, but with use comes comfort. Besides, one the beauties of roundabouts is that if you don't take your turn the first time around, just go around the circle again.

If you are seeking some of Ireland's out-of-the-way courses, like the lovely Cruit Island GC, you will eventually have to drive on narrow, single-track roads. There is a proper etiquette when passing oncoming vehicles. The car nearest the layby, or pullout, gives way. If the pullout is on your side (the left), pull into it and stop until the other car passes. If the pullout is on the other side (the right) but you are closest, stay on your side, but stop across from the center of the pullout and let the other car use it to get around you.

Driving in Ireland, especially in the rural areas, is a challenge, but not nearly the challenge of the excellent courses you'll get to on those small roads.

## FOOD AND EATING

Ireland is rapidly becoming a gourmet nation with fine restaurants, decent pub food, and interesting tearooms. Now that nonsmoking rules are in place, the pubs and restaurants are a pleasure to be in and eat in. As an island where you are never further than about 70 miles from the ocean, seafood and seafood chowders are specialties, as is lamb. Irish soda bread is a great treat, especially Michael Carroll's in Dingle (Milestone B&B). A couple of notes about food in Ireland are in order.

**1. B&B Breakfasts.** The breakfasts in Irish B&Bs are legendary. A typical breakfast will start with an open bar of fruit, cereal, juice, and yogurts. This will be followed by a fried breakfast of a combination of bacon (like Canadian bacon), sausages, black or white puddings (blood pudding), eggs, potatoes (usually potato scones), baked tomatoes, toast, and coffee or tea. It is enough food to fuel the golfer until dinner in most cases. The best B&Bs will vary the menu with special choices such as waffles or pancakes, cheese and meat trays, homemade jams and jellies (Maeve Fitzgerald's rhubarb/ginger jam in Doolin is to kill for), and special baked goods. One of the best reasons to stay in Irish B&Bs is for the breakfasts.

**2. Types of Eateries.** Eateries in Ireland consist of pubs, restaurants, and tearooms or cafes. We have stopped at chip shops or other fast food places, but we consider that necessity and not really eating. The differences between a pub and a restaurant are not large, but they can be significant. Often you will find an establishment has both a pub and a restaurant, sometimes with different menus. Most of the time, the restaurant menu will be higher priced for similar or comparable items. Price and atmosphere are the biggest differences between a pub and a restaurant, but some establishments we'd call restaurants have bars and are closer to pubs in price. For example, Crocket's on the Quay in Ballina and Yeat's Tavern in Drumcliff are both large family style restaurants with good bars and good prices in the restaurant. Average pubs prices for a decent main course meal would be between 8 and 11 or 12 euros. Fine dining restaurants, like O'Grady's in Barna or Oscar's in Enniskillen, would start at about 10 to 12 euro and go up rapidly. In between the two will be places like Stoop Your Head in Skerries, where you can get gourmet food at pub prices. Tearooms will be great stops for snacks or light lunches, and especially wonderful sweets.

**3. Sunday Dinner.** Finding food on Sunday evening is difficult. Pubs tend to have Sunday carveries (small buffets) until mid afternoon. On Sundays it's best to think and plan ahead with help of your B&B hosts. Also, early in the season (April and May) or late in the season (October and November) pubs often stop serving early (about 6 PM) weeknights.


*TOURING*

The tourist attractions in Ireland keep the island's economy alive and the tourists visiting. They range from geological delights (Cliffs of Moher, Giant's Causeway) to archeological sites (Ceidi Fields, Newgrange) to historical attractions (Cahir Castle, the Old Post Office in Dublin). Many of the attractions are under the auspices of Heritage Ireland, a national trust dedicated to preserving ancient and historical sites. If you intend to spend much time touring, it makes economic sense to join the trust at one of their sites and get free admissions to many of the country's best attractions. Be aware, though, that many small attractions, such as the Beehive Huts on the Dingle Peninsula or the stone fort in the Burren, are on private property and the owner charges a small fee to visit.

## IRELAND GOLF

Golf in Ireland is not the same as at home. Oh, some of the course, the parkland tracks, may be similar, but even they will have different trees and vegetation than you may be used to. Certainly, the links course will be new to most players who haven't traveled to Scotland or the UK. Golf, though, is golf. You use the same ball, hit with the same clubs, and try to get the ball into the same size hole as your used to. To help you come to grips with some of the distinctions of Irish golf, we present a brief discussion of Irish golf culture.

## THE COURSES

**1. How to Contact.** If you know where in Ireland you intend to go, the best way to find courses in the area, besides this guide, is online. The website www.irishgolfcourses.co.uk gets you information about most courses in Ireland, though not all. On the site will be some details about the courses and a link to the club's web site, if they have one. You can then contact the course through the web to book a tee time in advance, or just take the information with you so you can contact while on your trip. Other tourist information sites, like county visitor guides, will also have information about local courses. Finally, use your B&B hosts as resources for details on golf in the area.

**2. Prices and Paying.** In this book we list a general price with the course details. The price guide is for 18 holes (even at a 9-hole course) and is based on the most current prices, without trolleys, buggies, or club hire. Most of the 18-hole courses will take charge cards, but many of the smaller courses will be cash only, and often just ask you to put your money in an envelope and drop it in the honesty box and go play. Be forewarned that many of the small 9-hole courses have only an 18-hole or all-day price. If you can only play nine, be sure to at least try to negotiate a reduced rate.

**3. Yardage Markers.** The visiting player will find most courses in Ireland better marked with yardage markers than in Scotland.   Markers at 200, 150, and 100 will be found on about half the courses, and most others will have 150 markers. The problem is the markers aren't in yards, but in metres (meters). When playing on a course marked in metres (either check the score card or ask to be sure), use this easy formula for conversion: Add the first two numbers of metres to the distance and it will equal yards. For example, 150 metres plus 15 (the first two numbers) equals 165 yards. Another way is to simply add ten percent to the metres to get yards (10% of 150 metres is 15; 150 plus 15 is 165 yards).

**4. Toilets.** Most long courses in Ireland will either come back to the clubhouse at the turn or provide toilet facilities out on the course. Most, but not all. If it is a concern for you, be sure to ask.

**5. Amenities.** We try to provide information about what amenities (food, drink, practice facilities, golf supplies) are available at each course. Except at the resort style courses or the famous tracks, the amenities may be less than what you are used to. For instance, a snack wagon traveling around the course is practically unheard of. And only on the upscale courses will you find full driving range facilities. But at most courses you will find what you need.

**6. Type of Courses.** Finally, as in Scotland, the courses in Ireland are categorized by the type of terrain over which they play. In the states most of our courses are parkland or forested with a bunch of desert courses and a few links, like Bandon and Pacific Dunes in Oregon. We've noted, and used as descriptors, several types of courses you'll find in Ireland:

> **Parkland:** A mixture of pasture, meadows, and forest.
> **Linksland:** Played on and in the dunes land which links the sea to mainland.
> **Moorland or Heathland:** Combination of tough grasses, heather, gorse, and birch-type forests.
> **Clifftop or Seaside:** Parkland or moorland courses played beside the sea, often on high plateaus.

## PLAYING THE COURSES

**1. Alcohol.** At my club, it is not unusual for some players to pick up a six pack before they head out, and another at the turn. In Ireland, though, this would not be acceptable. The Irish love their whiskies, their Guinness, and their ales. In the pub after a round, but not on the golf course. We've seen a small flask pop out during a round or two, but generally the courses are alcohol free.

**2. Pace of Play.** Speed of play is a concern for golfers everywhere. In the states, five or six-hour rounds are not unheard of, and four-hour rounds seem to be the target. We find that the Irish play quickly and that four hours would be a long round, unless the rains hit—that slows everyone down. One of the reasons for the quicker play is that casual rounds in Ireland don't count toward your handicap, only official competition rounds. A lot of putts may be given since the round won't count. In Ireland, also, there will be a lot of twosomes on the course. They don't automatically pair you up. Finally, many friendly games are match play and once you've lost the hole you pick up and move on.

**3. Leave Space.** In the US, we tend to bunch up around tee boxes, whether the first or later in the round. The Irish tend to be very courteous and are reluctant to invade the space of other golfers. Often you will see a group on a green, another group half way between the green and the tee, and a group on the tee. When it's really crowded and groups keep meeting around the tee box, the Irish players have been very friendly and eager to visit. A time or two we've paired up with other players, but the norm is to play as twosomes. When you do get paired with locals, don't be surprised if the first thing they suggest, after introductions, is some sort of competition. Irish golfers, as well as Scots and Welsh, love to turn a casual round into a competition. Best ball pairs or alternate shot seem to be favorites. The stakes may be nothing more than bragging rights or drinks after the round. What matters is the competition rather than the bet.

**4. Course Quirks.** A fascinating feature of some of the older courses, especially the village 9-hole tracks, is that holes will often cross over other holes. For instance, at Ennis GC there is a junction where three holes cross each other; it almost calls for a traffic signal. Check the course map or ask in the clubhouse so that you are forewarned.

**5. Attitude is Everything.** Finally, our most important suggestion is to play "Vacation Golf." By this we mean have fun. Enjoy the golf and the surroundings. Don't be bothered by score or performance. Even a bad day of golf in Ireland is glorious, if you let it be. Whatever it takes to have fun is what we suggest you do: Take a mulligan (as long as it doesn't slow play), drop one instead of hunting through the heather, dismiss penalties for unknown hazards. Anne and I make a game trying to stay out of bunkers on a course. The first person in the bunker has the Orc for that day. Then at the end of the trip we see who accumulated the least Orcs. Golf is a game, meant to be fun. Enjoy!

## WHAT TO BRING FOR GOLF

**1. Clothes.** Think about the clothes you'll need to bring. Shorts can probably be left at home no matter what the time of year. It may be warm enough on occasion for shorts, but they are not a necessity. Pants with zip-off legs are a good option, though. Rain clothes and umbrellas are necessities any time of year. I generally take at least two rain tops (one jacket and one shirt) and rain pants. If playing in the spring or fall, long john tops or turtlenecks are not a bad idea; they're light weight and layer well. A sweater and/or fleece vest will probably be valuable items to take, along with a warm hat. Definitely invest in a good pair of rain gloves, the kind that grip even when wet. It's not a bad idea to bring a hat that will be waterproof and can strap to your head in the wind; you'll find lots of both rain and wind particularly on the west. Don't forget your golf shoes; many courses will not let you play in shoes other than specialized golf shoes. Plan to play in 70 degree sun, and at 45 degrees with a 30 mph wind and rain, all in one round. It helps if your golf clothes can do double-duty as touring clothes as well.

**2. Equipment.** If you plan to play only a couple of high end courses as a sidelight on your trip, you can probably rent clubs and skip the hassle and worry of traveling with your set. If you plan to play a lot or at the small courses, you need to bring either a full or short set of clubs, since the small course will mostly have crap to rent. Plan to bring plenty of ammunition with you—golf balls are expensive in Ireland, and you'll lose more than you expect. Also be sure to bring a supply of tees and a few pencils. Neither are provided free except at the upscale courses. A good rain cover for your bag will be useful any time of year. We also include a bungy cord to help attach our bags to trolleys (pull carts) we rent.

**3. Camera.** Plan to take a small camera with you out on the golf courses. A number of the courses you may play are drop dead gorgeous with unbelievable views. You will want to document the spectacle so that those at home will believe your stories.

**4. The One Thing to Leave at Home.** Leave at home your American expectations. Don't expect that the courses will be manicured to K-Club Ryder Cup standards. Don't expect the course to always be fair, links golf rarely is. Don't expect your game will be as good as at home. If you can leave your American expectations at home, you can be wonderfully surprised on every course, fancy or plain, that you play in Ireland.

**With these hints about getting around, food, touring, and golf in mind, let's now do some touring.**

# Chapter Two:
## Southeast — Golf, Pubs, and Attractions

Cork GC, Co. Cork

## *GOLF*

## WHAT YOU WILL FIND IN THESE CHAPTERS

In the next six chapters you will find detailed information on golf courses, eateries (pubs, restaurants, tearooms), and attractions in a specific geographic area. Golf courses are described in detail in the "Course Comments," while other salient information, including contact information, style of course, amenities, are presented first. Many courses will have a note "From the Forward Tees," wherein Anne, a 26-handicap player, gives her insights into playing the course from a woman's perspective. We don't rate individual courses because we've enjoyed playing them all, but we hope that the playing notes will help you decide if the course is one you would want to visit. For our favorites, see Chapter Nine.

We start our golfing tour of Ireland by heading south and west from the capitol city of Dublin. The most famous course in this region is one well known to all who follow professional golf, The K-Club in Co. Kildare (Kildare Hotel & Country Club). The K-Club was the venue for the 2006 Ryder Cup matches between the US team and the victorious European team, led by Irishmen Darren Clarke and Padraig Harrington. The K-Club will be a course on everybody's tour list which is one of the reasons we've passed it by. So much great golfing adventures await in this area that we try to seek out those experiences that are more unique—and definitely more affordable.

### *CILL DARA* GOLF CLUB (Kildare), Little Curraugh, Kildare, Co. Kildare
A short mile north of town on R415.
www.cilldaragolfclub.com (045) 521 295
9-hole parkland, 5852 metres, par 71, €10

**Amenities:** Modern clubhouse, built in 1986, has changing rooms and lounge. Small pro shop has all the essentials.

**Course Comments:** *Cill Dara* Golf Club is a fairly flat 9-hole parkland track with large patches of gorse which gives the course a linksy or moorland feel. Built in 1920, course improvements, including separate tee boxes for the second nine, have kept pace with the modern game. The fact that sheep still wander the course keeps players mindful that they are playing in rural Ireland. The course resides in the lovely Kildare farmlands with gentle hills around. Though the course is flat with wide fairways, bunkers around the greens, a pond, and the gorse keep a game at Kildare challenging. Whether you have time for 18 or only a quick 9, *Cill Dara* is worth a visit. The first, a 296-metre par 4, is a straight forward start to a round. Drive past patches of gorse to an expansive fairway guarded by more gorse left—you don't want a pull-hook here. A reasonable tee shot will leave a short approach to a green with one bunker right and gorse behind. Number two is a short par 3 of only 126 metres. To reach the green you hit over the corner of the patch of gorse to a small target protected by three bunkers. The 376-metre par 4 fourth, which plays as the 484-metre par 5 thirteenth, has the largest bunker at Kildare which protects the entire right side of the green. The tee box for the 13th is practically surrounded by gorse. The hardest hole is the 383-metre par 4 sixth. A pond crosses the fairway on your approach to the green with two bunkers on the right and one on the left.   The price of golf is for an 18-hole round as on many of Ireland's 9-hole courses, but the golf manager said that if you only have time for nine, he's always willing to discuss rates.

### CORK GOLF CLUB (aka Little Island), Little Island, Co. Cork

Off N25 road to Waterford about 6 miles east of the city. Take turnoff R623/Little Island exit and follow signs.

www.corkgolfclub.ie (021) 435 3451
Parkland/links, 6192 metres, par 72, €60

**Amenities:** A very complete pro shop and modern clubhouse complement one of Ireland's most venerable courses. The upstairs lounge serves food all day to members and players, but is not open to the non-golfing public. When you play Cork it's like becoming a member for the day, as often seen in Scotland.

**Course Comments:** Originally designed in 1888, today's course is much the work of Alister Mackenzie (designer of Augusta National where the US Masters is played). Situated outside Cork City along the shores of Lake Mahon (a wide area of the Lee River system), Cork GC (sometimes referred to as Little Island GC) is revered as one of the best courses in Ireland. The course is parkland, except that holes 5 through 12 play in and around the old Cork limestone quarry and have a definite links-like flavor. It is said that many of the skyscrapers in New York City were built from the limestone quarried at Cork. All 56 of the bunkers here are to be avoided, if possible, since most are deep and penal. So good is the Mackenzie layout, though, that it is possible to avoid the traps with reasonable shot making. The greens are moderate to large and play with quickness and undulations associated with his Augusta National course. Ponds on the course are not much of a condition of play, but the lake shore is definitely in your mind on four and five. Trees, gorse (or furze), and the ever-present wind will add challenge to an already spectacular track.

From start to finish Cork GC demands your undivided attention, which may be difficult with the captivating scenery. The par 5 second at 463 metres tees off over heavy rough to a right sloping fairway with OB on the right (only a problem for a very wild shot). Your approach to the moderate sized green must avoid the two fronting bunkers. The 4th, a 410-metre par 4, is considered by many one of the best and most testing holes in Ireland. The drive crosses a small bay where heavy gorse awaits shots too far right. Staying left lessens the distance across the water and sets up a better shot uphill to the raised green surrounded by three bunkers. The long par 5 fifth at 528 metres begins with an intimidating blind drive over a small canyon area (this is the start of the quarry holes) filled with gorse and the remains of an old stone tower. Ladies must tee off over an expanse of gorse—challenging, but fair. The rest of the hole plays like a seaside links hole; up and down over swales and hummocks and along the edge of the Lee estuary. The 6th, a par 4 of 302 metres, is my favorite on the course, for both its unique beauty and playability. The drive is blind to a landing area between the quarry on the left and gorse on the right. The large two-tiered green is backed by the bare rock wall of the quarry. The view as you approach the green, with the backdrop of gray granite wall topped with lush vegetation and an Irish cottage overlooking the hole, is a classic golf picture postcard. Teeing off (from any tee box) on the 374-metre par 4 tenth is like teeing off from an individual island in the middle of a quarry. From the back a drive of at least 200 metres is necessary to carry to the safety of the fairway. Your second shot must negotiate two fronting traps and two right side traps to reach the green. The 300-metre par 4 twelfth may be short, but it's not short of demands. The hole is a dogleg right where you can't cut the corner, but you do want to stay as much to the right as possible. The second shot will be steeply uphill with a large bunker in the middle of the fairway about 30 metres out from the front of the green. The green is further elevated and protected by bunkers on each side and with mounding behind. Five tough par 4s end the round at Cork. The 16th is another testing short hole. At only 315 metres, this par 4 begins with a steeply downhill tee shot over about 150 metres of gorse. Not a difficult shot, but intimidating. Try to stay to the left side of the fairway off the tee because from the right trees will block the approach to the green. The elevated green, tucked to the right, is guarded by a large trap on the left and two evil pot bunkers on the right. I thought the hole played much harder than its index of 16.

The day we played Cork Golf Club we played in front of Tom, a former men's captain. He, as was everyone we met at Cork GC, most courteous and helpful. Indeed, a stop at Cork GC, Little Island, should be near the top of any must play list.

**Comments from the Forward Tees:** This course has plenty of challenges, but it was fun to play. The setting is beautiful with great visual variety—water, hills, plantings, rock quarry. Holes like 4 and 5 adjust tee shots for ladies without taking away the challenge. I especially enjoyed the tee shots at 5 and 10. The par 3s on the front side were long and required careful shot placement.

### EAST CORK GOLF CLUB, Gortacrue, Midleton, Co. Cork

Off R626 at Tir Cluain (north of Midleton), follow signs.
www.eastcorkgolfclub.ie (021) 463 1687
Parkland, 5774 metres, par 69, €20

**Amenities:** Clubhouse opened in 1992 has changing rooms, a full service bar with limited food available, and sports a small pro shop.

**Course Comments:** In the busy area around Cork City is the town of Midleton, famous for its distillery [see Attractions]. The town also has an Eddie Hackett designed parkland 18-hole course called East Cork GC. The course is tightly tree lined, has light bunkering, a couple of stream crossings, but nothing too difficult. The biggest challenge at East Cork is the hard to read greens. They had much more break or borrow than I could see. Thankfully, they were of average size and speed. If they had been very fast, they would have been brutal. The configuration of the course is such that it plays in three distinct fields and crosses a road three times. The front nine is hillier and has one par 5 and three 3s. The flatter back nine has two 5s and three par 3s. A couple of holes cross other fairways (5 and 18). Although the course has not much to distinguish it, it is worth a visit for a relaxed round. Hole number six, a 319-metre par 4, is typical of the style of play at East Cork. the slight dogleg left to right has rough and trees at the corner. The green is protected by a large flat trap on the left. East Cork GC is kept in good condition, and it's easy to get on (just avoid competitions). The course, one of the first developed from a dairy farm, fits well into the countryside.

**Comments from the Forward Tees:** For me, the front definitely played harder than the flatter, more open back. A couple of the par 3s and a couple of the par 5s were quite long.

### FOTA ISLAND RESORT, Deerpark Course, Fota Island, Co. Cork

Follow signs from R625 off N25 about 10 miles east of Cork.
www.fotaisland.ie   (021) 488 3700
Parkland, 6100 yards, par 71, €70

**AMENITIES:** Luxury resort accommodations with a fine dining restaurant and a Spike Bar overlooking the 18th green at Deerpark. Excellent for light meals and snacks—we didn't try the restaurant. There's also a full service golf shop in the clubhouse. Besides the Deerpark Course, the facility has two other courses, Belvelly and Barryscourt, plus a golf Academy.

**COURSE COMMENTS:** Designed by Christy O'Conner Jnr in 1993 and then redesigned to European Tour standards in 1998, the Deerpark Course has hosted the Irish Open in 2001, 2003, and 2014. As a true championship course, Deerpark can be very busy, plan to book ahead. As a championship course, also, you will find much to challenge your game from whichever tee you play from (I played from the Society Tees, the Green Tees). A mix of more than 60 fairway and greenside bunkers are in play. Some are quite large and most are penal. Large ponds or loughs are in play on eight holes and will be trouble on all of those holes. The greens are moderate to large and have plenty of slopes—even the parts that seem flat will have interesting subtleties. Some greens are distinctly tiered. The course can be breezy and the winds at Fota Island tend to swirl. The lovely parkland course has pleasant views of the surrounding hillsides, but you're here for the golf more than the views.

Deerpark's 2nd is a 392-yard par 4 which plays to a narrow, slight dogleg right around a large bunker. One bunker sits on the right of the relatively flat green. The first of the water holes is the 3rd. On this 131-yard par 3 your tee shot is over a lough to an almost island green with a large trap on the right. There's not much bailout room on either side of the flat green. The trees behind make a good aiming point. Next come two par 5s—the 4th at 513 yards doglegs right, and the 5th at 480 yards doglegs left. The green on the 4th is two-tiered and the green on the 5th is quite swaled. An entertaining pair. Next is the 6th, a 330-yard par 4. Accuracy is the key to this short two-shotter with a stream bisecting the fairway about 180 yards out. A group of four traps on the right guards the green. After the 9th the course comes back to clubhouse. The 10th is a par 5 of 475 yards. It's a strong downhill narrow par 5 with a fairway that snakes down to a green tucked left and almost surrounded by lough. No bunkers are needed here. The 11th is a nice par 3 of 123 yards. Here the fairway is almost an island with water left, right, and behind the tee. The long green wraps around the lough on the right and has two bunkers, left and behind, for added challenge. The last hole is another good par 5. The 470-yard hole has trees right and left of the narrow fairway, but the real risk comes when approaching the small green which sticks out into the lough with water on three sides. A strong end to a fine course.

**FROM THE FORWARD TEES:** What a beautiful setting for a golf course. Besides beauty, the Deerpark Course will be a real challenge to ladies. Water is in play on eight holes, a wall on two, and bunkers everywhere. The course yardage from the forward tees is average length at 5509 yards—five par 5s with three on the front. They are not extremely long with the 10th being the longest at 452 yards, but with all the trees, water, and sand you will be challenged. There are also five par 3s—the 13th is the longest at 161 yards. The hardest hole for women is the 14th. It's difficult to get past the dogleg right into a green protected by water and traps. This course will require your full attention, but will surely bring a smile to your face as well.

### GOLD COAST GOLF CLUB, Ballinacourty, Dungarvan, Co. Waterford
From N25 between Cork and Waterford follow signs to the Coast Road at Ballincourty and then to the club.
www.golfcoastgolfclub.com  (058) 44 055
Seaside parkland, 6171 metres, par 72, €20

**Amenities:** Amenities at Gold Coast GC are excellent, with a lighthouse-design fully stocked pro shop. The modern clubhouse with lounge across the parking lot serves tasty meals, is fully licensed, and has wonderful views of the harbour.

**Course Comments:** In Co. Waterford, at the end of Ballinacourty Point overlooking Dungarvan harbour and the Celtic Sea, is the picturesque Golf Coast Golf Club. The first course on the point (9 holes) was built in 1924. The current parkland-by-the-sea track was redesigned in 1996 by Maurice Fives, who incorporated the older holes with nine new ones to create an 18-hole configuration. The amenities at Gold Coast are first rate, and the golf equals its other facilities. More than 50 bunkers will affect your play. Many of the bunkers front the greens making this more target golf than some courses, but none are too penal. The greens are large, fast, and mostly flat. Two holes play over bay inlets, but the shots are more visually intimidating than physically demanding. The wind, as always on a seaside course, can make shots more challenging. Finally, the course is dotted with stands of mature trees which can grab wayward shots, but add great beauty to Gold Coast. It adds up to a lovely golf course, filled with interesting shots. Comments from those who have played attest to its quality when they say: "I am drooling over it," "As good as playing anywhere in the world," and "A lamb when it's calm, a lion when the wind blows."

Holes seven, eight, and nine play on the tip of Ballinacourty Point near the lighthouse. You cross the road to the lighthouse and pass an OB area (the club's small practice ground) to play these three holes. Seven is a simple 150-metre par 3, but the views of the Celtic Sea (Atlantic) directly behind the green is a pleasurable distraction, even if it really isn't in play. Be careful as you tee off because the 7th fairway crosses over the 9th. Three bunkers guard the 7th green. The par 3 175-metre 8th does have the sea in play. You need a tee shot of about 125 metres to clear the chasm with crashing waves below. The green has one trap left, but a slice puts you in the water. The third of this fine trio is the moderate length par 4 ninth. A slight dogleg right to left with three bunkers protecting the green, this hole is not a great challenge. It is, though, a great beauty with the lighthouse behind the green and the sea beyond. We were reminded of this hole when we played Old Moray in Scotland which has a similar lighthouse view. Another ocean crossing (or rocks if the tide is out) comes on the 361-metre par 4 fifteenth. Your drive must clear about 130 metres of bay to find the safety of the fairway. Plenty of bailout room is to the right, but that will make the next shot degrees more difficult. Your approach must thread its way to a green protected by four bunkers. The 18th is a magnificent monster hole. The 505-metre double dogleg left then right plays to a large green with two equally large bunkers on the sides. With Dungarvan Bay as a backdrop, this is a fine finishing hole. The views, the quality course, and accommodating atmosphere are all reasons to put Gold Coast Golf Club on your agenda.

**Comments from the Forward Tees:** This is a great course. I love the views and playing by the sea and bay. It's long from the forward tees (5530 metres), but the trees and bunkers can be avoided. A couple of the par 5s are very long (442 and 454 metres), but the par 3s are all moderate length.

### HARBOUR POINT GOLF CLUB, Little Island, Cork, Co. Cork

On Clash Rd., off N25 road to Waterford about 6 miles east of the city. Take turnoff R623/Little Island exit and follow signs.

www.harbourpointgolfclub.com  (021) 435 3094

Parkland, 6102 metres, par 72, €40

**Amenities:** The clubhouse restaurant serves food all day and provides panoramic views over almost the entire course. The golf shop, Pointers Golf Emporium, is a complete shop which specializes in ladies' apparel. The club also has good practice facilities including a 16 bay driving range.

**Course Comments:** Set among the rolling limestone land on the banks of the River Lee, Harbour Point Golf Club is straight ahead golf with very few tricks. The undulating fairways are playable by all levels of golfers, if you can stay out of the trees. Hit the ball straight and you will be well rewarded; stray into the trees and it could be a long round. Don't let the open nature of the holes lull you into complacency. Harbour Point is a subtle challenge. Number five is a 180-metre one-shotter to a green that slopes severely back to front. With OB on the right, tall trees on the left, and two traps protecting the front, the hole demands an accurate shot. The next hole, a 421-metre par 4, needs a good drive to the left of the fairway to set up a view of the green on this dogleg right. The approach is complicated by two bunkers fronting the green. Don't be long, though, because a huge bunker sits behind the green. The 450-metre par 4 eleventh is a long tree-lined dogleg left (almost a mirror image of number six). Bunkers guard the long, back to front sloping green. The 18th, a 430-metre par 5 is a short par 5 with plenty of challenge. A fairway bunker on the left is within reach by big hitters (260 metres). The biggest challenges, though, are the two ponds and stream which cross the fairway about 90 metres from the large flat green. Only players confident in their shot should go for the green on their second shot. The 18th is a great risk/reward finish to a round at Harbour Point GC.

### KILKENNY GOLF CLUB, Glendine, Kilkenny, Co. Kilkenny

Off N72 in New Orchard, north of the main downtown area.

www.kilkennygolfclub.ie (056) 776 5400

Parkland, 5908 metres, par 71, €35

**Amenities:** Newly remodeled clubhouse lounge has food service all day and looks out onto the course. We played with a member, Tom Rothwell, owner of Dunromin House B&B, who commented on the fine reputation the clubhouse has for meals. Kilkenny also provides a small pro shop and changing rooms.

**Course Comments:** Even though the course is private, as are many of Ireland's town courses, visitors are accommodated if possible. If you are in the area, it's worthwhile to try to play this venerable (1896) parkland course. Pretty any time of year, Kilkenny Golf Club is especially beautiful in the spring when the course is dotted with flowering beds and numerous flowering trees brighten every fairway. Besides the beauty is plenty of challenge on this well bunkered track. Though most of the bunkers are only moderately penal, some large fairway traps are difficult to avoid. The greens at Kilkenny are mostly large, and none are small, all are well conditioned and heavily swaled. When we played the green speed was thankfully only moderately quick. I have a feeling the slopes could create tough putting conditions if the greens were fast. Although the course is flat, what elevation changes there are have been effectively used to add interest. All the one-shotters at Kilkenny are strong. Though none are outrageously long, each provides an interesting test. The 6th at 145 metres has four bunkers surrounding the green. The 10th is the longest at 192 metres and presents quite a challenge with a huge bunker fronting the green and two more on the sides. The 15th also has a trap fronting the green, but it's smaller than on the 10th, and the hole plays a little shorter at 182 metres. The final par 3, the 172-metre 17th, has three bunkers protecting the green, but the real challenge is to putt the undulating green. Come away with pars on the short holes and you know it's a great round.

The par 3s aren't the only holes of distinction on the course. The fifth, a 275-metre par 4, looks much longer than it plays—believe the card! Try to stay to the right with your drive because too far left means a blind shot to a multilevel, raised green. A large bunker protects the front right side of the green and a stone wall behind the green adds charm as well as difficulty. The 7th is a long two-shotter (364 metres) which has two fairway bunkers to collect miss hit second shots. A large horseshoe shaped depression sits to the left of the fairway. Nobody knows the reason behind the formation, but it leads to fanciful stories of leprechauns, fairies, or giant's horses. Though it serves no purpose, it should be noted that in more than 100 years of the club's existence, none have suggested removing the feature. The 9th is a short, but tricky par 5 of 443 metres. A large trap on the right side of the fairway is hidden from the tee, but reachable with a good drive. The green has more traps on both sides which will be especially in play for those who try for the green in two. Out of bounds down the right side complicates the drive on the 388-metre par 13th. You need to try to stay left on this slight dogleg right because the approach to the green from the right can be blocked by trees. A gully runs in front of the green, so try not to be short as you come into a green with one bunker on the left.

We had a great advantage when we played the course with Tom. He guided us around and let us know where to hit and where not to hit. Anne pays attention to directions well, but Tom had to say, "That's not where to be," too many times to me. Call ahead and try to arrange a round with a member on this fine parkland course.

**Comments from the Forward Tees:** Kilkenny is an enjoyable course. There's great variety in the scenery throughout the course, including hills, woodlands, and valleys. Most holes are fairly open, and the par 3s are reasonable length, except number ten which was 170 metres and requires a long carry over bunkers. I really don't like having to lay up on a par 3. The par 5s were long as well. All are over 400 metres, except the first which has other hazards.

### LISMORE GOLF CLUB, Ballyin, Lismore, Co. Waterford
Off R666, east of the village.
www.lismoregolf.org  (058) 54 026
9-hole Parkland, 5871 yards, par 69, €15

**Amenities:** Newly renovated clubhouse lounge looked very nice when we toured in spring of 2006. If nobody is in the clubhouse, put your money in the honesty box near the changing rooms and go play.

**Course Comments:** The course looks rather uninteresting from what can be seen from the clubhouse (basically, the 1st and the 9th). First looks, though, are often deceiving. Beyond the simple 357-yard first hole is some interesting golf. With only a few bunkers and moderately sized, mostly flat greens, it's trees and elevation changes that are causes for concern at Lismore. The 3rd, a short 135-yard one-shotter is semi-blind with only the top of a tall flag visible from the tee. Also hidden from the tee is a bunker which fronts the left of the green. As you come off the 2nd green take a look at the bunker and the green of the 3rd before you walk down to the tee. The 6th, the hardest hole for men and the fourth hardest for ladies (it's first hardest on the back nine), starts with an uphill tee shot on this 431-yard par 4. The hole also plays into the prevailing wind. With two good shots I couldn't quite reach the green. A stand of large trees on the left complicates the hole. The 8th, a par 4 of 359 yards, is a fantastic challenge. The downhill drive must thread between mature trees on a dogleg right. A long fade just missing the trees on the right is the perfect shot. First shot is downhill, and the second is uphill to the green. The grounds crew we met on the course were friendly and helpful as we made our way around. Lismore GC isn't a golf destination, but for a quick, stress-free round, it's on our list of play again courses.

**Comments from the Forward Tees:** Because the greens are small, approach shots have to be very accurate. The greens were fair and easy to putt. Par 3s were short enough to give a good chance for pars.

### MACROOM GOLF CLUB, Lackaduve, Macroom, Co. Cork
In the middle of town, through the castle arches.
www.macroomgolfclub.com (026) 41 072
Parkland, 5574 metres, par 72, €25

**Amenities:** Comfortable clubhouse with changing rooms downstairs and lounge upstairs which serves food most hours. No pro shop.

**Course Comments:** Macroom Golf Club is a Dr. Jekyll and Mr. Hyde course. The original nine, built in 1924 and redesigned by Eddie Hackett in 1976, is hilly with big elevation changes and plenty of sloping lies. The second nine, by designer Jack Kenneally in 1992, is mostly flat. Both nines are fairly well bunkered, especially around the greens. Though the bunkers aren't very deep, the sand is rough with many small stones, so you're never quite sure how the ball will come out. The greens are moderate to large and well conditioned. Green speed when we played was slow on the front and significantly quicker on the back. Water is a condition of play on both sides with a stream in play on three of the front holes, and the River Sullane and ponds on the back. Macroom GC offers great hillside views down to the village and the Kerry Mountains. The golf on both sides is as interesting as the views. Number one is a good lead off to your round at Macroom. The 442-metre par 5 begins with a downhill drive to a wide fairway with trees on the right. The second shot must contend with a stream and two bunkers on the left. The green is protected by an additional two bunkers. The 119-metre par 3 second is rather unique, though we did find a similar hole at Corrie GC on Isle Arran in Scotland. From an elevated tee you must drive over one of the few Irish oaks on the course. With no way around the tree you just have to go for it. The 8th also has an extremely tough tee shot of almost 200 metres downhill to reach the fairway. If you don't reach, I'm not sure what you do because the carry is over fenced off farmer's fields. The hilly front side ends at the 9th, a 369-metre par 4, where the drive is blind uphill over a creek with trees on the right. The second shot is downhill to a flat green protected by one trap. The 11th is a visually attractive hole. A par 3 of 140 metres, the hole has ponds on both sides of the green and a bunker on the left. Not difficult, but eye pleasing. Don't take a driver on the 302-metre par 4 twelfth. On this dogleg left over a long pond it's possible to drive through the fairway and into the River Sullane on the right side. The second shot is across the river to the green. Macroom Golf Club is an interesting and enjoyable course now, but some significant changes are planned for the next few years which will make the course even better.

**Comments from the Forward Tees:** This course looked to be hard with many side hill lies, trees, and much water in play for ladies. It wasn't as difficult as I thought it would be, and I scored well. Par 3s and 5s were reasonable length from the front tees.

### MOUNTAIN VIEW GOLF CLUB,  Kiltorcan, Ballyhale, Co. Kilkenny
Off R448, south of Ballyhale.
**www.mviewgolf.com** (056) 776 8122
Parkland, 5840 yards, par 71, €25

**Amenities:** The clubhouse has changing rooms and a cozy little pub called "The Summit Bar," with food available to societies or on special occasions. We happen to get invited to a society luncheon and enjoyed a delicious steak and chips dinner. The club also has a floodlit, covered driving range.

**Course Comments:** Set in the Co. Kilkenny hills about half way between Waterford and Kilkenny, Mountain View Golf Club is a naturally contoured parkland course with vistas out to the Comeragh, Slievenamon, and Blackstairs mountains. The course will challenge players of all abilities with elevation changes, ponds in play on three holes on the front and two holes on the back, and a plethora of bunkers. Several of the bunkers are hidden from view on tee boxes. The greens aren't large, but several have significant mounding, and all have subtle breaks. Mature trees on the front nine are more problematic than the younger trees on the back. The fairways at Mt. View are generous, but they need to be because most are sloped.

One of the features we liked at Mt. View was that three or four holes have greens which seem to hang in the sky, making it difficult to hit enough club to the green. While the whole course is top quality, we picked out several holes as typical of a round at Mt. View. The 2nd, a 302-yard par 4, begins with a drive over a large pond (in play on the first if you hit over the green) to a tree-lined fairway with OB on the right tee to green. The putting surface is multilevel and is well protected with bunkers. On the 5th you cross over a pond after your tee shot via two bridges. These special bridges are the ones used in the filming of one of Ireland's most famous movies, "Braveheart." Actually, the William Wallace epic is about Scotland, but most of it was filmed in Ireland. The 7th is a short 312-yard par 4 which doglegs left to right downhill with a line of trees on the right side. A large trap guards the left side of the green. Thirteen is a demanding par 3. It's only 153 yards downhill to the green, but it's hard to reach because it seems like there's no room behind. The one bunker that guards the left side sees plenty of action. A good long hole is the 533-yard 15th. Indexed as the hardest hole at Mt. View, the hole plays as an uphill dogleg left. The slope and trees lining both sides make it hard to pick out aiming points for your drive and second shots. I especially liked the 340-yard par 4 sixteenth. Aim over the trees on this downhill dogleg right to reach the middle of the fairway. The approach is difficult, again because the green seems to hang in the air. Take plenty of club as mounds behind the green will stop shots that are long.

If you are in the area in the wet season (which may be anytime in Ireland), Mountain View GC is a good choice. Built and run by the O'Neill family on their farmland in 1997, the course has great drainage because of a layer of limestone about two feet down. If Bea O'Grady, the owner's daughter, is fixing food, take advantage of some great Irish home cooking.

**Comments from the Forward Tees:** The course looks rather bleak and barren when you drive up, but it isn't at all. It's interesting visually with hills, water, and grand views. We played with a local, Leonard, who was keeping his score for a competition. He had driven some distance to get to the course, but had missed his starting time, so we said he could join us. When putting on the green, instead of saying, "I'll finish," like we would, he would say, "I'll stay with it." The par 3s are short enough to score on, if you avoid the bunkers. Most of the par 5s aren't too long (except for the 15th at 455 yards), but several were uphill.

### NEW ROSS GOLF CLUB, Tinneranny, New Ross, Co. Wexford
From N25 in town take R704 west to the course.

www.newrossgolfclub.ie  (051) 421 433
Parkland, 5568 yards, par 70, €20

**AMENITIES:** The clubhouse has the Tees Restaurant and a clubhouse bar with views of the 1st and 18th hole. Full range golf shop with helpful staff.

**COURSE COMMENTS:** Established in 1905 as a nine-hole course, New Ross was extended to eighteen by Des Smyth and Declan Brennigan in 1995. Some more recent updates to the course were completed by Gary Flood. With pleasant views of Barrow and Nove valleys and the Brandon and Backstairs mountains, the course is a lovely parkland track with tree-lined fairways. The best mountain views are from the 11th tee. Don't get too distracted by the views because the course demands your attention. More than forty-five greenside and fairway bunkers are in play, although a few are only in play for quite offline hits. Some are very large, but most are easy to play out of. Seven holes do have water hazards (ponds), but most are to the sides or behind the greens. The greens are moderate in size and well-conditioned with subtle slopes—some of the best greens in the area.

The course is very enjoyable to play, but there are challenges. The 3rd, a short (272 yards) par 4 is a good risk/reward hole. Big hitters can try for the green, but OB left and two bunkers fronting the green make it risky. The prudent play is a layup to about 100 yards out (avoid the bunker on the right) and a wedge into the wide, shallow green. The toughest hole for men is the 4th, a 408-yard par 4. This hole requires accuracy to stay in the narrow fairway and avoid two fairway bunkers. The green is protected by one bunker left and two ponds right. Another good short hole is the 309-yard par 4 sixth. The short dogleg right has a large bunker in the middle of the fairway after the turn. Smart play is a layup short of the bunker. The approach to a raised green is tricky because of a trap left and ponds right and behind. The 9th comes back to the clubhouse and the back starts with a par 5 of 465 yards. This par 5 doglegs less than 100 yards from the smallish green protected by two bunkers and a pond. The approach shot is key to the hole. One of the signature holes on the course is the 11th, a 173-yard par 3. This moderate one-shotter plays downhill to a green guarded by sand bunkers across the front and grass bunkers at the sides. Toughest on the back is the 15th, a par 4 of 343 yards. It's a tight hole with plenty of tree trouble on both sides and four bunkers surrounding the sloping green. New Ross GC is a great Irish bargain.

**FROM THE FORWARD TEES:** This is a good parkland course with nice views of the area. Holes have plenty of variety with ponds, bunkers, and trees. The yardage for ladies is shorter than some other courses, but there's still plenty of challenge. The course is 5194 yards long with a par of 73. The par 3s aren't too long, but bunkers, sloping greens, and ponds make them tough. The five par 5s on the course are divided; one on the front and four on the back. Save some energy for the end of your game because the last two are par 5s. The course, set in the rolling hills of the southeast, is fun to play.

### OLD HEAD GOLF LINKS, Kinsale, Co. Cork
Off R604 southwest of Kinsale town.
www.oldhead.com   (021) 477 8444
Seaside clifftop links, 7200 yards, par 72, €240

**AMENITIES:** The clubhouse has a Five Star ala cart restaurant and the Lusitania Bar which is an informal pub with great food. Both have excellent views. The course also has a fully equipped professional shop.

**COURSE COMMENTS:** Old Head Golf Links is a unique course designed by the team of Paddy Merrigan, Eddie Hackett, and Joe Carr on an almost island peninsula sticking out into the Celtic Sea south of the island. There are similar courses, such as Nefyn and District in Wales, but the experience at Old Head is class all the way. The setting with sea views from all 18 holes is, needless to say, dramatic. The play will also be dramatic with approximately 60 bunkers in play. The bunkers are a fine mix of fairway and greenside, very large and pot bunkers.  Although water is in the players eye on every shot, there really is no water in play on the course except for the few holes that play with the sea on a side—and on those holes the ocean is always on your mind. Greens are moderate to large and most have noticeable slopes.  Some holes are distinctly tiered and a few are flat as well.  Besides the bunkers and the ocean, the main defense of the course is the ever-present sea breeze that can be a mild zephyr or a howling gale.

The course has been called, "the most picturesque course in Ireland."  Regardless of how picturesque the course is also a strong challenge to play.  All the holes on the course are interesting and exciting, but since I played from the white tees (usually the middle tees) I'll describe the holes that most caught my attention.  The 2nd, *Gund Hole*, is a fine 376 yard, par 4.  This, the first of the dramatic sea holes, is a dogleg left with the the sea on the left and bunkers on each side of the corner.  Two sand traps and grass bunkers protect the false-fronted green.  The shortest of the par fives is the 6th, *Clough's Corner*.  This 468-yarder has OB all down the left of the dogleg right hole.  The green is protected by one bunker on the left and a set of four bunkers on the right.  The back-to-front sloped green is tricky to putt.  Next is a nice par 3 called *Legal Eagle*.  Not overly long at a 158 yards, with heavy rough on the right, tricky contours on the left, a bunker front left, and a mound in front, the hole is anything other than a pushover. On the back I liked the 10th, a par 5 of 485 yards called *Caddy View*.  The hole is a sharp dogleg right around a nest of grass bunkers.  The fairway snakes down toward the green and an old stone foundation on the right adds difficulty.  The green has very entertaining slopes.  *Haul's Leap*, the 15th, is the shortest par 4 on the course at 284 yards.    It's still a challenging hole.  The bending fairway is a tough target to find with trees and the sea on the right.  Five bunkers guard the fairly flat green.  The 18th is named *The Sanctuary*, but you aren't really safe until you finish the hole.   A par 4 of 385 yards, it's a magnificent and testing finish to your round.  Hit from the lighthouse over a corner of the sea to a dogleg left with a bunker at the inside corner (not reachable by most). The tiered green sitting just below the clubhouse is guarded by one bunker left.  No matter how you play or in what conditions you play, this course is definitely memorable.

### ROSSLARE GOLF CLUB, Old Course, Rosslare, Co. Wexford

Take N25 from Wexford to Rosslare.  In the village take a left on R740 and follow signs.
www.rosslaregolf.com   (053) 913 2032
Links, 6300 yards, par 72, €35

**AMENITIES:**  In the clubhouse, the Terrace Restaurant is open to members and visiting golfers.  The club has a full bar open from 10:00AM with bar meals available throughout the day.  Club professional Glen Robinson runs a fully-stocked golf shop. The 12-hole Burrow Course, designed by Christy O'Conner Jnr, is not just a practice course, but good for all levels of golfers who don't have time for the Old Course.

**COURSE COMMENTS:**  The course began as a nine-hole course in 1905.  In 1928 Fred Hawtree and John Taylor created the new course which has been continually modernized.  The course will challenge golfers with 90 bunkers (a good mix of fairway and greenside)—there are twelve just on the 18th.  Bunkers are a real mix of sizes and some will definitely be penal. There is no water on the course, but three holes play near the sea.  Greens are moderate to large and mostly flat with subtle breaks.  Greens were in excellent condition when we played and we heard they're that way most of the time.  Overriding all the other concerns will be the sea breezes which always seem to blowing against you. The view from the course is a lovely dunes landscape with some nice views out to the Irish Sea.

The challenges at Rosslare begin at the 350-yard par 4 first hole. This is an engaging opening hole.  It's a sharp dogleg left around two bunkers—approximately 210 yards to carry.  Four bunkers protect the relatively flat green.  The key here is to keep your tee shot safe.  A double dogleg left is the

3rd, a par 5 of 498 yards,  Traps on the right where most players will hit their second shots add difficulty.  The green is guarded by some mounding and bunkers left.  The 5th, a 363-yard par 4, is a demanding slight dogleg left which requires two good shots to reach in regulation.  Two fairway bunkers left are a bother to tee shots, while two fore bunkers, three geenside bunkers, and a hollow in front of the green bother your approach shots.  On the back I enjoyed the 11th which is listed as the hardest hole on the course—I liked it, I didn't say I played it well.  The 11th, a 436-yard par 4, demands all your attention.  The fairway is divided by a section of rough and a pot bunker about 150 yards out from the green.  The green is guarded by mounding and two bunkers.  The raised green is an inviting target at the 150-yard par 3 thirteenth, but hollows, rough, and four bunkers complicate what looks like an easy hole.  One of a set of good par 4s on the back is the 16th at 330 yards.  From an elevated tee hit to a fairway with bunkers on each side.  Second shots are to a back-to-front sloping green protected further by four surrounding bunkers.  At the 18th it's all about the bunkers—twelve of them.  Enough said. Rosslare Old is a lovely and challenging course that should not be missed.

**FROM THE FORWARD TEES:** This is a beautiful links course with wonderful views of the beach and sea.  The golf is fun, but needs your full attention.  The course is 5660 yards long and has a par of 37 on the front and 36 on the back for a 73.  For women bunkers around the greens are a major problem, as are the long par 5s.  The course has the usual links challenges with bushes, trees, mounds, and rough. There are a couple of longer walks; for instance, after the 3rd you have to walk around the 14th green to find the 4th tee and at 17 there is a long walk back to the 18th tee.  As tough as the course is, it's still a great course for ladies to play.

### ROUNDWOOD GOLF CLUB, Newtown-mountkennedy, Co. Wicklow

2-1/2 miles from the Catholic church in the center of the village, on the Glendalough/Roundwood Rd (R765).

www.roundwood.com (012) 818 488

Mountain top parkland/heathland, 6639 yards, par 72, €20

**Amenities:** Nice modern clubhouse which is very popular for dinner with locals and snacks available all day. Changing rooms and a small, but fully stocked pro shop in clubhouse as well.

**Course Comments:** Roundwood Golf Club plays up to the top of Slaughter Hill and then back down, and is a course on which you might want to take a cart or buggy. Players have to contend with lots of side hill lies and several blind shots. Bunkering, both fairway and greenside, is moderate, but entrances to the greens, some of which are quite sloped, are mostly open. The greens play very constant because they are built to US PGA specifications. A couple of lakes will affect play, as will a small creek which crosses several holes. Overriding any troubles on the course are the magnificent vistas out to the Irish Sea. Even on the stormy day we played the views were breathtaking, especially from 5 and 6.

Three holes stand out in our notes of Roundwood. The fifth is a 549-yard par 5 which begins with a blind uphill tee shot. The second shot is also blind as you keep going up. When you finally reach the crest you are rewarded with stunning views of the valley below stretching to Wicklow and the Irish Sea beyond. While on the top of the hill you next play the 332-yard par 4 sixth. The hole is a sharp dogleg left, but it is the second shot which is the real grabber. From the corner of the dogleg, your approach is to a green which seems to hang in air with nothing behind it (there is a little more room than it looks). As you get closer to the putting surface even more impressive vistas than on five come into focus. So enthralled was I with the views that I didn't notice much else about the hole. These two alone are worth the price of play. One hole we note for its challenge is the tenth. It's a 175-yard one-shotter with a pond left of the green and a stream in front and behind. Plenty of challenge here. Roundwood GC is relatively undiscovered and out-of-the-way enough to be easy to get on. The course and the views are definitely worth the effort to reach.

**Comments from the Forward Tees:** From a woman's perspective, the front nine seemed more difficult than the back. More trees, doglegs, blind shots, and bunkers on the front side. Distances on the par 3s were moderate, but the par 5s were extremely long (479, 461, and 442 yards).

### WATERFORD CASTLE HOTEL AND GOLF, The Island, Ballinakill, Waterford, Co. Waterford
Set on the River Suir about 5 km from downtown Waterford off R683.
www.waterfordcastleresort.com (051) 871633
Parkland, 6231 metres, par 72, €25

**Amenities:** Full hotel facilities nearby. The course has a licensed cafe which serves all day. The small pro shop has all the necessities plus specialized clothing.

**Course Comments:** Perhaps the only course in the world that is reached by private ferry, playing Waterford Castle Hotel and Golf Club is a unique experience from the very first. The four minute ferry ride (six vehicle ferry) across the River Suir begins your Waterford Castle experience. The 200-acre course, designed by Ryder Cup player Des Smyth in 1992, is set on a privately owned 320-acre island covered in mature woodlands. A 15C Norman keep forms part of the present castle which was enlarged in the mid-1800s. Smyth's design features include more than 70 fairway and greenside bunkers. Some of the bunkers are very large and a few are very deep. One problem when we played was that the large bunkers might have one rake and others had none at all; therefore, bunkers were often heavily foot-printed. We decided it was best just to stay out of them. The greens at Waterford Castle are moderately sized with reasonable slopes and borrows, but nothing too severe. Severe might be your reaction, though, if you end up in one of the ponds in play on four holes. Since Waterford Castle is a course in the middle of a river and only a few miles from the sea, the course can be quite windy. All the trouble on the course could get lost in the beautiful river views and tremendous variety of trees and flowers.

The ferry across the Suir (it's wise to check ahead on the ferry hours) is a good introduction to the Smyth layout. Number one, *Castle View*, a 385-metre par 4, is a slight dogleg left which wraps around a fairway trap with OB on the left. The approach is to an elevated green protected by mounding and three bunkers. I was well pleased to par this hole. I would have been pleased, as well, to par the difficult 176-metre par 3 second. Sadly, it didn't happen. The tee shot is over Drake's Pond which continues along the left. Smyth has thoughtfully placed a saving bunker on the left of the green to keep miss hits from visiting the frogs. *Bridge of Sighs*, the 374-metre par 4 third, is the number one index hole on the course for good reason. The drive is a downhill shot over a pond (a carry of 170 metres) to a narrow fairway with stands of trees left and right. It's a daunting shot! Your next shot is not much easier as the hole doglegs left up a small hill to an elevated green guarded by two traps and another pond. The 12th, *Sea Side*, is a long par 4 of 415 metres which begins with a drive downhill to a narrow fairway. The shot is made more difficult by OB right and a set of three bunkers left. For really big hitters or second shots for we mortals a second set of bunkers left and a large bunker right can be in play. The elevated green has one more trap on the right and mounds behind. Plenty of reason to mark the 12th as the second hardest hole. Though it's not long, the 13th, a 465-metre par 5 with five bunkers along the right side of a double dogleg right offers quite a challenge. Trees and a greenside trap add more challenge as you come in. *Des's Favorite* (the name of the hole) is the 187-metre par 3 sixteenth. The hole is a visual delight with a pond right and three bunkers around the green, one of them a saving bunker on the right side. The hole plays easier than it looks, but it still requires a precise first shot.

Although Waterford Castle GC may be a little rough around the edges, the course management is continually working to upgrade the facility. The course layout, though, is already five star and a joy to play. Besides the plethora of birds and wildlife on the course, one other feature we appreciated was on the scorecard. A color diagram of each green divided into six colored sections is presented on the card. At the start of the round is an indicator of which color will be used for pin placement. The system made it easy to know where the pin would be even though we'd never seen the course before. Waterford Castle GC is unique, interesting, challenging and worth a ferry ride or two to find.

**Comments from the Forward Tees:** The course is long, but wasn't too difficult. Many shots are downhill, in fact, it seemed like you played more down than up. Only 16 was a long par 3. The others were reasonable length. It's a fun course and a good golf challenge.

### WOODENBRIDGE GOLF CLUB, Vale of Avoca, Arklow, Co. Wicklow
Through the village of Woodenbridge on R747, then onto R752 toward Avoca.
www.woodenbridgegolfclub.com (012) 824 799
Parkland, 6393 yards, par 71, €40

**Amenities:** The pleasant clubhouse has changing rooms and a fully supplied golf shop downstairs, and a pub and restaurant upstairs. The views from the restaurant and lounge encompass most of the course. Food is served from 10:00 AM until 9:30 PM every day. When you are in the clubhouse be sure to take in the large display of historic photos giving the visual history of Woodenbridge GC.

**Course Comments:** The Woodenbridge Golf Club's original 9-hole course was designed by Patrick Merrigan and incorporated in 1884, making the club one of the oldest in Ireland. A major redesign of the 9-hole layout was accomplished by Tom Tavers in 1915. It wasn't until 1994 that the course was extended to the present 18-hole configuration. Known for its quality greens, Woodenbridge demands accurate shot-making as the course winds through lush forests, large bunkers, and the Avoca and Aughrim Rivers. The Merrigan design is as natural as they come with the course flowing from hole to hole in a smooth routing. The sixth, a 448-yard, par 4, is a long, slightly downhill dogleg left with a bunker about 190 yards from the tee on the right and OB down the left from tee to green. The curve of the hole will be felt on the approach over a road to the large green with one bunker guarding the right. The 8th is a dramatic one-shotter (121 yards) over an island in the river to a two-tiered green surrounded by four bunkers and mounds. The carry to the front edge of the green is only 110 yards, but it's a visually intimidating shot. A fun hole is the 353-yard par 4 twelfth. Again you drive over the river (it's not in play after the tee shot) to a right bending fairway with bunkers on both sides. The fairway is narrow with plenty of rough on both sides. Your approach needs to be accurate because the small elevated green is guarded by three large bunkers. Yet another tee shot over the river starts the 167-yard par 3 seventeenth. The elevated green on this hole has only two protecting bunkers. The river is an easy carry, but will come into play with a slice or a push. The 18th, a 551-yard par 5, requires an accurate tee shot with the river all the way down the left and three fairway bunkers right just where you want to hit. Eight more bunkers and OB left add plenty of challenge as you approach the two-tiered finishing green. Woodenbridge Golf Club is a course you could play all the time and still find interesting.

**Other courses in the region:**

Abbeyleix GC (18), Abbeyleix, Co. Laoise (057) 873 1450
Arklow GC, Arklow (18), Co. Wicklow (040) 232 492
Bray GC, (18), Bray, Co. Wicklow (071) 83 089
The Curragh GC (18), Curragh, Co. Kildare (045) 441 714

Druids Glen GC (18), Newtownmountkennedy, Co. Wicklow
(012) 873 600
Dungarvan GC (18), Knocknagranagh, Co. Waterford
(058) 41 605
Enniscorthy GC (18), Enniscorthy, Co. Wexford (054) 33 191
Faithlegg GC (18), Faithlegg House, Co. Waterford
(051) 382 000
Fermoy GC (18), Fermoy, Co. Cork (025) 31 472
The Heath GC (18), Portlaoise, Co. Laoise (057) 864 6533
Kinsale GC (18), Kinsale, Co. Cork (021) 477 4722
Lee Valley GC (18), Ovens, Co. Cork (021) 733 1721
Mallow GC (18), Mallow, Co. Cork (022) 21 145
Mount Juliet (18), Thomastown, Co. Kilkenny (056) 777 3000
Naas GC (18), Naas, Co. Kildare (045) 897 509
Waterford GC (18), Waterford, Co. Kilkenny (051) 876 748
West Waterford GC (18), Dungarvan, Co. Waterford
(058) 43 216
Youghal GC (18), Youghal, Co. Cork (024) 92 787

## PUBS AND EATERIES

The second section of each chapter, **Pubs and Eateries,** are our notes on places we've stopped for a bite or a brew. More than with golf courses, the food business is constantly in flux. A restaurant is there one year, sold, changed, or gone the next. We've checked on the eateries we list as close to publication as we can, but we can only tell you what our experience has been.

**Abbey Gate Bar and Restaurant** on Main Street in Abbeyleix, Co. Laoise, across from the abbey. Traditional pub with basic fare. Friendly spot popular with the locals. A local sculptor and teacher, Colin O'Reilly, came in and ordered the special leg of lamb: "Give me lots of potatoes, I'm really hungry today." He sat and read the paper until I engaged him in some conversation. When his meal arrived, it was heaped with potatoes. The manager came over to check that he had enough. The pub occupies the spot where a Cistercian abbey gateway once stood, hence the name.

**An Spalalpin Fanach** is located one block off Washington Street near the main shopping district of Cork, Co. Cork. One of Cork's oldest pubs, *An Spalalpin Fanach* is a drinking and music pub popular with college age. Good place to experience an old Irish pub.

**Blair's Inn** in the village of Cloghroe on R579 is about five miles from Blarney and five minutes from the castle. A picturesque family-style pub and restaurant decorated in hunting lodge fashion. There are extensive pub and restaurant menus at this award winning venue—awards include Dining Pub of the Year.

**D.W. Bollard's Bistro** in the heart of Kilkenny. Basic pub with a reputation for high quality. Bistro opened in 1973, but the restaurant has been there since 1904.

**Egan's** on the High Street in Portlaoise, Co. Laoise, at the east end of the village. Modern pub with an average sized menu. Not very distinguished, but the food was tasty and prices decent.

**Finn's Table** at No. 6 Main Street in the heart of Kinsale. Romantic fine dining off a limited menu. Everything is good. Check out the special early three course dinner.

**Lemon Tree Restaurant** in the heart of the village of Portlaoise, Co. Laoise. Known locally as Grellan Delaney & Sons, the restaurant is newly remodeled into four pub rooms and the adjacent restaurant. Very complete menu served all day. A first class pub.

**Jim Doyle and Sons** on the beach front of Bray, Co. Wicklow. Seaside resort pub with open area for good weather. Large inside pub. Small menu, but several unique item—we enjoyed the Mushy Bowl (similar to a poutine with chips, mushrooms, onions, ham, and melted cheese). Very lively pub.

**Kilkenny Design Cafe** across from the Kilkenny Castle and upstairs above the main Design Store. Pleasant cafeteria with chalkboard menu which includes many unusual items such as lamb in filo dough. A good stop after shopping or visiting the castle.

**Kytler's Inn** on Kieran Street, Kilkenny, just down from town center. Venerable pub decorated with antiques of all kinds. Lots of history to this pub in the oldest building in Kilkenny (1324). The pub was named for the famous Kilkenny Witch, Dame Alice Kyteler. She supposedly dressed in her maid's clothes and escaped, while the townspeople mistakenly burned the maid. The witch was never heard from again. Some say she haunts the kitchen, which is why the food quality is sometimes suspect. Traditional music almost every night.

**Langton's** on St John's Street in Kilkenny, Co. Kilkenny, a couple of blocks from the bridge. Modern pub with dining rooms and a formal restaurant in the back. Limited menu and fairly expensive. Very popular with young people and specialty parties (Hen Parties, Bachelor Parties). Music most weekends.

**The Marble City Bar** on High Street in Kilkenny, in the heart of town. A modern pub with excellent food and several specials. Good value.

**The Meetings** in Vale of Avoca, Co. Wicklow, two miles north of the Avoca Bridge where Avonmore and Avonbeg Rivers meet. Restaurant specializes in Irish dishes including Irish breakfast all day. Has received many awards including mention in Ireland's Top 100 Pubs and James Joyce Pubs. Lots of music.

**Muskery Arms Pub and Restaurant** on main street of Blarney, Co. Cork. Located directly across from the castle, the pub has no particular style, but does have a full menu. Good spot for a drink before or after a visit to the castle.

**Poet's Corner Cafe** on Main Street in Kinsale. Serves breakfast and lunch and sells used books (or exchanges one for two). Good sandwiches and coffee. Be aware, though, that they only take cash.

**Ristarante Rossini** at 33/34 Princes Street in the main downtown area of Cork. Italian Tuscan-style restaurant with a full range Italian menu. Food is outstanding.

**The Rising Tide** in Glounthaune is ten minutes east of Cork City on the old Cork/Waterford road. The restaurant is a modern nautical themed pub with lovely views of the River Lee estuary. Food is fine and the setting is lovely.

**Roundwood Inn** on the main street of Roundwood (Bray), in the heart of Co. Wicklow's highest village. The building dates back to 1623 and is nicely modernized without losing its lodge feel. Serves Irish food with German influences (Irish stew and Hungarian goulash). Very complete wine list.

**Scoozie's** off St. Patrick Street in downtown Cork. Modern, family Italian restaurant—it's a cross between Olive Garden and a pizza parlour with a little bit of ice cream parlour thrown in. A bit noisy, but the food is high quality.

**Silken Thomas Pub** on Main Street in Kildare, Co. Kildare, just down from the Tourist Centre. Old nicely decorated pub. Three menus starting at 10:30 with a dinner restaurant next door. Music on the weekends.

**Sir Walter Raleigh Pub** on the main street (N25) through Youghal, Co. Cork, just down from the lighthouse. Named for the famous explorer, the pub serves upscale food well prepared in a better pub setting.

**Tide's Gastro Pub** on Strand Road (the coast road) near the beach in Rosslare. Award winning restaurant in a good location—bright and lively.

**Wild and Native** on Strand Road (the coast road) in Rosslare. Serving from breakfast to early supper, Native & Wild serves amazing food reasonably priced.  Not a big menu, but interesting items.

## *ATTRACTIONS*

The third section in each chapter, **Attractions,** gives a brief description of the tourist attractions we've been able to visit in the area. The list is not comprehensive to all there is to see and do, but it does let you know what we've seen and done. For a list of "Must See Attractions," go to the last chapter.

The Southwest of Ireland is filled with an eclectic mix of worthy attractions to visit. Although this region may not have the physical beauty of sections further west, the history and grandeur of Ireland will be found in the area from Dublin to Cork and around. There's far more to see and do in this region than we've been able explore. Principal among our misses are the 18C Powerscourt House and Estate five miles inland from Bray, and the ancient religious centre at Glendalaugh in the Wicklow mountains. Regardless of what we have not been able to see, what we have seen leaves lasting impressions.

Kilkenny becomes our first area to explore. If you've stopped in at Kyteler's Inn for the music and story of the Kilkenny Witch, you've visited one of the more interesting sites in town. The most impressive attraction, though, is **Kilkenny Castle** in the center of town. The 14th Century (14C) castle you visit today, once the home of the Butlers, was begun in 1172 by the famous Strongbow, Earl of Clare. Wander the enjoyable gardens and park and revel in the view down the

River Noir, but be sure to take the castle tour. The hour long guided tour starts with a video history of the family and the castle and then proceeds to visit several rooms. This is one of the better tours we've taken at Irish historic sites. From the castle cross the street to the **Kilkenny Design Centre** housed in the massive former castle stables. The Centre houses several craft workshops and a series of fine shops. The goods sold here are not your normal tourist gifts, but instead quality Irish-made linens, pottery, wool, and other merchandise. Upstairs is the good cafeteria for lunch or a snack. Head next across town and uphill to **St. Candice's Cathedral.** The present 13C church and round tower overlook Kilkenny and is sited on the location of a 6C monastery. The trip up the hill is rewarded by the view and the impressive interior of St. Candice's.

South from Kilkenny heading in the direction of Waterford are several interesting stops. Important large religious locations are only a few miles apart, but as is often the case in Ireland, not easily connected by road. The first visit should be to the huge, but much ruined, **Kells Priory,** about nine miles south of Kilkenny on R697. The grounds contain the 1190 Augustinian priory, its defensive walled enclosure (partially intact), and a number of towers. It's an impressive sight, but a bit of disappointment because of vandalism and a lack of care. South of Kells Priory is a small early monastic ruin at **Kilree** (follow signs from Kells). The Kilree site contains the ruins of a small chapel, graveyard, round tower, and across a farmer's field (access allowed) a high cross. Anne and I wandered Kilree and I ventured out with the cows to see the high cross. The cows were friendly and I think they expected some kind of a handout from me. Heading east from the priory and Kilree, **Jerpoint Abbey,** a mile south of Thomastown on N9, is one of Ireland's most attractive ruined abbeys. The 10C Cistercian abbey is noted for fine detailed carvings. Look particularly for the knight and his lady and the bishop as you walk among the cloisters. It was at Jerpoint Abbey that we first purchased a **Heritage Ireland Pass.** Membership to Heritage Ireland allowed us further entrance to heritage properties without additional expense. It only takes visiting a few attractions to make membership pay for itself. Farther afield, but still south of Kilkenny and staying with the ancient religious theme, is the **Killamery Church and High Cross.** We found the cross by fortuitous accident one day when we stopped to photograph a particularly attractive Guinness sign on a roadside pub. After taking the picture I saw a sign for a High Cross pointing down the lane beside the pub. A mile down the road and a couple of hundred yards walk through a field we enjoyed a visit to the Killamery High Cross in the graveyard of an old church. On a pleasant spring day, we were the only visitors.

From Thomastown a drive of 30 miles brings the traveler to Waterford. The N9 is the easiest route, but we would suggest a slower more scenic path. Take R700 from Thomastown to New Ross, and then R733 south to the **John F. Kennedy Arboretum.** Dedicated in 1968 as a memorial to the late President's Irish connection, the 252-hectacre park (whatever the heck a hectare is, it's a big park) displays over 500 varieties of rhododendron as well as more than 6000 plant species. Absolutely gorgeous in the spring. **Dunbrody Abbey** and nearby castle are only a mile south the arboretum. The substantial ruins of the 12C **Tintern Abbey** sits on the bank of a tributary of the River Barrow a few miles away. Tintern Abbey, a sister house to the Welsh abbey of the same name made famous in a poem by William Wordsworth, was founded in 1200 and is open for visits. After visiting either or both abbeys, cross the Barrow River/Waterford Harbour on a small ferry which runs between Arthurstown on the east to Passage East on the west and continue toward Waterford. You will pass right by the entrance to Waterford Castle GC this way.

In Waterford are two attractions to visit. The first is **Reginald's Tower** on the waterfront. This three story defensive tower was once part of the city wall and now houses a museum of early Waterford history. Check behind the tower to see what restaurant might be there. For several years it was Reginald's Restaurant and Bar. On our last visit it was a Chinese parlour. Whatever is there, try to stop in for a look at the last remnant of the city wall which dates to 850 AD and was 12 foot thick. The next stop is on N25, the main route between Waterford and Cork, and is one of Ireland's most famous attractions. The **Waterford Crystal Factory** is a must stop whether you plan to buy the Rolls Royce of crystal or not. Waterford has been making crystal since 1783 and its designs are world famous. The tour can be very noisy when the factory is in production (Monday-Friday), but is more enjoyable on Saturday or Sunday (April-October) when only a small crew operates to show the steps in production. The showroom (visit either before or after the tour) is fascinating with great examples of crystal on display, including some lovely Waterford Crystal golf trophies.

On N25 from Waterford to Cork you drive right through the town of **Youghal** (pronounced, surprisingly, "you-all") which has an interesting town clock and the Moby Dick Pub which was used for scenes in the original movie and now houses movie memorabilia, with nary a white whale in sight. Closer to Cork you enter the town of Midleton which is the location of East Cork GC and one other slightly interesting attraction, the **Midleton Distillery.** Opened as the Cork Distillers in the 1820s, Midleton merged with Jameson and Powers in 1966. A modernized distillery was opened on the property in 1975. The audiovisual show and guided tour of the distillery with, of course, a tasting at the end is a worthwhile endeavor. Even if you've visited other distilleries, we find we learn something new at each one. One of the items you can learn is the difference between Irish whiskey and Scottish whisky, besides the spelling. The basic differences are that Irish whiskey is distilled three times (Scottish single malt only twice), that Irish is smoother because of the extra distillation, and that Scottish single malt may have more flavor (though the Irish won't say that). If you are really into whisky, when they ask for special volunteers get your hand up fast. At the end of the tour four people (the volunteers) are given a special comparison tasting of several different whiskeys (Irish, scotch, bourbon) and receive certificates as qualified tasters. I have certificates from Bushmills (in Northern Ireland) and Midleton. Be careful, though, if you are the driver!

Next we come to Ireland's second city, **Cork.** A bustling, crowded city, the first time we drove though trying to follow N25 which goes into the heart of town and out the other side. We held our breath as we tried to find our way in snarling traffic with few street signs. We felt lucky to get out alive. Or so it seemed in reflection. The reality is that with a good map Cork is not difficult to negotiate. Once we stopped to look around we discovered Cork to be a great city for shopping, pubs, and restaurants. A couple of special notes would be to stop at the **English Market** in the heart of the shopping district. Here local meat and produce have been sold daily since 1610. Another place to visit is **St. Fin Barre's Cathedral** located between the downtown area and the university district. Built in 1878 in 13C French Gothic style, the cathedral is ornately decorated.

A side trip from Cork goes north to a fine castle and one of the most captivating of Irish religious/political sites. North from Cork on N8 through Fermoy and Mitchelstown, it's about 50 miles to the village of Cahir (or Caher on some maps) where you visit **Cahir Castle.** Cahir Castle (in Irish *Cathair Dun Lascaigh,* "stone fort or the fortress of the fishery"), the most complete Medieval castle in Ireland, sits on an island in the River Suir. Built by the Butler family in the 13C, the castle was never seriously attacked (there is one cannon ball still lodged in an outer wall) because the Butlers were pragmatists who quickly changed political sides. Not an admirable character trait, but it did save the castle. Less than a mile (on R670) from the castle is another type of Butler lodging, the **Swiss Cottage.** This early 19C hunting/fishing lodge designed by John Nash for Lord Caher is a beautiful thatch roofed party house. The short tour is very interesting and the cottage is a photographer's dream. Eleven miles further on N8 is Cashel (CASH-el) and one of Ireland's premier religious attractions, **The Rock of Cashel.** The Rock of Cashel was a fortified stronghold of the Kings of Munster as early as 300 AD. The complex now consists of the ruins of the 12C Cormac's chapel

(German monks), a 12C round tower, and a 13C cathedral all of which overlook the 13C Benedictine Hore Abbey (sometimes Hoare of St Mary's). This site has been a seat of religious and political power for centuries. If you can arrange it, visit the Rock of Cashel again at night when the complex is beautifully floodlit.

Northwest from Cork and signposted off N20 is the most known attraction in Ireland, the **Blarney Castle.** More people probably know about about the Blarney Stone than know about Ireland itself. The castle, built in 1446, is a battlement keep which overlooks the River Martin. The fame of Blarney goes back to a story about its Lord, Dermott Laidhir McCarthy. When the Lord of Blarney was quizzed by Queen Elizabeth I's emissary, he waxed loquacious without ever answering directly. The Queen is reported to have said, "This is just more Blarney!" Everyone knows now that kissing the Blarney Stone (a stone set into the outer battlements) will confer upon the kisser the gift of gab. What you may not know is that to kiss the stone, you must climb seven stories of circular stairs and then lie on your back and hang over the edge with a guide holding your feet. The reason I didn't kiss the stone was because of something our Irish golfing friend told us. He said that teenage Irish boys sneak up to the stone at night and urinate on it. I wonder who's full of Blarney? Be warned, the climb down from the top of Blarney Castle is by way of the servants staircase, and is very narrow and steep. When we were there, a lady who had climbed to the top was having trouble coming down the servant's way. The guides had to stop the up traffic to allow her to go down the up staircase. Besides the castle (which is filled with graffiti), the grounds are a lovely park containing a Druidic site (rock garden), sacrificial stone, wishing staircase, a rock with a witch's face, and a pair of dolmens (burial chambers). Not far from the castle is the **Blarney Woolen Mills.** At the end of 18C the mill was a model community patterned after New Lanark in Scotland. Today, the Mills is a well stocked shop and pleasant tearoom.

Not far from Blarney Castle we spotted a ruined abbey signed from the main road. After the first turn off the main road, we saw no other signs, but could catch glimpses of the abbey through farms and trees. After several wrong guesses, we finally managed to find the road (by this time single track) that the abbey was on. We pulled to a stop on the road with the ruined abbey in the middle of a cow pasture that was pure muck, and the muckers were gathered all around the abbey. Sometimes in Ireland the attractions become not that attractive. In Macroom, west of Cork, one year we entered the busy market town on a market day. One side of the main street was filled with stalls selling various interesting products. We wandered from vendor to vendor tasting interesting cheeses, honey, breads, and even olives from the Continent. We've run across these **street markets** in Lisdoonvarna and Galway (as well as in Scottish villages) and stop to see what's on offer every chance we get.

# Chapter Three:
# Southwest — Golf, Pubs, and Attractions

Tralee GC, Co. Kerry

## GOLF

The drive out to *Galfchursa Ceann Sibeal* (Dingle Links) winds around the end of the peninsula, past 3000 year old beehive huts and iron-age stone forts, through villages seemingly untouched by time (except for the small road through them), and by vista points that beckon the photographer to burn memory so that people at home might believe how beautiful it is. When we arrived at *Ceann Sibeal* for our first visit to this most westerly golf course in Europe, we were struck by the beauty of not only the course, but the views of the Atlantic, the coastline, the Three Sisters peaks, and surrounding mountains. The most startling recognition, though, is that the same feeling of awe can be experienced at almost every one of the courses we describe in this section of the book. Whether you select an unknown eighteen hole gem like *Ceann Sibeal* or Dooks, a world renown track such as Killarney Mahony's Point or Arnold Palmer's Tralee, or a small beauty like Glengarriff or Casstlegregory, you won't be disappointed with golf offered in Ireland's northwest.

In this area, the Beara Peninsula is the least known in Ireland's southwest probably because it is the least developed. You can drive completely around the perimeter and meet nary a tour bus, though local traffic and tourists will still be seen. On our trip around the Beara we encountered an unusual sight—an unfriendly Irishman. Along the main road (R571) we saw a sign pointing inland to a waterfall and park. With time to kill, we decided to travel the five mile single track road to visit the park and falls. The drive was an adventure in itself, with the road narrow enough that we could barely find a place for two cars to pass without one of us putting wheels off the path that passed for a road. The scenery was worth the effort, though, as we drove down the center of a small valley with streams, loughs, hills, and forest all around us. We spotted the falls at the same time we spotted a sign asking for five euros a car to park and see the falls. As pretty as the waterfall was, we have many in Oregon and decided five euros (about seven dollars) was too much just to see another. Before we could get turned around in the parking lot, a woman came out yelling for us to pay up. We told her that we weren't staying. Now she started yelling that we had used the road they paid for to get here and we needed to pay. We hastened out back toward the main road. The last thing she shouted after us was to not stop and look at her waterfall. And to make sure we didn't stop, her husband drove his truck behind us honking all the way until we were out of sight of the falls. As I say, this unfriendly Irish experience is the exception. Definitely even the toughest golf will be far friendlier than the waterfall owners.

**BALLYBUNION GOLF CLUB, Old Course, Strandhill Road, Ballybunion, Co. Kerry (both courses)**
Take R553 through the village to R551 and the clubhouse. At the southwest edge of the village follow the signs (both courses).
www.ballybuniongolfclub.com (068) 27 146
Links, 6542 yards, par 72, €185

**Amenities (for both courses):** New plush clubhouse built in 1993 has changing rooms for members and visitors, two bars (food served all day), a well stocked pro shop with all the logoed souvenirs you'd want, and grand views to the Atlantic. The course also provides an excellent practice facility with greens, driving range, and sand bunkers.

**Course Comments:** The original Ballybunion course was designed by James McKenna in 1893 for the Lartique Railway. The railroad companies were the great expander of golf in Ireland and in Scotland. An Irish Times review in 1897 described the course as "a rabbit warren below the village, where a golfer requires limitless patience and an inexhaustible supply of golf balls." While patience and a good supply of ammunition is advisable when playing the Old Course today, it's due to the championship nature of the course, not the roughness. The original course folded because of financial problems in 1898 (I'm sure the Times review didn't help matters), and the course lay in disuse for eight years. In 1906 the course was reopened with a 9-hole layout by Lionel Hewson. The course was extended to 18 in 1926. Over the years more and more championships came to Ballybunion. In 1967 the Irish Professional tournament was won by Jimmy Kinsella, the recently (2006) retired pro at Skerries GC near Dublin. Ballybunion attracted international notice in 1970 when a Shell's Wonderful World of Golf match between Ireland's Christy O'Connor and American Bob Goalby was played on the links. The latest update to the course was in 1995 when Tom Watson, five time Open Champion and links golf enthusiast, modernized the course without changing the character of the Old Course.

Today, players can expect that it will be difficult to find a level lie on the fairways or around the very contoured greens. Plenty of bunkers provide challenges off the tees and as you approach the greens. At Ballybunion, as at other old style links courses, a premium is placed on accuracy around the greens, since there's more trouble left and right than front or back. But the biggest challenge at Ballybunion is the WIND, in capital letters. When we arrived to play the course from Limerick, we were told that the course was closed. The staff apologized as they explained that although a very rare occurrence, they had to close the course because of the heavy winds. We had played at Lahinch and Tralee with 40 mph gusts, but the 60 mph plus winds that day meant that balls would not stay on the lightning fast greens of either course. The wind was so strong that I couldn't get pictures even though it wasn't raining. The only picture I got was from outside the clubhouse braced against a wall, and then I had to take several to get one to turn out. We did walk parts of both courses so at least we could say we'd been to Ballybunion, but deeply regret (along with not spending enough time in the North and the southeast) getting to play the world renown course.

When you do play the Old Course, you are playing one of the truly classic links layouts in the world. The first hole gives a feel for what lay ahead. The 392- yard, par 4 is a dogleg left with carry of 230 yards needed to reach the fairway (the intervening rough is not too penal) and two bunkers on the inside of the corner. Four more bunkers protect the green which becomes a small target to approach. Number 3, a one-shotter of 220 yards, plays downhill with OB only six feet from the back right of the green. Three bunkers and a large rough-covered mound left add difficulty. Bunkers will scream at you on the par 5, 524-yard 5th—all 15 of them. To add challenge (yeah, right!) OB is all along the right side and it's hard to find a straight putt on what is the largest green on the course. In the wind the ball I dropped on this green would roll wildly from one slope to another. The 10th and 11th make a great start to the inward nine. Ten is a 359-yard par 4 where you must stay left to avoid being blocked from the green by mounds on the right. The left side also gives you a good view into the green next to the sea cliffs. The green affords great views up the coast. Eleven, a 453-yard par 4, has the sea cliffs (OB) all along the right. Not a slicer's hole! The hole needs no bunkers because mounds left and right will obscure the green which is perched on the cliff edge. Tom Watson called the 11th "one of the toughest holes in the world," but then, he'd be going for the green in two. The 13th is a short, but tricky dogleg left 484-yard par 5. Three bunkers are in play if you drive too far left. About a hundred yards from the green is a hard to see stream (Kitty's River) and three more bunkers guard the swaled green. A demanding drive is the start of the 16th, a 499-yard par 5. The hole is a dramatic dogleg left over a large mound with two bunkers in the prime landing area. Play to the right of the bunkers unless you're Tiger Woods who drove over the bunkers (360 yards) and had only a wedge to the green when he played in 1998. When you get to the green it's protected by three bunkers and big back-to-front slope.    Along with Waterville GC and Tralee GC, Ballybunion Old is the true class of Ireland's southwest.

### BALLYBUNION GOLF CLUB, Cashen Course
Links, 6278 yards, par 72, €65

**Course Comments:** Designed by American golf architect Robert Trent Jones and opened in 1980, the Cashen Course is a championship course (some say even tougher than the Old Course) in its own right. Played in the linksland between the Cashen River and the Atlantic Ocean, Cashen is a challenge worth your time.   With views of Cashen village, the par three 154-yard 3rd is a demanding short hole. Mounds on the right partially hide the green and two fronting bunkers add difficulty. Long isn't a good option either because a large bunker lurks behind the swaled and quick green. More good views follow on the 350-yard par 4 fourth which looks north to the mouth of the Shannon and south to Kerry Head. A drive of

200 yards is needed to reach the short grass and the six bunkers which await your drive. Avoid those bunkers and there are three more protecting a green surrounded by dunes. The 10th is a narrow dogleg right which plays between grass-covered dunes. Your approach shot is to a green backed by the Atlantic (though not in play) and guarded by a hidden pot bunker on the right. The 13th is a 395-yard par 4 straight ahead. Dunes on the left, mounds and ravine (which holds preserved remains of a Neolithic settlement) give the hole a timeless sense of beauty. The Cashen Course at Ballybunion is a world class challenge, but it may not remain the Cashen course for long. The club held a contest (winter 2006) to rename the course. Evidently, no winning name was selected and it's currently (winter 2015) still the Cashen Course. By the time you read this, the name may be different, but the course will be just as great.

**Comments from the Forward Tees:** Both courses are tough for ladies. Some of the carry's would be at my limit to reach the fairways. Bunkers were particularly deep and steep sided.

### BALLYNEETY GOLF CLUB (formerly Limerick County Golf Club), Ballyneety, Co. Limerick

Five miles south of Limerick on R512, just south of the village.

www.ballyneetygolfclub.com (061) 351 881

Parkland, 5876 metres, par 72, €25

**Amenities:** Modern clubhouse with comfortable changing rooms. Clubhouse also has the Ballyneety Bar which overlooks the back nine and serves pub food normal hours. The Fairways is a more formal restaurant with complete menu. A full pro shop and excellent practice facilities which includes a 20 bay covered driving range complete the complex.

**Course Comments:** The old Limerick County Course, now called Ballyneety GC, is a championship layout designed originally by touring pro Des Smyth. The facility has (2005) completed a €1.5 million remodel. Built on the old Croker

Estate, the ancestral home of the notorious "Boss" Croker of New York's Tammany Hall, Ballyneety will test golfers of all abilities with large, undulating greens, huge bunkers, and interesting water hazards. The course is an interesting layout with three one-shotters on the front and two on the back, and two par fives on the front and three on the back. The second is a good example of the testing par 3s at Ballyneety. Not exceedingly long at 152 metres, the two-tiered green is surrounded by bunkers and has a lake in play on the right. Number 5 is one of the longer par 4s on course (409 metres) and has two large bunkers on the left of the fairway just about where a good drive will want to go. The swaled green is guarded by three more bunkers. The turn holes are both tough. The 9th is a 466-metre par 5 which heads back to the clubhouse. From the elevated tee the fairway snakes past fairway bunkers right and then left toward the relatively flat green with a large bunker on the left. The 10th is a dogleg left with OB all along the right. The 326-metre hole has a stand of small trees which can cause problems for those trying to cut the corner. The sloped green is protected by plantings and a large bunker on the right. The 13th (143 metres) and the 15th (170 metres) are both par 3s where each green is situated between two lakes. Accuracy is key. The finishing hole is a short, but challenging 440-metre par 5 with a drive which must contend with a giant oak tree on the left and huge bunker on the right. A very undulating fairway will make approaching the humped green surrounded by four bunkers even more difficult. Ballyneety Golf Club is a reasonably priced first class facility.

**BANTRY BAY GOLF CLUB, Bantry, Co. Cork**
One and half miles north of Bantry on N71.
www.bantrygolf.com   (027) 50 579
Cliff top parkland, 5910 metres, par 71, €55

**AMENITIES:**   The clubhouse, built in 2000, presents great views of the course and the bay.  Also has a reputation for good food and it's open to visitors.  There's a well-stocked golf shop in the clubhouse.

**COURSE COMMENTS:**   In 1975 Eddie Hackett designed the first nine-hole Bantry Bay course.   In 1997 Christy O'Conner Jnr expanded the course to 18 holes.  Views from the course have been called "fantastic" and "spectacular," but there's more challenge than just distracting scenery.  A mix of 36 fairway and greenside bunkers will test your accuracy— most are greenside, visible, and not too penal.  The course's main defense, other than the ever-present wind, is water.  The bay is in play on four holes, seven have ponds in play, and there's one creek crossing.  Greens are medium to large with subtle slopes—none of the slopes are too dramatic.   We thought the greens were in great condition.  With views of the bay and Bird and Chapel Islands, it's sometimes difficult to keep your attention focused, but focus you should.

The challenging golf at Bantry Bay starts with the 1st, a 138-metre par 3, which ought to be named, "Don't Go Left." The moderately sized green is guarded on the left by a large pond and behind by a bunker.  There's not much room right of the green either because of trees.  An entertaining start.  A blind drive over a small hill starts the 310-metre 5th.  The hole doglegs left around trees. Find the fairway (it's pretty generous) and the approach shot only has to contend with a bunker front right and one left.  At the 362-metre par 4 eighth the aiming point for your drive is the pond 230 metres out (from the white tees).   Be careful, though, if downwind the pond is reachable.  The second shot is over the pond to a relatively small flat green with only one bunker right.  The best view on the course is from the 9th green; be sure to take a moment's pause before heading to the 10th.  The first hole on the back is a 371-metre par 4 which doglegs right along the bay.  The fairway runs out straight ahead at 235 metres—stay short or bend it right. Big hitters can cut the corner, but a miss right could be in heavy rough.   The green is unprotected except for the bay on the left.  On the 12th, a 402-metre par 4, you'll be rewarded for both distance and accuracy.  The hole doglegs right around a pond (about 100 metres from the green) and it's OB all along the left.   Second shots must contend with a large pond on the right and a fronting bunker.

Next is a 128-metre par 3 which some will call difficult. I call it diabolical. A large pond fronts the green which has two bunkers behind. Here it's easy to clear the pond, hit the green, and run off the back into the bunker. A good shot is one you'll always remember; a bad shot is one you'll want to forget. The finishing hole is a short (423-metre) par 5. The hole is a tree-lined dogleg left where it takes about 220 to reach the corner. Second (or third) shots must deal with a pond left for the fairway and five traps around the green. It makes a pretty picture—bunkers, the green, and the lovely clubhouse. A writer in the Irish Examiner said, "There are few more beautifully located or more delightful golf courses in the whole of Ireland." After our experience I'd say that isn't blarney.

**FROM THE FORWARD TEES:** This is a delightful course to play, especially on a dry sunny day. The course has wonderful views of the bay, and the bay and ponds will be in play on many holes. The course isn't particularly long from the front tees, but it is demanding. Overall distance is 4973 metres (5439 yards), and the front is a par 36 while the back is par 37. The longest par 5 on the course is the 11th at 432 yards. The par 3s on the front are both short, but they aren't easy since there are ponds on both. On the backside, the 13th is completely over a pond. Bantry Bay is a good challenge with lovely views. Have fun!

### CASTLEGREGORY GOLF & FISHING CLUB,
### Stradbally, Castlegregory, Co. Kerry
Follow signs off R560 off N86 on the north coast of
Dingle Peninsula.
www.castlegregorygolflinks.com (066) 713 9444
9-hole links, 5264 metres, par 68, €20/9. €40/18

**Amenities:** A caravan (trailer) serves as a small pro shop with tearoom (limited food available), and changing rooms.

**Course Comments:** According to early Irish golfing journals, golf was played at Castlegregory as early as 1897. Abandoned in 1907, the course was "rediscovered" by Dr.

Arthur Smith in the late 1980s. The course is definitely worth the effort to find. The first hole belies the true links nature of the course as it plays in the flats along Lough Gill (renowned for its fine fishing). From number two to the end you know you're in the linksland. Wonderful views of Lough Gill, Tralee Bay to the west, Brandon Bay to the east, and the Stradbally Mountains to the south assail your senses on practically every shot. While Castlegregory doesn't sport too many bunkers, several of those on the course are deep and penal. The greens have subtle borrows, and water is in play (lough, stream, pond) on five holes. Each hole at Castlegregory GC is unique which adds interest to the round. The 242-metre par 4 third is a short hole with a deep bunker guarding the left side side of the elevated green. The right is hard to hold as the fairway slopes severely left. From the raised tee box on the 368-metre par 4 fourth, you drive down to a generous fairway. Your approach to the green must negotiate a fairway made of natural bumps and hollows. The green has one bunker on the left. The 7th is a 394-metre par 4 dogleg left, which begins with a blind tee shot. The hole plays shorter than its yardage (metre-age?) because of the raised tee. The green is tucked left behind a dune covered in wispy grass. You can cut off distance by playing from the left rough, but the risk of a bad lie is much greater. The final hole is unusual for a links course, but fairly typical of American-style target golf. It's a 149-metre par 3 which plays directly over a pond to a flat green. One thing that does brand the hole as unique is that the pond and its shores are environmentally protected areas because it is home to a protected toad. Ireland's Natterjack Toad, mascot for the club, is elusive. You can hear the toad, with its distinctive yellow stripe down its back, on spring and summer evenings as it crawls quickly around instead of hopping.

A couple of years after we first played the course, we found out that Greg Norman designer of Doonbeg not too far away, had tried to buy the course to turn it into an 18-hole resort. Locals, who would have been shut out of their course, refused to make the deal. Play Castlegregory while you can. It's a definite gem.

**Comments from the Forward Tees:** Great course with a good variety of shots. The water on the course is always a problem, if only visually. While a challenge, Castlegregory is very playable with good course management being rewarded.

### GALFCHURSA CEANN SIBEAL (Irish for Sybil Head) aka Dingle Golf Club, Ballyoughterach, Ballyferriter, Co. Kerry

On the west coast of Dingle Peninsula off R559.
www.dinglelinks.com (066) 915 6255
Links, 6690 yards, par 72, €65

**Amenities:** The pro shop is one of the best stocked shops in western Ireland, and staff is both helpful and friendly. The upstairs lounge has one of the best views of any course we've played. You can have a pint or a bite off the complete menu and look out over the linksland to The Sisters (mountains) and the Atlantic beyond.

**Course Comments:** The Dingle Links course is the combined work of Eddie Hackett and Christy O'Connor Jnr, probably the two most respected golf architects of Ireland. The course, originally opened in 1924, is quite popular, but is isolated enough that it's still reasonably easy to get on. To be safe, though, call ahead to avoid societies or local competitions. Known to many as the St. Andrews of the Irish southwest, Dingle is a series of great golf holes, starting with *Poll na Cruaiche* (Hole in the Hill), the 386-yard 1st. This downhill par 4 begins with a drive to a generous fairway. The second shot needs to thread its way between two bunkers and over a burn. Take plenty of club, especially if you come in from the right since the water will be more in play from that angle. A fine par 3 is *An Giolcach* (Tall Reed-like Grass), the 202-yard 5th. [The translation of the Gaelic hole names into English was provided by Barbara Carroll, a *Ceann Sibeal* member and owner of Milestone B&B.] Even though the green is 36 yards deep, it's hard to hold because it usually plays firm. Four bunkers around the green and typical links bounces will add difficulty. The 7th, *An Mionnan* (Landmark), is a gentle left to right dogleg par 4 of 374 yards. Approach the green from the center or left, if you can, because a hidden bunker lurks on the front right, and the green has a severe slope left to right. The 8th hole is a visual delight with the peaks of The Three Sisters behind the green. The 10th at Dingle, a stunning 197-yard par 3, is the most westerly hole in Europe. The tee shot is uphill to a two-tiered green almost completely hidden by the slopes and dunes. Take an extra club to get up to the upper half of the putting surface. Another tough one-shotter is the 12th. At only 161 yards *Tuimin* (Small Spinning Wheel) is still a hard pin to find with three bunkers front and left and one more on the right. To find the pin on the back half you need to fly the ball at least 150 yards to clear the second bunker. The hardest hole for ladies and second hardest for men is the short (465-yard) par 5 thirteenth. Your drive on *Casadh Chosai* must stay short of the stream (about 220 yards). If you are a go-for-it player and the wind is light or helping, be warned that OB right, a hill, and deep stream are waiting for those whose shot doesn't match their ambition. The stream (which is in play on ten holes) crosses the fairway a second time just thirty yards short of the small green protected by the stream left and two bunkers right. Prudence ought to be the name of the hole— though, Barbara assures me that isn't the translation of the Gaelic *Casadh Chosai.*

As all over Ireland the locals are friendly and accommodating. We let two local ladies play through one year on number eight. Anne and I aren't slow players, but we wanted to slow down, take more photos, and have a snack. As we waited for the ladies to tee off, I broke out the snacks. The ladies saw that and asked what we had. When I said, "GORP," they were perplexed. I offered them some Good Old Raisins and Peanuts (actually raisins, peanuts, and M&Ms). They liked the GORP and wanted some more. Together, we munched our way through the rest of the round.

Cowslips and larks abound at Dingle GC; so do interesting views. Be sure to spot "The Giant with a Knife in His Throat"—an island which looks like a man lying on his back, another island behind looks like a knife lodged in the giant's throat. You can get the best image from the tee box of the fourth. As isolated as is *Ceann Sibeal,* it's a great course and should be on everyone's links itinerary.

**Comments from the Forward Tees:** Dingle is not an easy course for women; it's too easy to land in trouble (sand or water). Strategy is important, as well as compensating for links rolls. The course is long, but has a par of 73 for women. Number 11 is the longest at 531 yards, but it does play downhill.

### DOOKS GOLF LINKS, Glenbeigh (on the Ring of Kerry), Co. Kerry

Turn off N70 (Ring of Kerry Road) a mile east of
Glenbeigh, follow signs.
**www.dooks.com**  (066) 976 8205
Links, 6401 metres, par 71, €85

**Amenities:** The new clubhouse (2005) hosts a fully stocked pro shop and top grade changing facilities. The clubhouse lounge has a lovely horseshoe bar, nice views out toward the course on one side, and room for a piano for entertainment. Pub food is served most usual hours, and local members say the food has always been top drawer. Everyone we talked with said the Guinness is always perfect! A sign sets the tone at Dooks: "Mobile phones not permitted on course or in bar."

**Course Comments:** One of the oldest courses in Ireland (1889), Dooks GC is a world class links course set on a point of land at the head of Dingle Bay. It was the English Royal Horse Artillery using the nearby Glenbeigh Artillery Range who brought golf to the area. Not everything the English did in Ireland was bad. With much redesigning accomplished in the last few years, Dooks (Gaelic for "rabbit warren") retains its natural feel through the dunes. A first time visitor would not know the course isn't as it was laid out over a hundred years ago.  As natural as Dooks is, it still has teeth. A main difficulty for players at Dooks, even those who have played several times, is the distractingly beautiful scenery.

Once you get past the first hole, you'll have grand vistas of Dingle Bay, Inch Point, Rossbehy Cleek (estuary), the peaks of McGillycuddy Reeks (mountains), Slieve Mish and Dingle Mountains, and the whitewashed houses of Cromane fishing village. But it isn't the scenery alone which will challenge the golfer. Blind shots (drives as well as approaches), small greens which are quick with lots of undulations, ponds in play at 15 and 16, plenty of penal bunkers, especially around the par 3s, and the wind are enough to challenge even the best players on a good day. It is the wind, though, that will most affect the scores. On the Dingle Head the whole course is subject to significant breezes most of the time. But Dooks is designed to present golfers with a nice mix of upwind, downwind, and sidewind shots no matter which way the wind blows. The gorse which lines many of the fairways is ready to accept any offerings of Pro-V-1s or TopFlites blown its way. Dooks is a course for the thinking golfer.

Dooks challenges start on the first hole, a 393-yard par 4 rated the second most difficult on the course. The green is blind from the tee and, if you hit too short, blind from the fairway approach as well. The par 5 sixth at 477 yards is a dogleg right which plays longer into the prevailing wind. A series of three bunkers on the inside of the corner warn you to stay to the left. Two small, but dangerous, bunkers front the sloped green. A short and usually downwind gem is the 163-yard one-shot 11th. The hole is unusual because to reach the green you have to hit directly over an OB area. The green is protected by one small, mean-looking pot bunker. The tricky part was to try to hold the green with a 25 mph wind at your back. Normally, it would be a five-iron shot for me, but on this day an eight-iron was too much. Thankfully, there is room behind the green. The hardest hole at Dooks, according to the stroke index, is the 416-yard par 4 fourteenth. A straight forward tee shot downhill leads to a green fronted by four bunkers and with mounds of rough on both sides. It's a stunningly pretty hole from the tee with the bay in the background. A nice challenging finish to your round is the 18th, a 430-yard par 4 which usually plays against the wind.

The hole starts with a daunting blind shot when into the wind —aim at the two house chimneys in the distance. Mounds in front of the green point the way, but also provide trouble if you get hung up on them. Our playing partner, local member John O'Houlahan, told us that before renovations the dunes went completely across the fairway, making the approach shot also blind. It is tough enough as it is; it' hard to imagine how difficult it would be as a double-blind hole. Some say this is one of the finest finishing holes in Ireland. I wouldn't disagree with that.

As at nearby Castlegregory Golf and Fishing Club, the mascot of Dooks GC is the endangered Natterjack Toad. Golfers are requested not to go into the area around the ponds so as not to disturb the toad's habitat. Natterjack Toads, large Irish hares, grand scenery, and a testing course make Dooks Golf Club a must stop.

**Comments from the Forward Tees:** Dooks GC is a challenging, fun, but doable course from the forward tees. I felt I could be successful as well as challenged. Par 3s are reasonable distance for average women players. Bunker placement requires good course management to avoid.

### DUNLOE GOLF CLUB, Gap of Dunloe, Co. Kerry
Off N72, turn by Beaufort and follow signs to Gap of
    Dunloe or Kate Kearney's Cottage.
www.dunloegolfcourse.com  (064) 44 578
9-hole moorland, 4706 metres, par 68, €24/18, 9-hole
    price certain days

**Amenities:** The clubhouse is a pleasant coffee shop with snacks and sandwiches available. Attached to the coffee shop is a small, but well equipped pro shop. The course also has a covered multi-bay driving range.

**Course Comments:** This 1994 course offers spectacular scenery, even though it is not of the ocean or bay. From Dunloe GC you will find vistas of Killarney Lakes, the McGillycuddy Reeks (mountains), the Gap of Dunloe (a deep pass between the McGillycuddies and Thomas and Purple Mountains). [See Attractions] Dunloe GC is worth a visit for the golf as well as the views. All of the par 3s play to elevated greens where the top of the flag is just visible. Number five at 140 metres has a bunker which fronts the left half of the green. The 3rd (162 metres) and the 8th (158 metres) both have bunkers on either sides of the greens. Several of the bunkers at Dunloe come right to the edge of the green. We saw a pin placement about three yards from a bunker—not far beyond the pin, the green simply sloped into the sand. The second hole is a real gem. The 284-metre par 4 requires a precise drive to avoid a series of small bunkers left starting about 170 metres from the tee and a large bunker right. The putting surface is protected by rough and grass bunkers. The only drawback to a round at Dunloe Golf Club is that the course can be very wet. It didn't help that we played during the wettest May Ireland had seen in the last ten years, but on several holes we dug out our plugged drives.

**Comments from the Forward Tees:** Even though the course isn't long, it was very difficult to score when it was so wet. Hole 7 is a long (432 metres) par 5 which was particularly hard to play as a dogleg right with bunkers, gorse, and OB left. Par 3s are reasonable lengths. Even though there are some hills on the course, it was a comfortable walk.

### GLENGARRIFF GOLF CLUB ,Drumgarriff, Glengarriff, Co. Cork
On N71 at the south end of the village, south of Kenmore and north of Bantry.
**www.glengarriffgolfclub.com** (027) 63 150
9 hole parkland, 4094 metres, par 66, €20/18

**Amenities:** Small, pleasant clubhouse with changing rooms downstairs and a lounge/bar upstairs which serves good food all day. A few golf necessities at the bar.

**Course Comments:** Glengarriff Golf Club is a 9-hole 4514-yard par 66 gem with views of Glengarriff Harbour, Bantry Bay, and the islands. In the spring and early summer the course is ablaze with rhoddies and gorse in bloom. The course, founded in 1934, plays over and around a sizable hill, with several blind shots, a few bunkers in play, moderate to small speedy greens, and some of Ireland's last remaining Old Oak forest. A small stream crosses on the 6th, but most of the water you see isn't in play. A couple of the par 3s stuck with us. The third is a 170-yard one-shotter with a semi-blind tee shot over a canyon with trees blocking the view of the pin from the gent's tee. Only the top of the flag is visible. From the forward tee, it's a tough shot of 166 yards. The shorter 128-yard 5th also has a blind drive over a hill, but the top of the flag can be seen from the forward tee. Heavy rough all around protects the green. The 6th is a 281-yard par 4 which sharply doglegs left to right after yet another blind tee shot over a hill. The second shot crosses the only stream on the course. Glengarriff GC is a fun course well worth a visit and it has a celebrity connection—Maureen O'Hara-Blair, the actress, is Honorary President.

**Comments from the Forward Tees:** The course is fun with wonderful views from many holes. Hilly enough to be good exercise and to impact some shots. Two of the three par 3s are long for ladies.

### KILLARNEY GOLF & FISHING CLUB, Mahony's Point Course, Fossa, Killarney, Co. Kerry [for all three courses]

Three km from town center on the Ring of Kerry Road (N72).
www.killarneygolfclub.ie  (064) 31 034
Lakeside Parkland, 6164 metres, par 72, €60

**Amenities:** [for all three courses]: The lovely clubhouse was built in 1989 with a 240 degree view of the lake and the course. Clubhouse has changing rooms, an extensive dining room, with a wonderful horseshoe bar in the lounge. Very complete pro shop run when we played by Tony Coveney, three time Irish Open Champion, now pro David Keating runs the shop. An extensive practice facility serves all three of the Killarney courses.

**Course Comments:** Killarney Golf & Fishing Club is a busy golf resort with three great courses to choose from. The Mahony's Point Course was opened in 1939 (an original course at Deer Park served the club from 1906 until 1939) and was revised by Eddie Hackett in 1969. At that time nine of the holes were given over to the new Killeen Course, and a new nine created at Mahony's Point. Killarney Golf & Fishing Club has a rich, interesting history. In 1913 the original Deer Park clubhouse was burned to the ground, probably by three Irish suffragettes protesting the club's lack of equality for women players. A legend persists, most probably due to a specific photograph, that in the 1950s a trout rose from the lake to snap a dropping ball poorly hit from the 18th tee. The photo shows the suspect fish with ball in mouth being held up by a club member. Among the luminaries who have played at Killarney is South African Gary Player, who played his first professional tournament outside his native country at Mahony's Point. Mahony's Point is an outstanding course both for its beauty and its quality golf. The course boasts 45 bunkers, most greenside, some penal, and all in play. The multilevel and sloped greens are well conditioned and tend to be speedy. Water, in the form of streams, ponds, and Lough Leane, is in play on seven holes, but will be a major concern on the 17th and 18th. I believe the biggest challenge of the course is the drop dead gorgeous scenery. The mountains, old growth forests, and lake are distractingly pretty. As much distraction as the views will cause, on a nice day there's probably no more beautiful place to play golf.

The golf at Mahony's Point is as good as the vistas around the course. The second, a 404-metre par 4 is a strong dogleg left to right with two bunkers and a copse of trees on the inside of the dogleg and one bunker left. It takes a drive of about 250 metres to clear the right bunkers, so the prudent play is to stay short leaving about 175 metres to reach the green. The large green is protected by bunkers on each side. With a stroke index of 2, par is a great score on the the second. The 6th is a slightly downhill hole which plays shorter than its 360-metre length. The two-tiered green is severely sloped from back to front. We watched a player make a decent shot from the bunker behind the green, and then it rolled slowly past the pin and off the green into a small creek. On the 10th, a 344-metre two-shotter, aim for the trees that seem to be in the center of the fairway—they really are. Be careful, the tee box lines up to hit too far left. A drive of about 200 metres will keep you far enough back from the trees to make a good approach to a raised two-tiered green fronted by two dangerous bunkers. A short par 5 which should be birdie-able is the 435-metre 13th. The hole also has some interesting trouble. A creek runs across the fairway about 70 metres from the green which is quite elevated. The small green is guarded on the left by the deepest bunker on the course and two more bunkers on the right. Every course should have a hole like the 15th—a drivable par 4. This 284-metre hole plays downhill from the tee, and the two-tiered green is reachable even by moderate hitters. The hole isn't entirely defenseless as the green is slightly raised and is protected by four bunkers. The two finishing holes at Mahony's Point are simply delightful. The 17th, a 373-metre par 4, has trees left and the lake right the length of the hole. Leave your slice behind on this one. While all the par 3s at Mahony's Point are interesting, the 18th is considered one of the outstanding one-shotters anywhere. It makes a beautiful and challenging finish to your round. The hole is a 179-metre gem which plays over the corner of the lake on the right to a green protected by four pot bunkers on the left and brush and 150 ft. tall pines on the right. It's a fair challenge from any tee box, and will be a hole you will always remember regardless of your score.

Killarney Golf & Fishing Club, Mahony's Point Course has everything a visiting golfer would want in a five star experience: A wonderful, modern clubhouse, fantastic vistas your entire round, and a golfing challenge fitting the club's motto, The Queen of them All.

**Comments from the Forward Tees:** This course has it all: challenge, water, strategically placed bunkers, sloped greens, long par 5s, and grand views all over. I enjoyed the round at Mahony's Point, but had to be thinking from the first hole which started out over water to the last hole which had water, bunkers, and trees to contend with.

**Killarney Golf & Fishing Club, Killeen Course**
Lough side Parkland, 6566 metres, par 73, €80

**Course Comments:** Considered the flagship course at Killarney Golf & Fishing Club, the Killeen Course was recently made even more challenging (June, 2006) with added length, redesigned greens, and the addition of more water hazards. Water is now a feature of almost every hole. Already a championship track having hosted the 1996 Curtis Cup and two Irish Opens (1991 and 1992), the challenges are even stronger now. As testing as Killeen is, it is still playable by average players as long as you choose the appropriate tees to play from (Blue at 6566 metres, White 6047 metres, Green 5608 metres, and Red 5041 metres). Stray from the fairway, though, and the 36 strategically placed bunkers (plus a few waste areas), numerous ponds and streams, the lough, and thick stands of trees are ready to grab your wayward shots. The fescue/rye rough, as well, is waiting to eat up your score. The first four holes offer wonderful view of Lough Leane and on the spectacular par 3 tenth you play visually straight into the lough.

The 1st at Killeen is a great starting hole. The 345-metre two-shotter dogleg right has the lough ready to swallow up balls far enough right to clear the extra large bunker running the last hundred yards of the hole. Don't bail too far on your drive or you'll find the two fairway bunkers left. The large, quick, swaled green only needs the lough on the right for protection. The par 3 sixth, a one-shotter of 193 metres from the Blue (and a more reasonable 153 metres from the White) is quite a test of shot making. The long, narrow, tiered green is fronted by a stream which flows along the right side and behind. The bailout area left will leave a chip from uneven lies with the stream in front of you. Number 7 is a short 469-metre par 5 (which plays as a 315-metre par 4 from the Red tees). But don't let the lack of length fool you because plenty of difficulty will be found on the dogleg right. This classic hole has an undulating fairway and stands of trees surrounding the fairway leading to a wildly swaled large green. Another great par 3 is the 156-metre 10th. The trouble on this hole is the large pond which runs from the front all along the left of another large undulating green. The "Tiger" hole at Killeen (their name) is the 458-metre par 4 thirteenth. Rough, water (a stream), length, and a lightning quick green creates a test worthy of Tiger himself. The toughest hole on the course is followed by a shorter challenge of a different kind. The 356-metre par 4 fourteenth is a dogleg right around the oldest tree on the course, called the Turkey Oak (over 200 years old) on the inside of the turn. The green is protected by bunkers on both sides. The signature hole, on a course full of signature holes, is the 18th. The dogleg left has a trio of bunkers on the right side of the fairway and streams and ponds down the left. The fairway narrows on the second shot to a wildly tiered green with a large fronting bunker. The very undulating green will grab your attention. It is said that lots of euros (and/or drinks) are won or lost in clubhouse bets on how many putts it takes players to get down.

The Killeen Course at Killarney is intended to be the toughest of the three courses at the club. Regardless of what you score, you'll have a round to remember—the views, the shots, and the views.

### Killarney Golf & Fishing Club, Lackabane Course
Parkland, 6410 metres, par 72, €50

**Course Comments:** The newest of the courses at Killarney Golf & Fishing Club, the Lackabane Course is no weak sister. With plenty of lake and stream problems and at 6410 metres from the back tees, Lackabane will test all aspects of your game. The Donald Steel design, which opened in 2000, is known for its fast, undulating greens. The Lackabane Course starts with two fun, but challenging holes. Hole number 1, a 391-metre par 4, bends slightly around two large bunkers on the right. If you can start with a good drive you may catch the down slope and leave a short approach to a moderate green guarded by two bunkers left. Par or birdie gets your round off to an encouraging start. The short, 446-metre par 5 second plays as a dogleg right around two fairway bunkers. A well driven ball from whatever tee box will carry the bunkers, but length isn't as important as placement. Smart players will lay their second shot to the left to have an easier approach into the tricky green fronted by three bunkers. The tee boxes at the 4th and the 6th afford great views of Killarney Lake. Another well designed par 5 is the 507-metre 7th. The hole seems easy from the tee, but you must avoid the left bunkers on your second shot. The large bunker which fronts the green covers half the green on your approach and the pin seems always to be behind the bunker. The putting surface has the most severe slope (right to left) of any on the course. Don't be fooled by a stroke index of 11 on the 464-metre par 5 seventeenth—it's harder than that. A drive of 215 metres is needed to clear the stream and a precise lay-up short of the three large bunkers is required to set up your approach. Your third shot will probably be blind to a green which slopes to the left and away from you. The ultimate hole is the tough 391-metre par 4 eighteenth. A dogleg right with a long carry over rough with bunkers on the inside corner, the 18th plays as the hardest hole (stroke index 1) at Lackabane. The second shot to the left to right sloping green with two bunkers right always seems to play long.

Sometimes a third course at a venue is an afterthought or relief course (think Gullane #3 in East Lothian, Scotland). Instead, the Lackabane Course should be considered an additional championship track (think the Centenary Course at Gleneagles, Scotland). While it may not be the premier or favorite course at Killarney Golf & Fishing Club, Lackabane is a challenge worth your time.

**PARKNASILLA GOLF CLUB, Parknasilla Resort and Spa, Sneem, Co. Kerry**
On the south side of the Ring of Kerry (N70) near Sneem.

www.parknasillaresort.com (064) 667 5600
Parkland, 5161 yards, par 67, €25/18, €20/12 or 9

**Amenities:** Starter's bungalow has a small pro shop, serves snacks, and has changing rooms.  The course is part of a full service resort and spa with tons for families to do and at least two restaurants.

**Course Comments:** Parknasilla GC used to be on the grounds of the landmark Parknasilla Great Southern Hotel, but is now part of the Parknasilla Resort and Spa.  The course is a slightly unusual track near the colorful village of Sneem. The parkland course has attractive views of Bunnow Harbour, the Kenmare Bay (some maps call it Kenmare River, but it's three miles across to Ardgroom Harbour on the Ring of Beara), and Garnish and Sherky Islands, and plays in several configurations. You can play the original nine holes, or a redesign by Dr. Arthur Spring (who also did Castlegregory) as a 12-hole course. The third option is to play the 12 holes and then replay 1-4 and 11 and 12 to make an 18- hole round (the routing works comfortably). With rain looming on a late Sunday afternoon, we played the 12-hole course. Check in at the starter's bungalow, rather than up the road at the hotel where you would find a full service restaurant and bar. The views from Parknasilla GC certainly rival Glengarriff, or any course, and birds were in full song throughout our round. Parknasilla doesn't need many bunkers (the few it has have rough sand) because the forests the course plays through are thick and anything in the trees is probably lost. Several of the greens are elevated, but the slopes are easily playable.

The 3rd at Parknasilla is a 444-metre par 5 with a tight tee shot through the trees. The green is the most sloped on the course, which makes it a difficult target to hold in regulation. The 334-metre par 4 seventh begins with a challenging tee shot that is almost unfair to the first time visitor. From a raised tee you drive down to a narrow landing area between trees, and you can't see the landing area from the tee. Your approach shot is also blind over to a green protected by trees and a bunker. The double-blind hole is only rated fourth hardest for men, but number one for ladies. Another tight downhill tee shot begins the 11th, a par 4 of 386 metres. Trees and a fence are on the left, and a hill and rough are right. The second shot looks like you are hitting to a green in the bay—though not much, there is a little room behind the green. The tee on the 12th is fantastic! The tee box sits out on a finger of land in the bay. The drive doesn't have to cross the water, but it is blind uphill with forest on both sides. Parknasilla is a gorgeous bayside parkland track.

**Comments from the Forward Tees:** A good parkland course set beside the water. Not long, but still not easy to score. With trees, bunkers, and hills to deal with, the course forces you to think seriously about placement. Par 3s provide nice relief.

### SHANNON GOLF CLUB, Shannon, Co. Clare
Just outside the Shannon airport off N19, follow signs from the last roundabout.
www.shannongolfclub.ie   (061) 471 849
Parkland, 6448 yards, par 72, €40

**AMENITIES:** The modern clubhouse has a panoramic view over the Shannon estuary from the bar. Restaurant looks to the 1st tee and the 18th green. Both serve good food. In the clubhouse, also, is a fully equipped golf shop.

**COURSE COMMENTS:** Designed in 1966 by John Harris, Shannon GC is a course you can almost see from your plane as you land at the airport. It's a lovely forested course which has some views of the Shannon estuary. The course has plenty of challenges beside the swirling winds. There are almost 60 bunkers on the course, most of which are in play. Some bunkers are quite large, but none are too penal. Water, mostly ponds will be bothersome on five holes. One hole has a pond and a burn in play and one hole has the estuary all down the left. The course's moderate sized greens are mostly flat with subtle slopes. I found them very nice to putt on and we heard that they are usually in nice condition.

The course is fun to play with fair challenges. I liked the 2nd, a 497-yard, par 5, which doglegs left around a nest of bunkers (270 yards to clear), but there's plenty of room to the right. A fairway bunker further on the right about where average hitters land second shots adds to the difficulty. The flat green is surrounded by three bunkers. A nice par 3 is the 4th at 167-yards. Traps front and back guard a green set diagonally to the tee. It's a lovely challenge. Another par 5 I liked on the front is the 8th. This 501-yard hole is straight ahead and usually downwind with no bunkers to spoil your concentration. A pond on the left about 70 yards from the green and a burn running across the fairway from the pond will certainly command your attention. The flat green has one trap left if you need more challenge. On the back, the 11th, a 338-yard par 4, could be called a slight dogleg left then right or a fairway which snakes around a large bunker left and then another right. OB all down the left should only concern those who play a duck hook—you know, the kind you can't talk to. The slightly raised green tilts back to front and is protected by two bunkers. Next is the 12th, a 203-yard one-shotted where both accuracy and length are needed to score. Two small bunkers front the green right, but it is the dangerous pot bunker at the left side of the green that you need to fear most. A testing par three. The 17th is considered the signature hole at Shannon GC and at 203 yards it is indeed an intimidating hole. One bunker left is troublesome, it is the estuary encroaching on the right (35 yards from the green) that will really make you take notice. The course is fun and a great value.

**TRALEE GOLF CLUB, West Barrow, Ardfert, Co. Kerry**
A few miles west of Tralee village off R558 in West Barrow.
www.traleegolfclub.com (066) 713 6379
Links, 6975 yards, par 72, €135

**Amenities:** Wonderful modern clubhouse with changing rooms downstairs and a beautiful lounge/bar upstairs with views onto the course and the sea. Good food served all day. Be sure to look in on the Arnold Palmer Room (conference room) when upstairs. A snack shack next to the changing rooms downstairs allows easy access at the turn. The pro shop across from the reception desk is fully supplied with all the equipment you need and all the souvenirs you'd want.

**Course Comments:** The original Tralee 9-hole parkland course at Mounthawk (in town) wasn't playable in the winter. In the early 1980s, when the King, Arnold Palmer, came looking for a venue for his first Irish course, the club jumped at the chance. Palmer and co-designer Ed Seay put together a world-class links course in one of the most scenic locations in the world with views of the mountains of the Dingle Peninsula across the bay and the Atlantic which can be seen from every hole on the course. With all the water around the course, Tralee has no water crossings. Several holes play alongside the beach cliffs, notably 2, 3, 8, 15, 16, and 17. Tralee doesn't need water crossing because plenty of other challenges exist on the course. Tralee will test all level of golfers with typical links golf problems of tight lies, tough rough, blind shots, and elevation changes. Fifty-five bunkers will demand accurate shot-making to avoid. If you do find yourself in the sand, you'll need all your skill to get out of the often penal traps and fairway pot bunkers. Hitting out backwards will be your best option in some cases. The greens are fast and some are undulating, but none too severe. The biggest challenge, though, will be the wind which blows almost every day. If the wind is light, be thankful and enjoy the gift Mother Nature has given you. If the wind is up, be ready to face one of the fairest stern tests of golf you'll encounter. If the gale is blowing, as it was on the May afternoon we played, tie your hat on and have a go anyway. Even in 25 mph or higher winds, Tralee GC is a playable, fair course.

From the 1st to the 18th, Tralee GC provides quality golf on an immaculately groomed course. Number two, *The*

*Cuilin* , is a long (596-yard) par 5 dogleg right which plays along the sea cliffs overlooking the beach, which was used in the filming of David Lean's movie "Ryan's Daughter." It's too long for even big hitters to try to cut the corner. The green next to the cliffs is protected by three bunkers left and a drop to beach on the right. All of the par 3s at Tralee are strong, but *The Castle* (named for a nearby Tudor gun turret), the 194-yard 3rd, is backed much of the time by hay bales to keep sea water from splashing onto the green—functional, but not aesthetically pleasing. The 6th at 427 yards is another sharp dogleg left to right. Here a drive of 250 yards will reach the corner of a very mounded fairway. No bunkers are needed to protect the green which slopes to the left. *The Creek* [I have no idea why it's called that; there's no creek on the hole.] is the 8th hole and another dogleg. This time the dogleg is left along the beach (which is OB) with a narrow fairway snaking 399 yards to the green which is long and narrow and needs no bunkers to guard it. Six, seven, and eight are known as Palmer's Loop. The 11th is another long par 5. *Palmer's Peak* is 583 yards uphill with a blind second shot. Stay right off the tee to avoid the two bunkers at the inside of the left bend. Play through the gap in the dunes and try to stay center left. The green is visible from the top of the hill, as are the two bunkers on the left of the green. If the wind is against you, figure the hole is a par 6! When you finish the tough eleventh, you reach the 458-yard par 4 monster. The twelfth, the toughest hole on the course, begins with a semi-blind tee shot—the green is visible in the distance, but the landing area for your drive isn't. The green is tucked to the left of the fairway with dunes on the right and a deep gully left and fronting. Whether on your second or third shot, the severely sloped green is a hard target to find. The par 3, 159-yard 13th is both beautiful and intimidating. The hole is called *Brokers Hollow* because your tee shot must carry the hollow all the way to the green. Any ball short will imbed in the steep, rough covered, depression over which you hit. With a steep rough covered dune behind the green, the hole has no bailout area. If you manage to find the green, the swales will prove a challenge to putt. The 17th, which again plays alongside a "Ryan's Daughter" film beach, is a demanding hole whether played from the championship or members' tee. This 361-yard par 4 is a dogleg right with a landing area which can seem narrow in the wind. Three bunkers are in play for decent drives, and the green is two-tiered and will seem small. The finishing hole at Tralee is a gorgeous 486-yard par 5 playing slightly uphill towards the picturesque clubhouse. The hole is named *The Goat's Hole*, but should be called "Bunker Hell" for the thirteen bunkers in play. They can be avoided, but you must be very accurate or very lucky. The tiered green has five small, but nasty bunkers around it.

Tralee Golf Club is a course everyone wants to play, so be sure to book well in advance. The weather in this part of the country can be particularly fickle, and our day at Tralee is one of the best arguments for self-guided touring rather than with a golf group. We drove out to the club from our B&B to try to change a morning tee time to afternoon because the weather was supposed to be better later. It was no problem to change to a 2:00 PM start. We watched, though, a group of Americans putting on their wet weather gear in order to brave heavy rains and 25 mph winds on one of the toughest courses in Ireland. The 16 person group had no other options because their bus would be back to pick them up after the round to shuffle them off to their next destination. After a leisurely morning visit to the Famine Museum and Blennerville Windmill [see Attractions], we returned to the golf course for lunch. As we ate we watched the bedraggled, soaked tour group return to the clubhouse just about the time the clouds started to break up. Anne and I played in a stronger than normal (we asked) wind, but we were dry our entire round (and I've got the pictures to prove it).

Course architect Arnold Palmer said of his work at Tralee, "I designed the first nine, but surely God designed the back nine." Tralee Golf Club, with a layout by the King and the Almighty, is indeed one of the premier golf destinations in the world.

**Comments from the Forward Tees:** A real challenge that requires shot strategy, but it's worth the effort. Tralee, like other Arnold Palmer designed courses I've played, are designed well for women. Par 3s are short, but complex. Par 5s are very long and will play even longer if the wind is against you. My experience at Tralee, at times both frustrating and exhilarating, was rewarding. I can hardly wait to try it again.

### WATERVILLE GOLF CLUB, Waterville, Ring of Kerry, Co. Kerry
On N70 (the Ring of Kerry Road) just south of Waterville village.
www.watervillegolflinks.ie (066) 947 4102
Links, 7000 yards, par 72, €150

**Amenities:** The modern clubhouse with locker and changing rooms, has a well stocked pro shop, and restaurant and bar with views to the links and bay. High quality food served all day with fresh seafood the specialty. The comfortable lounge has real peat fires. The club also boasts an excellent practice facility with driving range and golf school. Waterville House on the grounds offers upscale accommodations.

**Course Comments:** Waterville Golf Club was the result of technology. In the 1890s the transAtlantic cable, modernizing communication between Europe and the US, meant hundreds of workers were stationed at Waterville as the last Cable Station was built. Workers seeking recreation structured golf at Waterville in 1889. Only a year later the club was formed and affiliated with the Golf Union of Ireland officially bringing golf to Waterville. Technology was also the undoing of the course when in the 1950s new technologies made the Cable Station obsolete. The 9-hole course lay dormant through the sixties until architects Eddie Hackett and Claude Harmon (Masters Champion and head pro at Winged Foot GC) were commissioned to build a new Waterville course. The new course and clubhouse were opened in 1973 with the original 9 holes reconfigured and expanded into the new front nine. Tom Fazio, Augusta National's current official architect, has recently completed an update of the original course and clubhouse.

Waterville GC plays along the shore of Ballinskelligs Bay and the River Inny estuary with views of the bay, river, and head lands. The course is a classic links layout with challenges from sand dunes, gorse, native grasses, firm fairways, sod-faced or revetted bunkers, undulating putting surfaces, and the ever changing, but always demanding, weather. To help play on this difficult, world class track, Waterville GC affords five tee boxes to play from. Whatever tee you choose, be ready for a stern test. To give an indication of what is to come, the first hole is named *Last Easy.* This 430-yard (yards are used instead of meters on the cards) par 4 begins with a drive to a generous fairway between low dunes. Three bunkers left and one right add challenge to the drive. The fairway narrows as you approach the tiered green protected by bunkers on each side. Number 3, a par 4 of 417 yards plays along the bay the whole way. Again, bunkers left and right challenge your drive, while the green tucks into the bay for protection. The 4th, *Dunes,* a 179-yard one-shotter, is the first of several testing par 3s. The hole has a different look from each of the different tees, but all face a narrow chute between rough clad dunes to a flat green fronted by one large bunker. A creek runs along the right side and dunes are on the left of the 424-yard par 4 seventh. The hole plays up and over a fairway rise to the tiered green fronted by traps and surrounded by rough. The 9th, which heads back to the clubhouse, is a dogleg right par 4 of 445 yards with three bunkers left and two right off the tee. The approach to the green is complicated by fairway mounds, bunkers, and depressions which look closer to the green than they really are. The 12th is another challenging par 3. This 200-yarder plays over dunes and a low fairway to an elevated green backed by grassy dunes. One pot bunker on the right makes the drive even more difficult. *Vale,* the 428-yard par 4 fifteenth, is a seemingly simple hole with no bunkers to bother you. The trouble is that the fairway snakes left and then right around dunes. A drive to the right of the fairway may leave a blind approach. A short, but tricky hole is the 386-yard par 4 sixteenth. The hole is a dogleg left with a series of dunes left and the bay right. The heavily swaled green needs no bunkers. The last of the wonderful par 3s is *Mulcahy's Peak,* the 196-yard 17th. The drive is over dunes and rough to a large undulating green. A slice on this hole will find the beach.

Play Waterville in the wind and the course can be brutal. Play it on a calm day and it will still be plenty of challenge. But play it you should.

**Comments from the Forward Tees:** Sometimes a course will move the ladies' tees so far up as to take all the fun away from the hole, but not at Waterville. The forward tees here give plenty of length advantage without changing the basic difficulties or challenges of the hole.

## Other Courses in the Region:

Adare Manor Hotel & Golf Resort (18), Adare, Co. Limerick
(061) 395 044
Ballyheigue Castle Golf Club (9), Ballyheigue, Co. Kerry
(066) 713 3555
Beaufort Golf Course, Beaufort (18), Co. Kerry (064) 44 440
Berehaven Golf Club, Castletownbere (9), Co. Cork
(027) 70 700
Castle Island GC (18), Castle Island, Co. Kerry
(066) 714 1709
Kenmare Golf Club (18), Kenmare, Co. Kerry (064) 41 291
Killorglin Golf Club (18), Killorglin, Co. Kerry (066) 976 1979
Limerick Golf Club (18), Ballyclough, Limerick, Co. Limerick
(061) 414 083
Listowel Golf Club (27), Listowel, Co. Kerry (068) 21 592
Ring of Kerry Golf & Country Club (18), Kenmare, Co. Kerry
(064) 42 000
Ross Golf Club, Killarney (9), Co. Kerry (064) 31 125

## PUBS AND EATERIES

In this section of Ireland good food and good music are plentiful. We've visited a number of upscale eateries, not always with pleasing results. We have also discovered some real gems. In one village pub we held a conversation with a local sitting at his normal spot, not at the bar but on the bar. Often the problem is not can we find a good place for a meal, but rather which of the good ones do we want to go back to. Especially in Dingle it's a matter of having only so many days, so which of the great places do we skip?

**Ashe's Pub** on Lower Main Street in Dingle, Co. Kerry, up from the harbour on the east end of the shopping district. Classic Irish pub and restaurant with plenty of memorabilia from *Ceann Sibeal* GC. The pub is over a hundred years old and has a tradition of well-prepared meals.

**The Atlantic Bar** on the square in Kenmare. This authentic Irish pub is popular with both tourists and locals. Food freshly prepared and available all day. In an area with a multitude of pub and restaurant choices, owners Margaret and Michael O'Sullivan continue to create a winning formula of service and quality.

**Betty's Bar** 101 Strand Street, a few blocks off the downtown area in an older residential section of Tralee. Old neighborhood drinking pub; "Cheers," where everyone knows everyone. Betty's is designed as a serious social and drinking pub. And serves no food. What's food? Guinness is food. I think some peanuts were available. When we first visited, before the ban on smoking in pubs, you could watch the level of smoke lower as the night got later. Most people were standing and talking, even though a great session was in progress. We visited with a local, who gave Anne his stool at the bar. We chatted about world politics and other unimportant matters until he looked at his watch and said, "Oops, time to go." With a quick good-bye he stumbled out of the bar into the darkness. We gave up our one stool and moved down to sit with the musicians who were warming up. A wonderful place to experience the local pub scene. We were the only visitors in the place.

*Curragower* **Seafood Bar** on Clancy Strand in Limerick overlooking King John's Castle. The atmosphere is that of a real Irish pub: friendly staff, local memorabilia on the walls, and lots of good craic. With a prime in-town location along the river, customers can enjoy the views from the terrace garden in good weather. The *Curragower* Seafood Bar may be small on the outside (it calls itself the smallest bar in Ireland), but with a maze of little rooms inside, the bar has plenty of room for visitors.

**Danny Mann's Restaurant and Pub** on New Street near the center of Killarney, Co. Kerry. This Super Pub (meaning big, with many areas for gathering) has a typical, but complete menu. Food is good. Danny Mann's is a popular pub with families and for the music later in the evening. A mix of locals and tourists were in the pub the evening we visited. Wait staff seemed disorganized, except for our server who was very good. We did get a strange impression of Danny Mann's. At 8:30 the band set up to play an hour later. Then at 8:45 a screen dropped down in front of the stage, and as the band warmed up behind the screen, a video/film about Irish dancing showed on the screen with no sound. At 9:00, as the movie continued, Irish music played with no relation to the film. Strange.

**Dolan's** along the waterfront (Shannon River) a few blocks from downtown Limerick. Traditional Irish pub first opened in 1878. Super busy when music is on the menu. People standing three deep at the bar. The crowd is made up of students, business people, and a few tourists. The food is very good at this pub better known for its music and Guinness. We had a good, generous lamb stew. Music was supposed to start at 9:30, and finally got going after 10:00. It was a typical example of a schedule according to Irish Time ("when we get around to it"). A great session in the evening we visited had an older drummer who sat under a sign which read, "Reserved for Musicians." His glasses slipped down his nose, his baseball cap was askew, and he seemed asleep when he wasn't playing. One sign of life was that every once in a while he'd sip his Guinness.

**Flesk's Restaurant** on High Street in Killarney.  Flesk's (named after a local river) is a restaurant with two themes. First, American Legion plates from local posts in America are hung around the room (the owner has an American Legion connection). Secondly, walls are decorated with paintings of local golf courses. A small bar is in the back. Flesk's offers a full restaurant menu with a page of Lite Bites (two lamb chops instead of three). The restaurant also offers an "Early Bird" special of three euros off an entree from 5:00 to 7:00 each day.

**Foley's Pub** on the main street of Kenmare.  Typical pub set up around a horseshoe bar has a small pub menu, but specializes in pizza.  We sat at the bar with an American microbiology professor from a college on the east coast and his wife on their first trip to Ireland (they loved the country). They had a pizza and said it was great. The next night we went back to try the seafood pizza. It was excellent. The music was good each night, too. A folk singer one night (even got some John Denver tunes) and a traditional duo the next. Traditional or folk most evenings.

**John Benny's Pub and Restaurant** on Strand Street in Dingle, Co. Kerry, across from the harbour.  A traditional pub and a great venue for traditional music. Owner John Benny is a musician and often plays. Music almost every night. Monday is Traditional Irish and Set Dancing, and on Wednesday the emphasis is on singing. Food it tasty and plentiful.  Can get quite raucous in season on weekends.

**Mickey Ned's Pub and Restaurant** in Kenmare, Co. Kerry, at the end of town across from the Tourist Office. Modern, upscale bar and restaurant has a very broad selection of elegant starters and mains. Fine dining in simple, elegant surroundings. When we visited, the big screen TV was showing Olympic Show Jumping and an Irish participant was up for the gold. The TV didn't intrude on our dining (in the front room), but when the back room erupted in cheers we had to go see what the commotion was about. We found that Olympic spirit exhibited all over Ireland that trip. Every village with any connection to an Olympian had signs of support proudly in display. The show of support in this pub was particularly appropriate for a bar named for the owner Mickey Ned, one of Ireland's famous rugby players.

**Molly Darcy's Traditional Irish Pub and Restaurant** is south of Killarney on N71 about a half mile from Muckross House. This old coaching inn has a large restaurant menu except on Sunday when they offer a "carvery" all afternoon. Has received many awards including Dining Pub of the Year.

**Ned Natterjacks** in the village of Castlegregory, Co. Kerry. The name of the pub derives from the indigenous endangered Natterjack Toad (at home on both Castlegregory and Dooks golf courses). A lively place all through summer, Ned Natterjacks is a good stop for a pint, meal, or craic any time of the year. "Ol, *ceol agus craic"* - "Good drink, music, and fun."

**The Old Smokehouse** in Dingle where Lower Main Street meets Mall Street. The Old Smokehouse is a very good choice in a town with many good choices. The atmosphere is typical Irish with efficient, friendly service and generous portions. The quality of the food is outstanding. The clientele is usually a mix of locals and tourists. On one visit we saw across the room an older gentleman in an Aran sweater eating. He looked like an Irish "character" until he pulled out his mobile phone (cell phone to us) and started texting as fast as any teenager. Proof that Ireland is changing.

**Out of the Blue** on the waterfront in Dingle across from the pier. Don't come here unless you want fish; nothing else is on the menu. But if you love fresh, well-prepared seafood, don't miss an opportunity to visit Out of the Blue. We've been a couple of times and the service was outstanding and the food delicious. The place is small; book ahead or be prepared to wait. If the weather is pleasant, the waiting wouldn't be bad since the restaurant is located on lovely Dingle harbour. Has won "Best Seafood in Ireland" awards more than once.

**The Oyster Tavern & Seafood Restaurant** three miles west of Tralee on R558. Extensive seafood menu including local catches and a fish from New Zealand (Red Emperor). The menu also contains a full page of meat dishes. Prices were reasonable for fine dining and portions were large. Comes highly recommended.

**The Queen's Hotel** on the main street of Newcastle West village, Co. Limerick. A pleasantly comfortable pub with good food. We shared a couple of sandwich specials which were tasty. Mostly locals and shoppers. Be careful when driving in this narrow streeted town.

**Sheehan's Traditional Irish Pub** on Main Street in Killarney near the church. Tradition pub—what tourists would expect to see—which doesn't serve food, only drinks and music. The Guinness is as good as anyplace, and the music is better than most.

**Stoker's Lodge** on N69 as you come into Tralee from the north. Railroad themed restaurant with photos, prints, and railroad memorabilia. Popular with locals, therefore very busy and noisy. Good service even though busy. Food was well prepared and high quality. The name, Stoker's, comes from stoking the engines of steam trains.

**The Tankard Bar and Restaurant** in Fenit about five miles out of Tralee on R558. The tavern gets its name from the mugs or steins (tankards) people used to bring in for their beer. These tankards were then hung over the bar until their next use. The tankards are now gone, but the name remains. Separate menus for the bar and the restaurant, but in the pub you can order off either. Typical pub menu, but it did include a Salmon Boxty (smoked salmon with a potato pancake and salad). Restaurant menu is extensive (two pages of "New Beginnings" or starters), specializing in seafood and steaks. Recommended by Tralee GC staff.

*Tish 'n tSaorsaig* in the center of the small village of Ballyferriter on the Dingle Peninsula. *Tish 'n tSaorsaig* (House of Seers) pub is an old local establishment. It's small with several seating areas and a small bar. Besides local area maps, the unusual decoration is paper money from around the world pinned over the bar. A limited pub menu is served all day (mostly soup and sandwiches). The food was very tasty. On a Sunday afternoon in May, we were outnumbered by the five locals at the bar (one literally sitting on the bar). A few unusual signs caught our attention: "Do you want to talk to the man in charge, or the lady who knows what's going on," "Eat, drink and be fat and drunk." And our favorite, "I've spent most of my life playing golf; the rest of the time I've wasted."

*Ua Flatbeartais* **(O'Flaherty's)** on Bridge Street in Dingle, Co. Kerry, at the south end of town. O'Flaherty's is a drinking (no food) and music pub. It's both a local's hangout and an attraction for tourists. There's nothing fancy about the pub: cement floors, benches and stools, bright, stark lighting. Walls are decorated with old posters including a Gerry Adams (Sinn Fein) Before the Dawn (autobiography) poster. You've got to stop by O'Flaherty's if you are visiting Dingle—more than once. Stop in a quiet afternoon so you can really see the place. Stop in the early evening to see the pub in action. Stop late at night to be there for the end of a session. You never know what might happen. One night we saw a young girl (and her mother) from Arizona stop in to try to play with some session players. The cordial Irish players invited her to grab her guitar and play. She only knew bluegrass (which she thought was Irish), but the local players followed her lead, and then gently left her in their dust. It was slightly painful to see that she didn't know how badly she was outclassed, but musically it was exciting.

**The Wild Onion Bakeshop and Cafe** on High Street in Limerick. Famous for its American-style breakfast (including French toast, American pork sausage with eggs and hashbrowns), lunch (American hamburgers), and sweets (American carrot cake with cream cheese frosting). Several years ago Bob and Ruth DiGirolamo moved from Chicago to bring a bit of America to Ireland. They succeeded well. The cafe is still Irish enough to be recommended by the Bridgestone Guide.

## *ATTRACTIONS*

For the non-golfer, those non-golfing days, or for before or after golf, the southwest of Ireland offers a variety of attractions with emphasis upon scenic beauty. We'll begin on the **Beara Peninsula.** The peninsula, partly in Co. Cork and mostly in Co. Kerry, is less spoiled by tourism than the Ring of Kerry or the Dingle Peninsula. That also means that the area is less developed. Begin your tour at Kenmare and drive southwest on R571 as it skirts lovely Kenmare River to Coulagh Bay. Just past the brightly painted Eyeries Village, turn right on R575 which heads out toward the wide open Atlantic. A short side trip on R572 will bring you to one of Ireland's unique attractions, the **Cable Railway to Dursey Island.** Built in 1970 and designed to carry six people or one man and his cow the 250 yards from the mainland to the island, the cable car runs every fifteen minutes for two hours in the morning and again in the afternoon. On the island the ruins of St. Michael's Chapel and a 16C monastery are within easy walking distance. Continuing around the Beara Peninsula to visit the village of **Castletown,** the largest spot of civilization on the peninsula, where Russian factory ships moor in the harbour. Nearby is the **Derrintaggart stone circle,** a bronze age alignment on farmland signposted just west of the village. Like many of the antiquities on private land in Ireland, the farmer asks for a small fee or donation, which in this case is promised to charity. Also nearby is **Dunboy Castle** (admission fee), a park containing ruins of both Puxley's Castle and Dunboy Castle. Continue on R572 to Glengarriff with a side trip from Adrigole up to the **Healy Pass** with a spectacular panorama of Glanmore Lake below; or skip Glengarriff (hopefully you've already played the course) and continue over the pass to hook up again with R571 back to Kenmare. All around the perimeter of Beara be sure to stop at the numerous **vista points** for some of Ireland's most dramatic scenery. Kenmare, between the Beara Peninsula and the Ring of Kerry, has more in town than good eateries and great music pubs. Kenmare has it own stone circle a few hundred yards from the main town square. The **Kenmare stone circle** is the largest in the area consisting of several large boulders set in an egg-shaped configuration more than fifty feet across.

Kenmare is a good point from which to start a tour of the **Ring of Kerry** (the common name for the *Iveragh* Peninsula). When contemplating a visit to the Ring, most guides suggest you travel counterclockwise around the Ring (Kenmare - Sneem - Waterville - Killorglin - Killarney) in order to not have to follow the myriad tour buses traveling the Ring. On advice from locals, we did just the opposite and were happy with our decision. By traveling the same route as the buses we avoid having to meet a large greyhound bus head-on on corners that would be tight for two cars to pass. The Ring road is well paved, but at some points is very narrow especially along steep cliffs. We actually saw a tour bus push two cars off the road (they literally had to back up into a ditch) because the bus was coming through and he was a great deal larger than the cars. We've put up with a slower pace and some diesel exhaust fumes, but that was better than a head on encounter with something that takes up three-fourths of the road at its widest. The exception to this suggestion is if you are heading to Waterville or Valencia Island and expect to get to your destination before about 1 PM. It takes the tour buses from Killarney about that long to get to those spots. If you can get there before the buses and come back with them, counterclockwise is okay for the first part.

From Kenmare it's 29 km (18 miles) on N71 to Killarney. Along the way stop first at **Moll's Gap** where R568 from Sneem junctions with N71. Here is a typical tourist stop at the Avoca Restaurant and Gift Shop, but here also are some fine vistas. On the way into Killarney you will pass numerous pullouts which will provide opportunities for views of streams and Upper Lake in the **Killarney National Park.** The park, Ireland's first designated national park, encompasses three lovely, rhoddy enriched lakes: Lower Lake known as Lough Leane, Middle Lake known as Muckross Lake, and Upper Lake known simply as Upper Lake. Also in the park, just before reaching Killarney, is the **Muckross House and Gardens** complex. The neo-Tudor style mansion, the 1448 home of clan chieftain MacCarthy Mor, is available for touring and is surrounded by a gorgeous garden/park with horse and buggy tours also available. The house and gardens are definitely worth your time to visit, and the buggy ride is a nice tour, if you're into that kind of thing. The grounds are home as well to the fine 15C ruins of **Muckross Friary.** A couple of miles closer to town **Ross Castle,** set beside Lough Leane, is open for touring and worth a visit. It was here we saw a holder for a reed that had been dipped in tallow. The reed candle was then set on the horizontal holder and both ends were lighted. Thus, we have the expression, burning your candle at both ends. The tourist town **Killarney** is quite an attraction itself. Plenty of opportunities exist to hear good session music in the evenings, and plenty of tourist shops are available during the day.

Leaving Killarney on N72 heading toward Killorglin, it's only about 9 miles to the turnoff to Dunloe GC, Kate Kearney's

Cottage and the Gap of Dunloe. **Kate Kearney's Cottage,** part pub and part gift shop, sits at the parking lot entrance to the Gap of Dunloe. You should take the time to visit Kate's Cottage for a pint, a coffee or a tea, and to see the old coaching inn that has remained unchanged for years. The **Gap of Dunloe** is a road (vehicle traffic is limited to locals or horse and buggy) from Kate's Cottage to Moll's Gap or Upper Lake on the other side of the park. The path through the narrow rock strewn gorge affords wonderful views of lakes, peat bogs, the MacGillycuddy Reeks, and the Tomes and Purple Mountains. The 20 plus mile trip is worth it for those with the time. For the rest of us, don't be tempted to take the buggy trip (short and expensive), instead walk a couple of miles into the Gap to get a feel and some alluring views.

Back out on N72, turn left onto N70 at Killorglin. The road which takes you to Dooks GC also passes **Kerry Bog Village,** a commercial representation of what an early small Irish village near a peat bog would be like. Although the village is a model with an admission fee, it is interesting and educational. Our visit was less expensive than normal because we pulled in just behind a tour bus. When paying our entrance fee, it was assumed that we were part of the group and so got the group rate. Regardless, it's worth paying the full price. From here to Valencia Island, the Ring road passes some lovely beaches (particularly Kells Beach near King's Head) and spectacular panoramas. Leave N70 a few miles past Cahersiveen Village on R565 to Portmagee and Valencia Island. Just across the bridge from Portmagee on the island is the **Skellig Heritage Centre.** The centre explains the history of Skellig Michael (Greater) and Little Skellig, two small islands about seven miles off shore where St. Finian established an early Christian monastery in the 6C. **Skellig Michael** can be visited by boat from Portmagee, but the crossing is often rough and the island has 2300 steps cut into the rock by St. Finian's followers. The heritage centre is a good place to learn about the many seabirds in the area.

Continuing on N70 through Waterville (An *CoireAn,* meaning Little Whirlpool)), a village known for its golf course, fine angling, and celebrities such as Charlie Chaplin who have made it a stopping point, starts the swing back inland along the Kenmare River. About 28 km (16 miles) from Waterville is a turnoff (signed) to **Staigue Fort,** a splendid round stone fort dating to between 300 and 400 AD. The fort is probably the defensive residence of a local king, but nobody knows for sure. When we visited in 2002, we ran into an example of the "ugly tourist." With signs every few yards asking visitors not to climb on the stones, a car load of tourists arrived behind us and immediately started climbing up every wall they could find. I tried hard to get a picture of one standing above a sign, but they moved too quickly. Please remember, just because an antiquity has lasted 1700 years is no reason to believe it can stand up to anything. Aside from the colorful village of Sneem, the rest of the Ring is just a pleasant drive on a narrow country road. From Sneem we'd suggest taking R568 to Moll's Gap rather than continuing on N70 to Kenmare, if you started in Killarney. The road to Moll's Gap is more scenic especially as you near the Gap. The Ring of Kerry can certainly be a full day trip, although you can see most of the attractions and still have time for nine at Parknasilla or Glengarriff. If the weather is bad, cloudy or foggy, wait for better conditions to tour the Ring of Kerry, because it's really all about the views.

The next peninsula over is the Dingle Peninsula, which offers as dramatic views as the Ring and has many more ancient attractions. From Castlemaine on the N70 north of Killorglin, turn onto R561 and drive along the cliffs above Castlemaine Harbour. A view point at Inch offers visitors views of the harbour, Inch Beach, and Dingle Bay. From this viewpoint you can actually see Dooks GC with binoculars. The road winds along the coast until moving inland to meet up with N86 near Anascaul. An interesting stop in the village is the **South Pole Inn,** a pub of rather special distinction. Tom Crean established the pub in 1920 when he retired as second officer to famous Irish explorer Sir Ernest Shackleton (born in Co. Kildare). The pub is almost a museum of Crean and Shackleton memorabilia. West on N86 it's 18 km (11 miles) to one of Ireland's most popular tourist town, **Dingle.** Dingle, or

*An Daigean* in Gaelic, is a town of about 1500 residents and, at any time of year, at least that many tourists. The town offers great shopping, lots of pubs, the harbour, and the dolphin Fungie, a resident in the harbour since 1983. Two places we would suggest as Must Stops are first **An Cafe Liteartha,** on Dykegate Street. This cafe/bookshop specializes in all things Gaelic, including the language. We've watched a group of Americans sit down in the cafe, try to read the Gaelic menu on the wall, hear the Gaelic conversations around them, and get up and walk out in frustration. We find the place and the people charming, and the soup very tasty. We asked in English about the menu and were responded to in English. I love going back there just to listen to the beautiful Gaelic dialect. A second stop, **Dingle Record Shop** on Green Street, is for anyone interested in Irish music. Owner Mazz O'Flaherty is a fascinating character. She is a player, singer, songwriter, artist, and mystic. We walked in one bitterly cold spring afternoon after a round at Dooks. Anne had her arms crossed in front of her for warmth. Mazz asked what kind of body language that was. Anne said her hands were so cold. Mazz took Anne's hands in hers and chanted in Gaelic while rubbing Anne's hands. After about a minute, she said that should help. Anne said her hands weren't cold the rest of the day. Mazz knows her music as well, and set me up with some wonderful recordings I couldn't get at home. I took a couple of pictures of Mazz, and she scoffed and said those won't turn out. When I got home and downloaded all my photos, two were missing. The two I'd taken of Mazz O'Flaherty in Dingle Record Shop. Whether you're in the market for CDs or not, stop in Mazz's shop, just for the experience. You should also stop into one of three special pubs in Dingle. These establishments are merchants by day and pubs at night. Foxy John's is a cobbler's shop during the day; Curran's is a clothier; and Dick Mack's is a hardware store. Stop in for a pint at one or all— they are very lively places in the evening.

The Dingle Peninsula's main road is almost as narrow as the Ring of Kerry road, but affords more and better vistas. From Dingle take R559 in a counterclockwise loop (you would run into very few tour buses) and at Fahan stop to explore one of two sets of **beehive huts** (clochans), stone dwellings from the early Christian days. The first set is easier to find, but a little more commercial. Just past the beehive huts is **Dunbeg Promontory Fort** which seems to hang out on the edge of the sea cliffs. Stonehouse Restaurant, the completely stone pub across from the fort is fascinating, but we've always visited too early in the day to find it open. I'd think it would be worth a visit. Continuing around the peninsula, ford the stream (that's right, a stream crosses over the road and not under it) and be sure to stop at one or all the vista points by Slea Head, which all look out to the Blasket Islands. Just a little ways further that's our next stop, the **Blasket Island Centre.** The centre is a museum dedicated to the Blasket Islands and people and the writers who populated the islands. Displays and a great audiovisual show tell the story of why the Blaskets were abandoned in the 1950s. Ballyferriter is a good place to stop for a coffee, tea, or pint before seeking out one of Ireland's special treasures, the **Gallarus Oratory.** The oratory is a 1200 year old stone chapel in the shape of an inverted boat. The chapel was built just by fitting the stones together, no mortar was used. Amazingly, the chapel hasn't leaked in 1200 years —the floor is bone dry even in the nastiest of weather. Not far from Gallarus is **Kilmakedar Church,** built in the 12C and whose cemetery houses an ancient sundial and an Ogham stone (early Celtic writing system). Make sure you have the correct church. One down the road from Kilmakedar has a sign on it saying in effect: "This isn't the church you want; it's down the road." N86 then returns to Dingle and heads toward Tralee.

You can either take the more major N86 to Tralee from Dingle or, if the weather is decent, drive the **Conner Pass** (*conair*) road, the highest pass in Ireland at about 1500 feet. The road is fine, but especially heading down toward Tralee it's not for the faint of heart. On a clear day the views are literally breathtaking, because even on a good day the wind howls on the pass. About a mile east of the summit is a turnout for a waterfall. It's a pretty spot, but if you scramble up the rocks you find a lovely small lake.

Tralee's attractions aren't really in Tralee. Just south of town is the **Blennerville Visitor's Centre and Windmill.** We had always bypassed the windmill and centre as looking too touristy. That was a mistake. The windmill is still in operating condition (if the wind isn't too strong) and the Visitor's Centre houses a museum dedicated to the emigrant ships, such as the "Jeanie Johnson." Both were very informative. On the other side of Tralee near the golf course is the **Ardfert Cathedral and Friary.** The 13C cathedral occupies ground that once was a monastery founded by St. Brenden the Navigator, and the friary is 13C Franciscan.

The two final attractions we describe in no way exhausts all there is to see and do in this section of Ireland. All the attractions we list are simply our picks from what we've been able to see and do. A place where we've stopped several different times is the thatched roof village of **Adare** on N69, the route from Tralee to Limerick. The main street of town is lined with quaint beautiful houses and shops, most with thatched roofs (which we understand last as long as 80 years). The large church on Main Street is a transformation of a 13C Trinitarian Abbey, and behind are ruins of a 14C Augustinian Priory and a 15C Franciscan Friary. Across from the church is a beautiful and peaceful village park, whose trees will provide shelter from the rain if you leave your umbrella in the car as we did. Finally, we come to Limerick, the Republic's fourth largest city after Dublin, Cork, and Galway. Limerick has been made even more famous by Frank McCourt's book *Angela's Ashes* (Pulitzer Prize winner in 1997), a story about growing up in the city in the 1930s and 1940s. The main attraction in town, other than the Shannon River, is **King John's Castle.** Located in the center of town, the castle was begun in the 1200s on the site of a Viking settlement. The self-guided tour of the castle is informative and the views out over the city are worth the admission.

# Chapter Four:
# The West — Golf, Pubs and Attractions

Ennis GC, Co. Clare

## GOLF

If you are heading north from Tralee, you have two possible routes. First, you could take N20 east and then north to Limerick through Abbeyfeale and Adare. A more direct route is to drive N69 from Tralee through Listowel to Tarbert where you pick up the ferry across the Shannon River to Kilrush. But whatever way you go, there's great golf (some little known and some world known) in the west of Ireland.

**ATHENRY GOLF CLUB, Palmerstown, Oranmore, Co. Galway**

Take the Athenry exit (R348) off M6 to Derrydonnell road towards Oranmore, course is on the left.

www.athenrygolfclub.net (091) 794 466

Parkland, 5602 yards, par 70, €25

**Amenities:** Nice clubhouse (1991) has changing rooms and lounge which serves pub meals most usual hours. Small pro shop with most of your golfing needs.

**Course Comments:** Two interesting features to note about Athenry (ATH-en-rye) Golf Club are the club's history and its archeology. First, the history of Athenry is the story of a club looking for a place to play. The original club was located in Rodefield in 1902, then moved to Raheen in the 1930s, and Mounbawn in 1957, and finally came to Palmerstown in 1977. The Palmerstown course was redesigned by famed Irish architect Eddie Hackett in 1991. Hackett's design was upgraded in 1995 with new 17th and 18th holes. It certainly hasn't been a club to stand still. In fact, the first greens at the current course were compacted by foot power—club members walking the greens over and over. Another interesting historical note is that in 1952 Santa Claus landed on the course by helicopter. It was the first Santa for the town. The second feature of the club is the archeology of the course area. On the course are four ring-barrows ("circular ditch or fosse, the material from which has been thrown up outside it forming an enclosing circular bank," *100 Years of Golf*, Rynne). These are roughly aligned SW to NE for a distance of 240 metres. The ring-barrows are believed to be Celtic burial monuments dated to around the birth of Christ. One is in the middle of the 9th fairway, one was a bunker near the first green (the bunker was relocated), the others are on the 13th and 14th fairways.

Besides its interesting historical and archeological features, the course features some good golf holes as well. The 1st, a 349-yard par 4, is a good starting hole. It has a tight fairway, but the rough is not too penal on this slight dogleg left. Bunkers protect the green as do trees on the right. The 7th is the longest par 4 at 417 yards and the hole is rated the toughest on the course. The long two-shotter has plenty of room for your drive. The trouble comes from the bunkers fronting the green and on the sides. The green is a small target to approach with a mid to long iron. A sharp dogleg left, the par 4, 377-yard 13th has a copse of mature trees protecting the inside corner. Typical of the course, traps on each side of the green make accuracy the key to scoring well. The par 3 17th (143 yards) has trees all along the left which encroach on the entry to the green. Bunkers on both sides again protect the green which has a definite right to left slope. The finishing hole is not the longest par 4 on the course at 331 yards, but it's still a challenging end to your round. Trees line both sides of the fairway and bunkers can cause trouble on both your drive and approach to the green which is tricky to putt. Athenry Golf Club is interesting for several reasons: the history of the course, its ancient sites, and well designed holes.

### BEARNA (*Bhearna*) GOLF CLUB, Corboley, Bearna, Co. Galway

Take R336 (the coast road) west from Galway to the village of Barna and turn right at the only stop light in town. Course is 2.5 km up the road.
www.bearnagolfclub.com  (091) 592 677
Mountain top moorland, 6174 metres, par 72, €30

**Amenities:** *Thawnaghard* ("a green fertile place in high wasteland"), the Bearna clubhouse, affords views of 16 of the 18 greens from the lovely lounge. Locals point out that the clubhouse is 265 feet above the sea, but that in the lounge you can get as high as you like. The lounge serves meals all day from an interesting menu. Changing rooms and a small gift/pro shop with golfer essentials are below the lounge.

**Course Comments:** The motto of Bearna Golf and Country Club (pronounced "BARN-a") is: "Failte *agus Ceol na*

*Fuiseuige leat"* meaning "Welcome, and may the lark song accompany you." It's a very nice wish since larks only sing when it's not raining. The course, a 1996 design by Bobby Browne, the pro at Laytown and Bettystown Golf Club near Dublin, is a moorland track set on a hill top with grand vistas of Galway Bay, The Burren, Aran Islands, and the Clare hills. Bearna is a sea of green and yellow in the spring when the gorse blooms, and a sea of red and green in the fall when the heather blooms. Although the layout provides generous fairways, plenty of challenges await. Set on a hill top only a couple of miles from the ocean, the wind can be a factor even on calm days. The rough is tough grass and heather surrounding large patches of unforgiving gorse. The 27 bunkers at Bearna are almost all greenside and fairly flat. Most of the greens are large and quick, with some undulations, false fronts, or side roll-offs. Water in the form of creeks, ponds, and Lough Inch, is in play on 13 holes. A nice feature of the Bearna scorecard is that *Na Poill* (the holes) are given with their Gaelic names and English translations.

The 6th, *Sean-Bhother na Mona* ("The Old Bog Road") is typical of the interesting holes at Bearna. Water and heavy grass rough are the problems on this long, 405-metre, two-shotter. The first shot needs to avoid the creek and pond on the left. The elevated green is protected by a bunker on the right. As on many of the holes at Bearna, extra tee boxes are provided so that the grounds crew can alternate tees and keep them in good shape. *Ionnsai na Hinse* ("The Attack on Lough Inch") is the 350-metre par 4 eleventh. With a pond on the right in the rough (in play with a slice), a corner of the lough and the creek flowing into it endangering your approach, the 11th is a demanding hole. The green, guarded by large bunkers on both sides, is severely sloped at the front. Another slope-front green is on *Loch Toirmeasctha* ("The Forbidden Lake"), the 120-metre par 3 thirteenth. Short but testing is the best description of this hole. Your tee shot must clear a corner of a pond to reach the large green. Bailout room is to the right, but two bunkers are on that side as well. The 15th, *An Tulan Cleasach* ("The Mischievous Mound") is a sharp dogleg left around a mound covered in heavy rough. It's too far to cut the corner on this 345-metre par 4, so being long enough to get past the corner and short enough not to run out of fairway (250 metres) is the key to the hole. The green is narrow and guarded by two traps. Eleven, 13, and 15 are three holes that designer Bobby Browne ranks as his favorites. I believe that *Ladhar na Bo Bradai* ("The High Ground of the Thieving Cow, Between Two Valleys") should make a favorites list for its name, if for no other reason. This 170-metre par 3 makes an interesting finish with a creek and whins (gorse) fronting a very raised, two-tiered green protected by slopes and two bunkers on the right. Left is the safe miss on this hole. Bearna Golf Club is a top notch facility from the spectacular clubhouse to the well conditioned, interestingly designed course. Near the popular Galway City area, the course can be busy. Be sure to plan a round at Bearna well in advance.

### BALLINROBE GOLF CLUB, Cloonacastle, Ballinrobe, Co. Mayo
Three km northeast of the village on R331.
www.ballinrobegolfclub.com (094) 954 1118
Parkland, 6354 metres, par 73, €20

**Amenities:** The old farmhouse and stone outbuildings provide a wonderful rustic lounge, changing rooms, and small pro shop. The club has a nice lighted driving range and short game practice area, as well. Good quality food is served in the pub usual hours. It was here that our playing partners, two ladies from Dublin, told us about Rock Shandies, a mix of special orange club and lemon club (special Coke products only available in Ireland). It makes the most refreshing nonalcoholic drink for after a round. The closest I can get to it in the states is a mix of orange juice and ginger ale with a dash of bitters. Give it a try in Ireland.

**Course Comments:** For the centenary of Ballinrobe Golf Club (1995) the lovely parkland course received a major face-lift by famed architect Eddie Hackett. The beautifully landscaped and manicured course gives players views of the

Robe River on several holes. The course also boasts the ruins of 13C Cloonacastle Tower, a lime kiln, ancient stone fences, and a set of sculptured stones representing the history of County Mayo. And then there are the trees of Ballinrobe GC. The registry of plantings at Cloonacastle Estate (1803) shows the planting details for 24,200 trees (firs, oak, ash, beech, alder, elm, birch, mountain ash, sycamore, whitethorn, aspen, and various fruit trees). I think my ball found most of them as I played Ballinrobe. Besides the trees to challenge your play are 29 bunkers, mostly greenside and large. Most of the bunkers are very much in play, with good sand. Greens are moderately large, and though some are undulating, all have subtle breaks. Ponds come into play on eight holes, most significantly on 6, 8, 9, 10, and 13.

Playable all year because of its limestone base, Ballinrobe is both tough and fair. The par 5, 487-metre 4th is a double dogleg right and then left with a fairway that makes its way between two sections of stone fence. Stay to the middle to avoid the trees and OB on the left. As you approach the green avoid the huge fronting bunker on the left side of a large green with more bunkers right and behind. The 302-metre 9th starts with a drive over the pond in front of the forward tee (a true concern for the ladies) to a wide fairway. Avoid the two fairway traps on the right and one on the left. A pond further to the right is only in play for the wildest slices. The green has trees left and a large bunker right. As you pass, be sure to notice the decorative standing stones to the left of the first pond. The 10th, a short par 4 of 365 metres, is rated the second most difficult hole for good reason. Tee off beside a 13C tower house to a broad fairway with OB all along the left. The biggest problem will be to try from a downhill lie to cross a pond which fronts the entire green. The water is all the defense the green needs. The hole plays as a par 5 for ladies because of the water. The 16th is a tremendous par 3 of 160 metres. To reach the lifted green you must defy a huge penal bunker which runs the length of the green. The finishing hole is a short par 5 (455-metres) where you tee off from an elevated box next to an old lime kiln. The fairway doglegs left and you want to stay left because a line of mature trees runs down the right side of the hole and overhang the green. The hole is particularly lovely with the trees framing the green and clubhouse behind. Ballinrobe Golf Club is a popular, busy course. It's a fine parkland track that deserves to be on every golfer's agenda when in Co. Mayo. Even Padraic Harrington has said that Ballinrobe is one of the finest courses in the west of Ireland.

**Comments from the Forward Tees:** A difficult course for ladies because of the water, trees, and bunkers to give trouble. Nice variety in the views and holes. Tee shots are fair and challenging. We played with two ladies from Dublin whole were playing in a golf tour tournament in the area. On their free day, they chose to play Ballinrobe.

### CONNEMARA CHAMPIONSHIP GOLF LINKS (aka Ballyconneely),Ballyconneely, Clifden, Co. Galway

Take N59 west from Galway or N59 south from Westport to Clifton. Follow signs on the coast road then right at Ballyconneely (Keongh's Pub). Take the first right past Bunsen Castle to club entrance.

www.connemaragolflinks.com  (095) 23 502
Links, 7055 yards, par 72, €85

**Amenities:** The 1983 modern clubhouse has changing rooms downstairs and a lounge/bar upstairs which serves quality food the usual hours (8 AM to 11 PM). Also downstairs is a well stocked pro shop with helpful and friendly staff.

**Course Comments:** Connemara Championship Golf Links must be considered one of Ireland's premier links courses. Actually, two courses (an 18 and a 9-hole—the club now lists them as three nines, A, B, and C) occupy some of Ireland's most beautiful gently undulating linksland with views of quaint Irish farmhouses, loughs, the Atlantic, islands, mountains of the Connemara Peninsula, and the Twelve Ben Mountains. On a sunny day no more beautiful place in the world exists, unspoiled and uncluttered. The Eddie Hackett and Tom Craddock designed Old Course (A and B nines), if 1973 could be considered "old," plays through the rock strewn links, while the new nine (C nine), built in 1997, plays more on higher ground and nearer the water. Neither are easy. If you are lucky enough to play on a windless day (which means the wind blowing 10 mph or less), you will not see the real teeth of Connemara, but the course will still present plenty of challenges. On the Championship Links (nines A and B) are 78 bunkers, all in play, but all can be avoided. Watch out for the pot bunkers—we've heard that some golfers will spend hours trying to get out. The Old Course has moderate sized greens, but those on the third nine tend to be large. The greens at Ballyconneely are quick, as are most links greens, and have interesting twists and turns. The Championship course has three creeks in play, while the second course has water on four holes (mostly ponds). The other challenge at Connemara is the links grass which is very tight on the fairways and tall and tough off the fairways.

The Championship course at Connemara treats you kindly at first, and then tests you on the back (B) nine. Not that the front is all that easy. For example, the 6th is 213-yard par 3 which usually plays into the wind. The hole plays from a slightly elevated tee across to a slightly elevated undulating green with four fronting bunkers. And the hole is stoke index 10! The 9th, a par 4 of 436 yards, plays from a raised tee box to a rolling fairway. Your approach is uphill to a green protected by three bunkers and a rock outcropping. Stay to the right of the green because locals say even Seve Ballesteros couldn't get up and down from left of the green. The most difficult hole at Connemara (at least according to the stroke index) is the 445-yard par 4 twelfth. The narrow fairway doglegs uphill left to right. The raised green, which slopes back to front, is guarded by three fronting traps. This hole is followed by a 212-yard par 3 some call brutal. On the 13th you hit from one hilltop across to another with plenty of rocks and heavy rough in between. The left to right sloping green has bunkers left, right, and behind. The 15th is one of two holes at

Connemara without bunkers (the 17th is the other). Drive down to a wide fairway, then up to a raised green protected by mounds with heavy rough on this 412-yard par 4. For moderate hitters, the second shot should be a lay-up to the base of the hill leading to the green. The chances of losing a ball in the heavy dune grass is too great to go for it, unless you know you can make it. Yeah, right! Following another par 5, the 526-yard par 5 eighteenth is a challenging finish. Drive from an elevated tee to a generous landing area. A small creek crosses the fairway 100 yards from the green. Four traps front the elevated green and another protects the right side. We haven't played the third nine (C), but from the look of it, we'd love it as much as the older course.

With or without wind, Connemara Championship Golf Links will engage the best golfers with different challenges at every hole. The course, though, is eminently fair to all ability levels. The views are world class, as is the shot-making required to score well. As wonderful as the course is, the people make it even better. We almost missed our start because I was so busy discussing the American PGA Tour with the club's assistant pro. After a leisurely round (still under four hours) on a beautiful day, we were bought beers by the foursome in front of us as an apology for slowing us up. We gratefully drank the beers, but honestly hadn't noticed we were going slowly. That's how beautiful the course and the views are.

**Comments from the Forward Tees:** This is a difficult course for ladies even though distance is adjusted to be fair. Because it's links golf I found myself in trouble on some second and third shots. It was still great fun and the views were good compensation.

### CONNEMARA ISLES GOLF CLUB, Annaghuane, Lettermore, Connemara, Co. Galway
From Galway take R336 (coast road) to Costelloe, turn left onto R343 and then immediately right onto R374. Course is about 5 km west of Costelloe.

No active website  (091) 572 498
9-hole links, 5042 yards, par 70, €20

**Amenities:** When you arrive, you'll discover Ireland's only thatched-roof clubhouse, which houses a small bar (serves meals) and changing rooms. The clubhouse was originally the farmhouse on the land now used for the golf course.

**Course Comments:** If the address of the golf course doesn't put you off, finding the course might. But believe me, Connemara Isles Golf Club (Galf *Chumann Oileain Chonamara,* Golf Mara to the locals) is worth the considerable effort to find. The course is a 9-hole links layout which plays to a par of 70.  As rustic as it seems, the course was actually built by Tom Craddock and Pat Ruddy in 1995. Connemara Isles plays around and over the Atlantic which you cross four times as you play from island to island and back. With the sea affecting your shots on four of the nine holes, there wasn't a need for bunkers. The greens are moderate in size and play slow, which is good because many are severely sloped. Several blind shots and very heavy rough (made more difficult by the damp conditions often found on the peninsula) add to the challenge. The course is roughly maintained, but that just enhances its charm. Some players say they like Connemara Isles better than many of the big name courses.

The times we've played, both in spring and fall, the weather has been a combination of mist and fog. It means we haven't been able to enjoy the fine views of the bays, the mountains, and islands that good weather would afford, but it does give Connemara Isles a *"Golf in the Kingdom"* mystical quality. It is a fun course to play, whatever the weather. The 3rd, a 159-yard par 3, is an easy one-shotter, except that it's all ocean carry from tee to green. You actually are hitting over to the next island to a green steeply sloped back to front. And, Tin Cup, no drop area is provided—hit your wedge with the wind and your driver against it, and hit it again if you don't make it. You get another chance to cross the sea at the 412-yard par 5 fifth (as you go back to the first island). That's correct, only 412 yards, but a par 5 for good reason. The hole is a dogleg left where your second shot is over the water. The carry is about 110 yards, but the fairway on the other side is steeply uphill. Your approach will be to a raised green from an uphill lie. A longer par 5 is the 481-yard 8th. A blind drive starts this longest hole on the course, and the fairway narrows as you get closer to the green. A rock wall indicates OB left and thick rough awaits right. A large swale in front of the green stops run-up shots.

Connemara Isles Golf Club is a must play course in this corner of Ireland. It has everything you want in a great course (except length). The staff and members are some of the friendliest we've come across. In fact, the feeling of the club is expressed on the golf card: *"Coinnigh d'ait ar an gcursa le do thoil* (We hope you enjoy your game of golf)."* For an out-of-the-way course, Connemara Isles is busy; plan to call ahead so you won't be disappointed.

**Comments from the Forward Tees:** What a beautiful setting. This course is a challenge, especially because of the water. It was a great feeling to hit across the water successfully more than once.

### EAST CLARE GOLF CLUB, Coolreagh, Bodyke, Co. Clare
In the village of Bodyke.
www.eastclare.com (061) 921 322
Parkland, 6031 metres, par 71, €30

**Amenities:** Modern clubhouse with changing rooms downstairs and lounge upstairs. Very nice bar serves meals all day (until 9 PM). Small, but well equipped pro shop.

**Course Comments:** The parkland East Clare Golf Club, a Dr. Arthur Spring design (he also designed Woodstock GC and Castle Island GC in the area), opened as a 9-hole course in 1991. In 1997 the course expanded to the present 18-hole configuration. The course is undiscovered enough to be easy to get on, but societies have found it, and it is becoming a popular venue for their outings. Being fairly flat, the course is a good choice for a relaxing round, although enough challenge exists to make your round interesting. Thirty-four greenside bunkers mean approach shots need to be accurate. If you do find the sand, the traps are quite playable. The moderate to large greens have some significant undulations which will make putting a challenge. Water, mostly ponds to cross off tees, is in play on seven holes. East Clare's hilltop location means that it can be quite windy, and most days will have enough breeze to affect shot-making. East Clare has pleasant views out to farmland and forests, as well as views of a large peat (turf) bog beside three and four. It is this last feature that keeps East Clare from being an outstanding course. The course is built on part of the nearby peat bog, and thus can be damp. If you have a chance, play the course after a spell of dry weather. Okay, it's Ireland. Play the course after a spell of "relatively" dry weather.

The middle of the course has an interesting set of holes in seven through ten. The 419-metre par 4 seventh is the only one of the central set that doesn't involve water. A dogleg left with mature trees on the inside corner, the tee shot is downhill and the approach is slightly up to a green with no bunkers. Birdie is possible on this long hole. While three of the par 3s at East Clare have drives over natural ponds to greens guarded by bunkers, the 8th (145 metres) is another drive-over-the-water par 3, but this time it's over a water feature which would make the BBC's Ground Force team proud. Trees encroach on the green from the left as well. A tough, but pretty hole. The 9th, a 419-metre par 4, begins with a downhill first shot toward a stream and a lake. A little over 200 metres is all you can go without risking trouble. The second shot is across a large pond to a green with traps on both sides. If you don't feel like challenging the pond, plenty of bailout room exists to the left of the green. The 9th is a classic risk/reward hole. The 10th is a strong 346-metre par 4 with an acute dogleg left to right after your tee shot over yet another pond. The second shot is again over a pond and uphill to a green protected by two bunkers. A tee shot of about 185 metres will put you in position for the approach. It was on this hole that we met Red (our name), the course's resident red fox. We had been warned that Red might seek us out and beg for a handout, but we weren't prepared for how tame he/she seemed. Of course, Red is not tame, but is a wild animal and should be treated as such. Red walked within about ten feet of Anne and about five feet of me (great for photos) begging for chocolate. That's right, Red is a choc-o-holic! After seeing that we had no chocolate offerings, Red continued his/her meanderings. Although fox still can be seen on the course, sadly Red is no longer one of them.

One of the holes I liked best at East Clare is the 387-metre par 4 fifteenth. This classic two-shotter begins with a downhill drive to a wide fairway. The second shot is slightly uphill to a plateau green protected by traps on each side. The 15th isn't tricky, but good straight ahead golf. The 16th is another hole which begins with a tee shot over a lake. The 469-metre par 5 starts with a drive to an uphill fairway. It's an easy shot, but the lake makes it intimidating. The second shot is blind because of the hill. The green and two bunkers are tucked to the right of the fairway. Before our round we met a local who gave us some helpful advice. He said that you usually can't feel the wind on the tee of the par 3 second, but that it's usually against you. Also, that regardless of the distances on the card, whatever club you successfully used on two is the one to use on four. Both suggestions made a difference in my score. East Clare Golf Club is even more of a holiday destination now. East Clare Golf Holiday Village opened next to the course. The village offers ownership of fully furnished, luxury two bedroom villas (sleep 6). I would call the units Time Share, but the moniker is or has been illegal in Ireland. You can resort exchange (for instance, through RCI) into the Golf Holiday Village units. Talking to representatives of both the course and the Holiday Village, I found out that the two will cooperate to make staying at the resort attractive to golfers.

**Comments from the Forward Tees:** Water made for difficult tee shots with long carries, but the course is lovely.

**ENNIS GOLF CLUB, Drumbiggle, Ennis, Co. Clare**
In the heart of Ennis village (on R474).
www.ennisgolfclub.com (065) 682 4074
Parkland, 5612 metres, par 71, €25

**Amenities:** Well appointed 1999 bar and separate dining room. Excellent food available most usual hours at the 19th Hole Restaurant which offers a very complete pub menu. Small, but nicely equipped pro shop with friendly, helpful staff.

**Course Comments:** The drawback to the venerable (1907) Ennis Golf Club is that it is short. One of its charms is that it is short. Ennis is a lovely parkland track with a variety of native flowering deciduous and evergreen trees and pretty flower beds. Even though the course is in the heart of a bustling town, the proximity doesn't really intrude onto the course. To get a full 18 holes in the space of a big 9-hole track (90 acres) is tricky. Ennis accomplishes this by judiciously using the land it has. In a round you would cross over other holes six times. Number nine crosses eight and 13, so at times three groups may be waiting for each other to play. If you are lucky enough to play with locals (some of the most enjoyable folks we've ever played with), they will help direct you. If you're on your own, proceed with caution and don't be afraid to ask. Besides being a tight course, Ennis has other defenses. The course is well bunkered; mostly greenside and not too penal. At least on one hole I saw a saving bunker at the side of a fairway to keep shots from going OB. The greens are small, of course, with some undulations, but are never unfair. The course has no water on it, but a dry creek bed crosses in front of the 14th and 18th greens. I asked Noreen, the Lady's Captain, if they call it a burn, stream or creek. She said that most members just call it a nuisance. Stream, creek or nuisance, it's still a concern of play on those holes.

The men's Captain, John Finn, said that between 1997 and 2006 the club spent three million euros on course upgrades. The spending shows in the quality golf at Ennis.

Number five, a 333-metre par 4, is a slight dogleg right with an uphill drive that needs to go around or over a set of stones on the left side of the fairway (it takes a carry of about 185 metres to clear the stones). Legend says that Finn McCoul placed the stones there, since it is certain that no Ennis man could have done it. The second shot is downhill to a green protected by a large bunker on the left. Even though I didn't play it well, I do like the 140-metre 7th. Your downhill tee shot must avoid the rocks and trees left of the narrow green. Don't stray too far right or the slope will kick your ball further right leaving a difficult chip to the green. The 11th is a par 4 of 311 metres. It's one of two holes (along with the 10th) in an area called Finn's Land for the farmer who sold the plot to the club. This dogleg right has a tight tee shot with woods left and a hill and trees right. Stay left as you approach the green from any angle because a trap on the right of the green can't be seen if you are more than 100 metres out. The 16th is a picturesque downhill 176-metre par 3 which starts with a tough drive between two sets of tees. Because of the angle of trees near the tee box, it's natural to pull the ball left where a bunker guards one of the larger greens on the course. Jack, the Men's Club President, told us that the club had only about 40 visitors (not counting societies) last year. What a shame others haven't yet discovered the charms of friendly, venerable Ennis Golf Club.

**Comments from the Forward Tees:** Very little difference in distance between ladies' and men's tees, except on the par 5s. Longer distances makes the course a challenge for ladies.

### GALWAY BAY GOLF RESORT, Renville, Oranmore, Co. Galway

Southeast of Galway off the N18 toward the bay, well signed.

www.galwaybaygolfresort.com (091) 790 70711

Bay side parkland with links feel, approx. 6535 metres, par 72, €110

**Amenities:** The beautiful newly designed clubhouse is part of a Five Star resort complex. Full restaurant and bar serving quality food all day. Completely stocked pro shop to serve all your golfing needs.

**Course Comments:** Galway Bay's then Director of Golf, John Cassidy said that the goal of the remake of the course is to turn a nice facility into a true 5 Star resort destination. The resort is designed around one of the finest championship golf courses in Ireland, a course which architect Christy O'Connor Jnr hopes will soon host an Irish Open. The completed reconstruction includes a total rebuild of 11 holes, all tee boxes redone, most bunkers rebuilt changing many into pot bunkers or links style bunkers. Also, the course has a new irrigation and drainage system, and all greens rebuilt to USGA specifications, which will increase all-year playability. The course boasts close to a hundred bunkers in a good mix of fairway and greenside. The new O'Connor design makes judicious use of saving bunkers behind the greens, especially when long might lead to more trouble. The greens are a mix of medium to large, with several elevated and many with multi-levels and great potential for exciting pin placements. A couple of things about the course weren't changed in the makeover. First, no changes have been made to the stupendous views across Galway Bay to the city. Five holes play on the edge of the bay, and you approach number 12 green over a pond with the bay as backdrop. Secondly, O'Connor maintained his commitment to highlight and preserve the ancient historic features of the Renville Peninsula. Several ancient sites are part of the course, including remains of small circular stone huts (beehive huts), Rathapours ring fort ("the fort of the potatoes"), ancient stone walls, and part of an old (15C) copper and lead mine.

Our visit to the course was in 2007 in the middle of the renovation. We haven't had the opportunity yet to play the updated course, but reports by those who have say the course is superb. Comments such as "great test for any golfer," "excellent layout," and "one of the most scenic courses anywhere," are common.

**GORT GOLF CLUB, Castlequarter, Gort, Co. Galway**
Two miles west of Gort off R460 on the edge of the
    Burren.
www.gortgolf.com (091) 632 244
Parkland, 5974 metres, par 71, €20

**Amenities:** Modern clubhouse with changing rooms
and small pro shop downstairs. Upstairs lounge has pleasant
views over course and out to The Burren.

**Course Comments:** The original 9-hole course for
Gort Golf Club was built during the golf boom in 1924. Christy
O'Connor Jnr, redesigned the course to an 18-hole track in
1996. The parkland course plays through gentle hills and a
combination of mature and young trees. Though the course is
undulating, it's still an easy walk. The prevailing wind, though,
will make it play longer than the distance on the card.
Generous fairways and moderate sized greens are protected
by 41 bunkers, some large and a few evil pot bunkers. Only
holes two and four have no traps, while 14 has seven, four
around the green. Ponds are in play on three holes, but only
on the fourth is it a real concern.

Gort GC starts with a serious test. Number one is a
346-metre par 4 with great views from the tee. A downhill drive
to a wide landing area starts the round. A lake on the left
should only be a concern for the wildest of pull-hooks. Second
shot doglegs left around a huge bunker to an elevated green
guarded by a second bunker left. If your first shot is good, you
can cut the corner to the green. Remember to subtract
distance since you are cutting rather than following the
fairway. The 418-metre par 4 second is another dogleg left
which starts with a blind tee shot downhill to a fairway sloping
right. Your second shot from a side-slope lie should avoid the
grassy hollow on the right fronting the green. No bunkers are
needed; the sloping fairways provides plenty of difficulty. The
combination of one and two makes a challenging start to a fine
course. The 4th is a great driving hole with water left and trees

and bushes right. With a good first shot on this 333-metre two-shotter, the approach should be a pitch to the bunkerless green, but don't ignore the water still on the left. The 9th is my favorite hole at Gort. It's a classic par 5, long and narrow. The fairway, less than 20 metres wide, snakes between a hillside on the right and a drop-off left all the way to the green. The green has the same hill and drop-off protections as the rest of the hole, with the addition of a small bunker front left.

Leave your clubs by the bushes as you come off 11 and walk back to the 12th tee. Three fairway traps make the 303-metre par 4 eleventh an interesting challenge. If you avoid the fairway bunkers and the two more greenside, the hole is a birdie opportunity. The 168-metre 13th is very difficult into the normal wind. The two-tiered green is guarded by a bunker which fronts the entire green and one more on the right. Club selection is key on this hole which is more uphill than it appears. If the wind has hurt your shot to the 13th, it will help you on the 495-metre par 5 fourteenth. Even though three fairway bunkers and four more by the green can give you lots of trouble, the hole is wide open enough that you can tee it high and let it fly. As you reach the mown grass of the fairway, look to the right and you can see the outlined base of an ancient ringed fort. Gort Golf Club is a fun, challenging course out-of-the-way enough to still be relatively unknown. Its reputation for quality golf means it won't remain undiscovered for long.

**Comments from the Forward Tees:** Tee shots at 1, 5, and 14 are shortened for ladies, but aren't as interesting as from tees further back.

**KILKEE GOLF CLUB, East End, Kilkee, Co. Clare**
North of the village overlooking Chimney Bay.
**www.kilkeegolfclub.ie** (065) 905 6977
Seaside parkland, 5555 metres, par 70, €20

**Amenities:** The modern clubhouse has changing rooms and a lounge, but no pro shop. The lounge has a full bar and serves sandwiches and light meals all day, with a full dinner menu available in evenings. A ball crack in the pub window also suggested that some member has a vicious hook.

**Course Comments:** Kilkee Golf Club (in Kilkee village turn north on the scenic drive along the shore) has been called, "A little pot of gold in County Clare," by golf writer Keil Christiansen. It is certainly a course deserving wider recognition for the quality of the holes at this seaside parkland course. It is also deserving of recognition for the club's efforts to improve the course. Located less than an hour from some of Ireland's finest golf destinations (Lahinch, Doonbeg, Ballybunnion), this 5555-metre par 70 offers some of the finest views of any course. The Atlantic Ocean, George's Head, the Pallock Holes (natural swimming holes formed along the edge of the sea), Chimney Bay, sea cliffs, and the village of Kilkee all draw a golfer's attention away from the game. But on a fine day out of the busy season (July and August), you may be the only one on the course to enjoy those views.

Kilkee may be short, but it is challenging, especially if the wind is blowing as it usually does. Bunkers will be in play on several holes, but none are too worrisome. Water, though, is a different matter. A burn crosses several holes, and five holes have ponds in play. Number three crosses a corner of the bay (more about this later). Greens are mostly flat and small, except the 9th which is quite large and double-tiered. We played when it was very wet which slowed the greens considerably, but in the dry I believe they would play fast. A couple of holes have small grass dykes fronting the greens to create an additional hazard. Two and three are a fantastic pair of testing holes. The 2nd is a par 5 of 443 metres which begins with a blind drive. The third shot on this slight dogleg left (second for long hitters) must cross a burn which connects several ponds to reach the elevated green with a small bunker in front. After playing the 2nd, climb farther up the headland to the tee box of the 3rd, where you tee off over a section of Chimney Bay. It only requires a shot of 160 metres to clear the chasm, but short and you're in the ocean and too long means you're in heavy rough. Some of the best views are available at the 15th tee. This 387-metre dogleg right two-shotter plays downhill and even moderate hitters can reach the corner. A small stream left and pond right protect the green. On holes with blind tee shots, white stones in the fairway indicate the line of play.  When we played, the course wasn't in the best condition. Fairways and greens on the 2nd through 6th were heavily damaged by a violent storm and freak waves a month before. Talking with local members in the pleasant clubhouse after our round convinced us that the course is usually kept in excellent shape.

**Comments from the Forward Tees:** A good scoring course for ladies. Water crossing can be a problem, but the par 3s are reasonable length. The back side is longer, but played drier.

### LAHINCH GOLF CLUB, Castle Course, Lahinch, Co. Clare
On the set side of Lahinch village on the road to the
　　　Cliffs of Moher (R478).
www.lahinchgolf.com (065) 708 1003
Links, 5594 yards, par 70, €35

**Amenities:** A fine modern clubhouse at the Old Course, serves both the Old and Castle courses. Clubhouse has nice lounge with views onto the course, but must be playing the course or a guest to visit. Very complete separate pro shop. Changing rooms for the Castle course are near its first tee and a snack shop (in high season) is there as well.

**Course Comments:** Along Liscannor Bay on the west coast of Ireland is one of golf's sacred places. Winding its way among the dunes and beside the sea is Lahinch Golf Club, one of the oldest courses in Ireland. Like other old Irish courses, the original links course was the result of a Scottish Regiment of British Army officers who heard about an area of meandering dunes just waiting to become a golf course. In 1893 this enchanting land saw its first course developed. Two years later none other than Old Tom Morris (St. Andrews, Scotland) designed a full course at Lahinch (two of those original Morris' holes exist today as four and five). Much revision has been done to Lahinch in the intervening years. First, Dr. Alaster MacKenzie (Augusta National and Cyprus Point) made extensive revisions in 1928. Finally, Martin Hawtree worked the course over to rediscover the spirit of the MacKenzie design. Today, Lahinch Golf Club deserves to be included in the world's great golfing destinations. As to be expected, Old Lahinch is not an easy test. With a dunes system so large and complicated it seems possible for golfers to get lost for weeks, tough multilevel sloped greens, large and deep bunkers, and coastal winds which seem like a gale on a calm day, Lahinch is a stern taskmaster. Old Lahinch is a magnificent course, a must play on every golf tour, and a course where in the busy season (April to October) five hour rounds tend to be the norm.

All of which brought Anne and I to the Castle Course, the 1975 Lahinch second eighteen. At much less than half the price of Old Lahinch, the Castle Course can be almost empty while the tour groups are stacked five deep waiting for a crack at Old Lahinch. Play the Old Course, by all means. Enjoy the magnificent Morris-MacKenzie-Hawtree layout, but don't ignore the small jewel next door just because its less expensive and more relaxed. The Castle Course will still give a challenge to every level of golfer, but maybe with a little less frustration thrown in. The Castle Course, an 18-hole mostly flat links course, provides some nice views of the Old Course, the beach, and the bay from an elevated section. The ruins of 14C Dough or O'Brian's Castle come into play on both seven and eight, and give the course its name. The greens, some elevated, are mostly flat and medium speed. Castle is well bunkered with numerous fore-bunkers, but none are too severe. A lake and OB come into play on number eight. As a whole, the course seems simple, but plays tougher than it looks. Taken too lightly, the Castle Course can bite.

As we played, a heavy rain squall hit on the third hole with gusts close to 50 mph (it's fun to check the conditions with a Skymaster hand-held weather gauge by Speedtech Instruments, Great Falls, VA). We put up our Gustbuster umbrellas and stood by our bags for about 10 minutes. Everything not covered by our umbrellas was soaked through. The wind continued after the squall had ended, the sun came out, and three holes later we were dry. Such is life on the Irish links. Seven and eight are typical of the quality holes at Lahinch Castle. The 7th is a par 3 of 115 yards. The tee shot on this short hole is partially blind with only the top of the flag in view. A bunker fronts the green and the castle ruins loom right. Our impression after our round was that all the par 3s had been well designed and fun to play. The 8th is the most challenging hole on the course. A short par 4 of 268 yards, the fairway bends left around the edge of a lake estuary. From the tee, the green looks invitingly close, but with water (OB) left and prevailing winds (20-30 mph when we played) pushing everything towards the water, it's a wonderfully difficult shot. As we played up the 15th, a helicopter landed in a field adjacent to the course. We figured someone was dropping in for a round at Old Lahinch. We continued our round with no one in front of us and no one for two holes behind us. Such is the glory of golf at Lahinch—at least at the Castle Course.

**Comments from the Forward Tees:** Great course with many challenging holes. Par 3s are of reasonable length, except two which is 182 yards. Overall, the course isn't extremely long off the front tees. Ladies get good distance adjustments, but still have enough challenges.

### LAHINCH GOLF CLUB, Old Course, Lahinch, Co. Clare

Links, 6613 yards, par 72, €170

**AMENITIES:** Same as for the Castle Course.

**COURSE COMMENTS:** Called "The St Andrews of Ireland," by writer Herbert Warren, the Old Course at Lahinch is one of the sternest test of links golf there is. Designed originally by Scotland's Old Tom Morris in 1894, the links course was redesigned by Dr. Alister MacKenzie in 1927 (retaining some of the Morris holes), and then modernized in 1999 Martin Hawtree without losing the Morris/MacKenzie character.  The course is one of the toughest in Ireland (or anywhere for that matter) and not just because of the tough rough or wind.  The more than sixty mixed fairway and greenside bunkers are quite penal and all in play.  There's no real water in play on the course, although the 12th does play alongside the Inagh River (OB).  The greens are the next major defense the course has.  Greens are large with plenty of slopes—many are double and even triple tiered.

All the holes are great, interesting and intriguing, but we did pick out some to show the character of Old Lahinch from the white tees.  The 3rd is a 412-yard par 4 where the drive is a long carry (about 170 yards) to a raised fairway which bends left—big hitters need to be aware that the fairway runs out about 270 yards out.  The long approach shot (second or third) is over rough to a raised green with two traps in front. The 4th and 5th are two of the remaining original Old Tom Morris holes and they show the genius of his design.  The 4th, *Klondike*, is a 472-yard par 5.  Drive from the beach (practically) to a narrow fairway nestled between large dunes. Second shots play over another large dune toward the distant swaled green.  Shorter hitters who try going around the middle dune to the right need to be wary of set of bunkers there which can be troublesome.  It's a classic hole.  A second Old Tom Morris hole is next.  *Dell* is short (148-yard), blind one-shotter. Tee off over the hill which hides the green—aim over the stone on the hill.  Hit and hope on this venerable hole.  Another great par 3 with an uphill tee shot to a very sloping green is the 156-yard eighth.  The green is protected by three penal bunkers. On the back the 12th, a 514-yard par 5, grabbed my attention. Playing with the Inagh River OB on the left, the 12th is a relatively narrow par 5.  Hit out towards the castle (on the Castle Course) to a fairway which bends left and has bunkers left and right—trouble for big drivers.  The smallish green is a difficult find with three traps protecting it.  Stroke Index #1 at Lahinch Old is the 15th for good reason.  The hummocky fairway will cause problems as will a fairway bunker left and deep rough on both sides.  The large undulating green is surrounded by three bunkers.  A fun and challenging hole is next. At the 192-yard par 3 sixteenth you hit from an elevated tee to an undulating green protected by four bunkers. Hitting the green on your tee shot is key. As tough as the course is, it's still a lovely challenge.

When you play, look for the Goats of Lahinch. The goats originally belong to longtime caddy, Tommy Walsh, who lived nearby. The legend now is that you can predict the weather by the movement of the goats—if they're around the clubhouse prospects aren't good, but if they're out in the sandhills it's going to be a fine day. But even the roughest weather, a day at Lahinch is a fine day.

### Galfchumann Uachtar Ard (Oughterard Golf Club), Oughterard, Co. Galway

On N59, the main Galway/Clifden road, approximately 25 km from Galway City.
www.oughterardgolf.com (091) 552131
Parkland, 5964 metres, par 70, €25

**Amenities:** Modern clubhouse with changing rooms downstairs and a large lounge upstairs which serves bar meals usual hours. Beside the clubhouse is a fairly complete pro shop.

**Course Comments:** Oughterard (OOk-ta-rard) Golf Club is near enough to the large golfing population of Galway City that the course might be busy, yet it's far enough off the beaten path to be able to call in the morning and be playing in the afternoon. The interesting configuration comes back to the clubhouse after 12, making a short round possible. Thirteen through 18 play on the other side of the golf course road. A very typical parkland track, with lots of trees and a couple of forest walks between holes, Oughterard is beautifully landscaped with plantings and wild flowers. A mixture of fairway and greenside bunkers (50 in all) will add challenge to your round. Some of the bunkers are large and a few penal, but all are difficult to play out of because of inconsistent sand. It's better to play Oughterard in the dry because the course doesn't have the best drainage. The moderately undulating greens are the exception being newly remodeled to USGA standards. Ponds come into play on a total of five holes, though most of the time more as a visual then physical challenge. The water on the 10th will be a serious test off the forward tee.

On a recent trip to Ireland, we hadn't planned to play Oughterard GC, but when we found a free afternoon we were glad to grab a chance to play the Harris and Hackett 1974 design. Among the quality holes at Oughterard is the 376-metre par 4 fourth. The hole is a long dogleg right which begins with a blind drive to a tight fairway with thick forest left and a more open row of trees right. The second shot is slightly downhill to a swaled green with a trap left. A fore bunker and copse just left of the green complicates the approach. The 8th, a 444-metre par 5, is a dogleg left which starts with a drive out towards a bunker on the right that is reachable with a decent shot. Trees and a hill line the left of the fairway. A small ditch fronts the green (it's playable with no water) which is protected by three bunkers. It's a birdie opportunity even for moderate hitters who stay out of trouble. The signature hole at Oughterard is the 167-metre 9th. It's a long carry over a pond which comes within five metres of the green and bunkers are on both sides. Be sure to be long. Another carry over a pond starts the par 4, 353-metre 10th. Your tee shot must carry 125 metres to reach the fairway. What looks from the tee like a pile of leaves on the right is an ancient marker stone. A large fairway bunker and big greenside bunker will affect your approach to the green. A sign off the 11th tee says, "Refreshments: Ice Cream, Drinks, Ring Bell." A path is mowed over to the edge of the course, where some neighbor and the club have come to a mutually beneficial arrangement. On the finishing hole it is the traps which make a difference. The 393-metre par 4 has a fairway trap on the right which can catch wayward long drives. An approach bunker left and three more around the green make the flag a hard target to find. It was at Oughterard that Anne noted that at times it hits you that you're not just playing anywhere. You look around and realize you're in Ireland. And when in the Emerald Isle, Oughterard Golf Club is not a bad place to be.

**Comments from the Forward Tees:** Tee boxes are set up for fair distances for ladies, but still keep the holes interesting.

### SPANISH POINT GOLF CLUB, Spanish Point, Milltown Malbay, Co. Clare

Located 3 km south of Miltown Malbay off N67.
www.spanishpointgolfing.com  (065) 708 4198
Links, 4624 metres, par 64, €20

**Amenities:** The cozy, rustic clubhouse fits beautifully into the seaside setting and serves a limited food menu. In the summer, the clubhouse is open as late as 11 PM.

**Course Comments:** One of Co. Clare's most unheralded golf courses is a short 9-hole track set two miles south of Milltown Malbay (ten miles south of Lahinch) at the village of Spanish Point. With a clubhouse opened in 1981 by Dr. P.D. Hillary, the President of Ireland, the hundred year old Spanish Point Golf and Sports Club is a true gem. With wonderful views of Mal Bay, the course plays over and around large dunes. Spanish Point is a true links course with wind and tough grass rough always conditions of play. As on other seaside links courses, each hole often creates a new spectacular view, but many times you have to pay the price of playing in the wind and rain. The course is well bunkered, with most in play and several very deep. The bunker sand is filled with sea shells which are interesting to hit out of. The greens are moderate to small, and have been in good condition whenever we've played. Though a few have slopes, none are too severe. The blind shots, three blind drives and one approach, are all fair, but do add to the challenge.

All the holes at Spanish Point are interesting, but some have become our favorites. The 5th is a medium length par 4 of 360 metres, which begins with a blind drive. On this longest hole on the course, aim at the white rock at the top of the hill (and hope you don't hit it). Your second shot is downhill to a green protected by four bunkers. The 287-metre par 4 seventh is the hardest hole at Spanish Point. It's also a kick to play. The tee shot must cross over a low stone wall on this left to right dogleg. A large bunker on the outside of the dogleg waits to catch shots that run through the fairway. The second shot is no easier than the drive. It's a blind uphill approach with the pin hidden from view. Walk up to get a view of the pin placement. Wherever the pin is, don't be left of the green or you'll find a big drop-off into unforgiving rough. A nice finish to a round is the 150-metre par 3 ninth. Part of the green is visible on your tee shot over a rough-covered dune. Between the bottom of the dune and the green is about 20 metres of fairway (cut grass), so being a little under clubbed is acceptable. The people at Spanish Point, players and staff, have always been friendly and courteous. One player, teaching his wife or girlfriend, let us play through. When Anne hit her usual straight-up-the-middle shot, he turned to his partner and said, "See what you could do with practice." While the course isn't the test of its neighbor, Lahinch, you'll find yourself, as we did, wanting to play Spanish Point Golf Club over and over.

**Comments from the Forward Tees:** The views on a clear day are so spectacular that keeping focused on golf is difficult. Two of the par 3s are very long at 170 and 190 metres. I agree with Bob that the 7th is the hardest hole to play. It was actually harder when I played it the second time and was hitting longer. It made club choice harder: go for it or lay up? Lay up. I also liked the challenge of the blind shots here. Fun, but not unfair.

**Other Courses in the Region:**

Ballinasloe GC (18), Ballinasloe, Co. Galway (090) 964 2126
Dromoland Castle GC (18), Newton-on-Fergus, Co. Clare
        (061) 368 144
Dunmore (Demesne) GC (18), Dunmore, Co. Galway
        (093) 38 709
Kilrush GC (18), Parknamoney, Co. Clare (065) 905 2633

Loughrea GC (18), Loughrea, Co. Galway (091) 841 049
Tuam GC (18), Tuam, Co. Galway (093) 28 993
Woodstock Golf & Country Club (18), Ennis, Co. Clare
        (065) 682 9463

## PUBS AND EATERIES

*An Cruiscan Lan* **Hotel** in Spiddal, Co. Galway, on R336 the main coast highway. A hotel and restaurant complex (snug bar, lounge, dining conservatory) in the heart of Irish speaking village of Spiddal (also spelled Spiddle on some maps). After a misty round of golf at Connemara Isles GC, *An Cruiscin Lan* with its warm fires was a welcome respite. The food (seafood chowder, tuna and macaroni salad) was excellent, and was served quickly by friendly staff. Throw in the bonus of decent prices and you have a winner.

*An Fear Gorta* **Tea Room** in Ballyvaghan across from the bay. The Hungry Grass (*An Fear Gorta*) is an elegant garden spot tea room across from Ballyvaghan Bay. A front room and a conservatory room complete with passion flowers hanging above. Formal garden in back. Serves light lunches, soups, and sweets.

**Brogan's** on O'Connell Street in Ennis, Co. Clare. Brogan's is very popular with locals and tourists. The food is well prepared and the service is friendly and efficient. The pub can be quite crowded at lunch and dinner.

**Cafe on the Quay** in Kinvarra, Co. Galway. Cafe a couple of doors up from Murphy Store serves more substantial food, such as sandwiches, soups, and specialty pizzas.

**Donnelly's Seafood Bar and Restaurant** on the coast highway (Spiddal road) in Barna. The small village of Barna (don't blink or you'll miss it) on the coast road about four miles from Galway City is blessed with two fine eateries. Of the two, Donnelly's Seafood Bar and Restaurant is the larger, the older, and the more pub-like. This very popular establishment is worth seeking out for a drink or a meal. The food is excellent, but neither as gourmet nor as expensive as O'Grady's. When you visit, search around and find the traditional snug which now has a window where once drinks were passed through to ladies.

**Flannery's Pub and Restaurant** on the pedestrian mall at Ballinrobe's famous Cornmarket. The epitome of an Irish pub with traditional decor and plenty of friendly locals. Winner of numerous pub and restaurant awards and listed in the Top 100 Pubs in Ireland, Flannery's has a cozy bar atmosphere with top class service, quality food, and good pints.

**Fogerty's Restaurant** on Market Street in Clifton. Fogerty's Restaurant has a good reputation and a lovely interior. The wait staff were generally friendly and efficient. We were rather disappointed on our visit as the food was not top quality nor prepared well (fake crab in the seafood soup, strong fishy taste to broth on seafood pasta, chicken overcooked and dry). Check with locals.

**Hungary Monk Cafe** in Cong, Co. Galway, across from the abbey. Small (four tables) coffee shop across from Cong Abbey and around the corner from the Quiet Man Cottage. Popular with locals on the Sunday morning we stopped. Serves light lunches and sweets.

**The Huntsman Inn** at 164 College Road (the main Dublin to Galway road) about 10 minutes from Galway City center. Empty the Huntsman Inn might seem stark, but filled with patrons, as it usually is, it is light and airy. The Huntsman Inn is an effective combination of good food, good drinks, great atmosphere, and fine entertainment.

**Keane's Oyster Bar** on Kilrush Road five minutes from Kilkee, Co. Clare. The Oyster Bar site has been in the Keane family since 1641. Today, the pub and restaurant is one of the most popular gathering places and eateries in the area. Keane's Oyster Bar also offers special deals for golfers at local courses, including Kilkee GC.

**Ma Murphy's** on New Street in the center of Bantry one block up from N71. Have a drink (no food) in an authentic old Irish pub with the other tourists gawking at the locals.

**McDermott's Pub** on the main road (R479) up from the harbour in Doolin. A mix of locals and tourists, most in for the music. Crowded, even off season. You'd think the food might be an afterthought, but that's not the case at MacDermott's. We had roast lamb with dressing that was as good or better than anywhere else, and Anne had the best beef stew of her life. Traditional music starts between 9:30 and 10:00 PM every night.

**McDonaugh's of Ireland** at the harbour end of downtown pedestrian shopping mall in Galway. Fish & Chip shop in front with restaurant to the side. Fish and more fish. Plenty of interesting selections straight off the boats onto your table. There are non-seafood items on the menu, but who notices. Loud and lively is McDonagh's Seafood Bar, Fish & Chip Shop, and Fish Market. We've had both lunch and dinner in the restaurant and been well pleased both times.

**Mitchell's Restaurant** on Market Street in Clifton, Co. Galway, in the center of town. On our first visit to Clifden, we asked a shopkeeper for a recommendation for seafood chowder. Without hesitation she directed us to Mitchell's. We had noticed signs for it on our way into town. We certainly weren't disappointed in our selection. Another year, Mitchell's was the first recommendation by our B&B. Too bad we didn't go back instead of trying a new place.

**Murphy Store and Coffee Shop** on The Quay in Kinvarra across from the bay and Dunguaire Castle. Coffees, teas, sweets and arts and craft gifts.

**O'Conner's Seafood Restaurant** in the middle of Bantry village. Lots of awards: Taste of Ireland, Good Food Ireland, Seafood Restaurant of the Year for 2009. Seafood, steaks, and specials based on what the boats brought in that day.

**O'Grady's on the Pier** in Barna on the coast road (R336) four miles west of Galway City. A fine seafood restaurant which blends an old-style facility with contemporary cuisine in a spectacular harbour setting along Galway Bay. Small room downstairs and another up keep the traditional harbour-side theme with simple decor and lovely views. Owner Michael O'Grady has made O'Grady's on the Pier a go-to-place for Galway visitors, as well as a favorite stop for locals. The food is outrageously fine with large portions and reasonable prices, though they aren't pub prices. The two dinners we had at O'Grady's are at the top of our list for meals we've had in Ireland (along with Out of the Blue in Dingle and Stoop Your Head in Skerries). Service is as spectacular as the sunset views. It all begins with Michael himself. On our last visit, I dropped Anne off at the door and went to park several blocks away (it's always busy, be sure to call ahead). As I ordered a whisky, Michael acted as bartender and brought me a quite generous pour and said, "Don't tell the girls I didn't measure it; they give me a bad time when I do this." That's the overall impression we have of O'Grady's—the ambiance, the food, the service—it's all about the customer.

**The Pantry Restaurant and Bakery** on O'Curry Street (village's main street) in Kilkee. Winner of a Bridgestone Best of Ireland Award, The Pantry is the 1982 brainchild of two ex-home economics teachers, Imelda Bourke and Siobhan McKeever. They opened the current larger premises in 1991 and continue to specialize in value for money.

**The Poet's Corner Pub** in the Old Ground Hotel on O'Connell Street in Ennis. The Poet's Corner looks like a typical Irish pub with a rich wood bar and tables with benches. Pub menu is small with several starters and an adequate selection of main courses. On an early weekday evening, the Poet's Corner was packed with local business people stopping for a pint on their way home, and tourists out for the evening. Singles were eating at the bar and a businessman was reading his evening paper over a pint. The food was very good and the service efficient.

**The Roadside Tavern** on N67 from Lahinch about a block off the Lisdoonverna village square. The Roadside Tavern is over 100 years old and retains its old tavern style with low lights and coal fire. Typical pub fare and a page of sandwiches. Look for the unusual smoked fish dishes, of which several are on the menu. The tavern specializes in smoked fish from Burren Smoke House down the road. Serves Wines of the Glen (one of the few Irish wineries) including Elderberry, Apple and Elderflower, Gooseberry, and Ginger. This was one of the finest pub meals we've ever had.

**The Shamrock Inn Hotel** on the main street (N67) of Lahinch. Modern, bright hotel pub with complete menu including nightly specials.

**Vaughan's Pub** in Kilfenora (the Burren) up from the Burren Centre and church on R476. Small village pub which serves great food. We've eaten here twice for lunch; the fish chowder is one of the best we've had. Off season the clientele is mostly local. The tourists who drop in are mostly those who know the place. Very friendly staff, interested in our travels.

## *ATTRACTIONS*

The tourist attractions in the West region of Ireland are a blend of big city and small village, of magnificent natural wonders and mysterious human-made wonders, of power and religion and music and literature. All will find much to interest them in the counties of Clare, Galway, and Roscommon.

We start our look at the attractions of the West where Anne and I began our exploration on our last trip, in Tralee. We stay in Tralee at *Teach an Phiobaire* Guest House, the House of the Piper, with Patricia and Michael Dooley. Michael is a world renown uileann pipe (Irish bagpipe) maker and in demand session player. We planned to leave Tralee in the morning to catch an early ferry across the Shannon (from Tralee it's straight on N69 to the Tarbert ferry terminal). We discovered that we had the wrong sailing time; the ferry sails one way on the hour and the other direction on the half hour. We hurried because we had a tee time set up at East Clare GC, but Patricia didn't hold out much hope. She said that she advises at least 45 minutes for the 45 km (27 miles) to Tarbert. Even waiting behind school buses, I made it to the ferry in 25 minutes and we had to wait 5 minutes for the **Shannon River ferry.** Keep in mind, though, that I've made many trips to Ireland, many more to Scotland, and four to Wales, so I don't exactly drive like a tourist. Forty-five minutes was really a more reasonable time. If you don't have to go to Limerick, the Shannon River ferry is a pleasant way to head north. Just off the ferry and heading west on N68, an alluring stop for anyone with a literary bent is to turn onto R484 and visit **Kilmihil** Village. The nondescript village has been made quasi-famous by a series of four books written by Niall Williams and Christine Breen about their transplant from New York City to rural Ireland. The first in the series is *O Come Ye Back to Ireland: Our First Year in County Clare.*

Ennis is our first destination in the West. A progressive, small city, with good eateries, Ennis also is home to the engrossing **Ennis Franciscan friary.** Built by the O'Brien's in the 13C, by the end of the 14C the friary was home to over 600 students and a hundred monks. On a quiet May morning, we got a personal tour by the steward of the fascinating carvings of the friary. You do get special treatment when you have joined the Irish Heritage. Before playing golf at Ennis in the afternoon, we drove out (R476) to visit **Dysert O'Dea.** This site includes an 8C monastery, an 11C church, a 12C high cross, and a castle which now houses an Archeology Centre. All are worth a visit.

Traveling over to the coast just a few miles north of Lahinch GC, you must visit the **Cliffs of Moher.** From Lahinch stay on the golf course road for about 7 miles to reach the Visitor's Centre. We had heard about the spectacular cliffs, and sort of pooh-poohed the reports. After all, we have some great sea cliffs in Oregon. We weren't prepared for the nearly 5 miles of cliffs over 600 feet high with pounding surf at their base. The view from the vantage point near 1853 O'Brien's Tower (don't bother going into the tower) is truly unworldly. So too is the view of (mostly) young people who climb over the protective fencing and crawl out to hang over cliff edges. I believe that a local sport is watching to see the next dumb one fall to their death. Oh well, some people were never meant to reproduce. The Visitor's Centre closes and they stop charging admission to the parking lot at 5:00 PM. The light on the cliffs happens to be the most photogenic in the early evening, so if you can time your visit right, there's no cost (but you will miss the Visitor's Centre exhibits which we've never seen in three visits). Continue north on R478 to R479 to the village of **Doolin.** Not much is in Doolin except boats out to the Aran Islands, a few touristy shops (including a couple of great CD shops), and, oh yes, three fantastic music pubs! Doolin seems to be home to Irish session music (at least for tourists). The three pubs, O'Connor's near the harbour, and McCann's and McDermott's on R479 about a half mile from the harbour, offer traditional music sessions almost every night of the year. You can walk from one to the next to the next to hear mostly good sessions. Some say that the sessions tend to be touristy, but we've enjoyed nice music at each one several times. One night we were in McCann's talking to a local for about an hour before we discovered he was the owner of the pub. Doolin is great for music and great also as a base for touring one of Ireland's most impressive geological features.

**The Burren** (the Place of Rock) is an area of approximately 100 square miles of classic limestone pavements. A "wild, barren, unreclaimable waste" which

Cromwell noted had neither a tree to hang a man nor water to drown him. What it does have are starkly beautiful landscapes of rock laced with stone fences and more than 1000 species of flowers and plants. The Burren and The Burren National Park can be explored from several routes. A dramatic combination of sea and landscape is viewed as you travel the coast road (R477) from Doolin or Lisdoonvarna to Ballyvaghan. You can go directly from Lisdoonvarna to Ballyvaghan on N67. Or you can go from Lisdoonvarna to Kilfenora on R476 and then through The Burren on R480. And that doesn't exhaust all the possibilities for routing. To really understand the archeology and geology of the Burren, a stop at the **Burren Centre** in Kilfenora is mandatory. Through informative film and displays, you can get a better sense of what you are seeing. The gift shop has a good selection of books and maps to help. While in Kilfenora visit the partially ruined cathedral and the well protected display of three 12C **high crosses.** A fourth high cross in the field next door has an excellent depiction of the Crucifixion.

On R480 is one of the most famous ancient monuments in Ireland, the **Poulnabrone Dolmen** (the name means "hole of sorrow"). This 5000 year old portal tomb is a hundred yards off the road and is a classic example of this type of megalithic structure. Excavations found the bones of 16 individuals (men and women, adult and children) buried in the tomb. The trick is to explore and photograph the dolmen with as few people around as possible. You have to time your visit correctly to avoid the bus after bus of tourists who visit. A little south of the dolmen is **Cahercommaunell Stone Fort** where you can explore a dramatic hill fort from about 800 AD. The fort is on private land and the landowner usually charges a fee. At the north end of R480 is the **Aillwee Cave** and Visitor Centre. The cave system, discovered in 1987, is small by the standards of caves such as Carlsbad Caverns in New Mexico, but still can be an enlightening sight to those who haven't had the opportunity to view stalactites, stalagmites, and underground waterfalls. A gift shop and cafe are just down the hill from the cave. On N67 at the north end of The Burren, make the effort to visit **Corcomroe Abbey,** St. Mary of the Fertile Rock, signed on a side road past Bealaclugga. We first visited this 12C Cistercian ruin in the spring of 2002. The day was quite squally and we pulled into the parking lot behind a tour bus in a downpour. The tour group got off the bus, hustled around the abbey grounds, and climbed back into their transport as quickly as they could. After they drove off, we waited until the shower passed and the sun came out. We then leisurely strolled the grounds as the only visitors. Such are the joys of touring on our own. The abbey is rich in interesting carvings and three 12C churches can be seen on the Burren hills overlooking the abbey. The last attraction in the area of The Burren we'd suggest you visit, but certainly not the last possibility, is the **Kilmacduagh Early Monastic Site** sign posted from R353 south of Gort. The complex contains a small cathedral from the 1200s, a leaning round tower (two foot out of vertical), a small church thought to be for women, the 13C O'Heyne's church, an abbot's house or Glebe by the car park, and a graveyard still in use. If you're on any kind of a schedule, watch your time. So captivating is the site that the twice we've stopped we've spent longer than we meant to.

The road (N67) from The Burren to Ireland's third city, Galway, passes through the harbour town of Kinvarra where **Dunguaire Castle** sits on a small peninsula in Kinvarra Bay, an inlet of Galway Bay. The 1520 castle was completely restored in 1970 and is good for touring the rooms up to the narrow rooftop battlements which afford grand views of the bay. The castle is one of three in Ireland in which you can partake an evening of Medieval food and entertainment. The other two castles are Bunratty near Shannon and Knoppogue between Ennis and Shannon. We had always thought a Medieval evening sounded hokey, but thought we ought to have the experience. We were mistaken. The evening's meal was delicious and the performances by young people were charming. The evening of song, poetry, plays, dinner and drinks is not cheap (about $50 per person), but nor is it expensive for what you get. In high season you must sign up early, but even off season all the seating was sold out by dinner time.

There is much to see and do in **Galway City,** the City of Tribes, founded in the 12C. Most of it in the 21C involves shopping. The long two-street pedestrian mall downtown is host to a formidable array of shops, the most famous of which used to be Kenny's Bookstore and Art Gallery. It was our first stop the first three times we'd been to Galway. Sadly, on our last trip we were stopped short as we walked into Kenny's and found no books. Instead of three floors of new and used tomes with pictures of practically everyone known in literary circles for the last 75 years hanging by the hundreds, Kenny's is now a very smart gallery for all types of art. They still have all their books, but now they warehouse them and sell via the internet. Technology isn't always our friend. About every third establishment on the mall is a pub of some kind, and most of them host traditional sessions. Galway is the only place outside of Dublin we've heard afternoon sessions midweek. For music and shopping, downtown Galway is a great place. For historical attractions head practically any direction out of town.

To the east of Galway via N6 and R348 is **Athenry Castle** in the village of Athenry. Athenry Castle is an early Anglo-Norman Tower (13C) in ruin since 1597. The tour of the castle is self-guided, but the steward in the information centre took the time to give us a half hour History of Ireland 101. Very informative and we could tell he loved his job. We could tell, too, that Padraig O'Toole, the guide at **Aughnanure Castle** northwest of Galway near Oughterard (N59), also loved his job and "his" castle. In both Ireland and Scotland we find many endearing tourist guides at sites who love to share their sites with the visitor. The castle is beautifully situated a short walk along a stream from the car park. Padraig told us the history of the the O'Flaherty's formidable ruins of the six floor tower house with views over Lough Corrib. To the north of Galway along N84 and R334 is the village of **Cong,** best known for the 1952 Oscar winning (Best Director, John Ford) film, "The Quiet Man," staring John Wayne and Maureen O'Hara. Once the home to the Kings of Connaght, one of the main attractions in the village is the 12C Augustinian Cong Abbey with interesting doorway, part of the cloisters, and a fairly intact monk's fishing house. The fishing house is situated in the middle of a river and has a hole in the floor where monks could net dinner as it swam by. Besides the abbey, the village draws tourists to the Quiet Man Heritage Centre, a replica of the cottage used in the film, which now contains movie memorabilia.

To the east of Cong someplace is **Ross Errilly friary,** one of the best preserved Franciscan friaries in Ireland. I say somewhere because we found it, but we don't know how we found it. Directions say its 10 miles southeast of Cong off R346 and R344. So many small unmarked roads are in the area that we had no idea what road we were on, but just stumbled onto the friary. It's a worthwhile find because, for a ruin, it's in very good condition.

Our last suggestion is to take a trip we have yet to take. As much as we love visiting all the golf courses we've been to, golf has gotten in the way of seeing parts of Ireland we know really should not be missed. The **Aran Islands,** which watch over the mouth of Galway Bay, is one of those trips we must take. The islands of Inishmore (the largest), Inishmann, and Inisheer (the smallest) are similar geologically to The Burren, being limestone slabs. The islands are crisscrossed by stone fences as small parcels of land were cleared for sustenance agriculture by the islanders. Today, the islands and people represent the living past. Besides being a tourist destination, the Aran Islands are also famous for Aran knitwear, particularly sweaters in symbolic stitches. The main archeological attraction on the islands is *Dun Aonghase* on Inishmore. This great drystone fort sits on the cliff edge 200 feet above the crashing waves of the Atlantic. The islands can be reached by ferries from Galway docks, from Rossaveel near Spiddal, and from Doolin. Or they can be reached by air from Connemara Regional Airport, 20 miles west of Galway. A visit to the Aran Islands is definitely on schedule for our next trip.

# Chapter Five:
## Northwest — Golf, Pubs, and Attractions

Carne GC, Co. Mayo

## GOLF

The Northwest of Ireland, counties Mayo, Sligo, Donegal, and the west of Roscommon, is the most remote. Here, too, is where the visitor will find some of the most scenic courses. Beautiful and remote creates a problem. You will want to visit as many as you can, but even in our numerous trips dedicated to tracking down these great hidden gems we've managed to miss several courses we know are world class. That just gives us reason to make our next trip.

The well known links courses, such as Ballyliffin, Murvagh, and Rosses Point, are the main draw for golfers. Don't be so quick to pass by the unknown or short courses. Anne and I spent a glorious sun-filled day playing Cruit Island, a 9-hole track that will rival the world's best at holding your interest and demanding your best shots. Though links courses get most of the attention, you would do yourself a disservice if you skipped some of the areas wonderful parkland courses.

### ACHILL ISLAND GOLF CLUB, Keel, Achill Island, Co. Mayo

On the beach side of R319, the main road on the island, just before the village of Keel.

www.achillgolf.com  (098) 43 456

Links 9-hole, 5416 yards, par 67, €15/18, but will negotiate on 9 hole price

**Amenities:** Small, single-wide caravan (trailer) acts as club office. Honesty box for when no one is around. Changing rooms and toilets behind.

**Course Comments:** Achill Island Golf Club is one of the most unique courses you'd ever want to visit. And visit it you should. It's a rough course which is barely manicured. The sheep on the course, lots of them, keep the grass short, and the one-man maintenance force drags a large screen behind a tractor to break up the sheep droppings (instant fertilizer). Fairways are outlined for each hole by rows of white rocks. The local rule is: stay within the "marked fairway" and play lift-clean-and-place; outside the white rocks, play your ball from whatever it lands in. Greenside or fairway bunkers with heavy beach sand are trouble on almost every hole. The greens are small and flat with subtle undulations. The greens were in surprisingly good condition considering the roughness of the rest of the course; they putt very true. While the sheep have the run of the course, the greens were fenced to keep out cows and cars (we didn't ask). A stream is in play on five and six, and the wind and tight links grass can always add difficulty. With the afore-description, why did I say you should play Achill GC? Several reasons come to mind. First, it is certainly unique. It's very reminiscent of Leadhills in Scotland; golf on a mountain top sheep field. Second, Achill sits in a breathtakingly beautiful location. The island (the largest in

Ireland and reached via a 300-yard bridge over the Atlantic) is full of picture postcard villages, like Keel. The course is a 9-iron shot away from the pristine Keel Beach, and surrounded with views of the village, the headlands, the Atlantic, Slievemore Mountain, and lambs gamboling about in the spring. Third, the club will give you a 9-hole price; reasonable for a quick round and a story to take home that will only get better with telling. Finally, even though short and flat, the golf is still interesting enough to keep your attention. I love the courses at Carne, Tralee, Rosses Point, Killarney, Headfort, and Skerries, but the story I told first upon returning from Ireland was of playing golf in the sheep field at Achill Island.

The holes at Achill are just straight ahead (between the white rocks), but a few are worth mentioning. The 4th, a 250-yard par 4 has a drive toward the beach rocks, the headlands, and the ocean. On the 5th, a 295-yard two-shotter, you start with your back to the great view you drove down toward on the 4th. Your tee shot must cross a corner of the creek and avoid it as it is in play just right of the green. The 6th also has the stream in play on the right side. You'll find that any hole with sheep in the way will be interesting. We found that the sheep, even young lambs, get quickly out of the way of a bounding golf ball. We found no evidence of sheep injured by golf balls. Though, come to think of it, the pub across the street did have a lamb chop special. Achill GC is a course to write home about, albeit for a different than the usual reasons. We got around in an hour and a half, and it was as enjoyable as any hour and half we spent on the trip.

**Comments from the Forward Tees:** Women get 398 metres (427 yards) advantage on this 9-hole course, but we face the same challenges. I discovered it hard to tee off into sheep and lambs, even if they do run when a ball approaches. Playing here is a totally unique experience.

## BALLINA GOLF CLUB, Mossgrove, Ballina, Co. Mayo

On the east side of the village on R294.
www.ballina-golf.com (096) 21050
Parkland, 6175 yards, par 72, €20

**Amenities:** New clubhouse built in 2005 has changing rooms downstairs and lounge and restaurant upstairs with excellent views over the course. The restaurant serves great meals morning to early evening with later bar hours. A small full service pro shop is also downstairs.

**Course Comments:** Built in 1924 as a 9-hole course in the heart of the Moy Valley and expanded to 18 holes in 1996, Ballina Golf Club (pronounced BALL-in-ah) is a lovely parkland course which is more difficult than it looks. A well landscaped course with pleasant views of the Ox Mountains, it plays well all year because of good drainage. We played after a very wet spell and in the rain for 9 holes and found only a few soft spots near tee boxes or between holes. The rough, wet and high, was tough to get out of. The course is smartly bunkered with mostly flat, greenside bunkers. A few looked small and tricky. Thankfully, those weren't the ones I ended up in. Several grass bunkers add difficulty to holes. The greens are an interesting mix of small to large of various shapes and levels. Several have unusual shapes, particularly the 16th and 18th, which reminded me of a square overturned bowl. A stream is in play on several holes. We were also told by Padhraig Connelly, the Honorable Secretary, that most days the wind would at least be a consideration. Unique for the courses we've played in Ireland, signage for the holes was in both yards and metres.

Ballina GC has its fair share of interesting holes. The 2nd, a par 4 of 304 yards, is a dogleg left with trees and OB on the inside of the bend. The fairway slopes down to a green with a bunker on the right, a false front, and a high plateau at back. The 7th begins with a wide open tee shot, if you avoid the OB left. The 416-yard par 4 has plenty of bailout room to the right. Your second shot must clear a wide stream just in front of the green to be safe. The uphill par 5 eighth (517 yards) has water in play on the first shot. It will be hard to find a level lie on the sloping fairway for your approach to the small, elevated, almost gun-turret green. The par 3, 187-yard 16th is great. It's a long shot downhill to a green with OB and a stream left, back, and right. The green is unusual; a platform green with run off on three sides, like a hat with a brim on three sides. Padhraig told a story of one of the better local players who took a twelve on this par 3 in competition. He hit two OB left, two OB right, one in the bunker, and two putted for a twelve.   With all the famous or getting famous links courses in Co. Mayo, Ballina Golf Club provides a pleasant change. The friendly staff, particularly Tina the club's office manager, and members add to the quality golf at Ballina.

**Comments from the Forward Tees:** One slight criticism of the layout is that placement of the forward tees took some of the interest out of some holes. Easier is not always more fun.

### BALLYLIFFIN GOLF CLUB, Old Links, Ballyliffin, Inishowen, Co. Donegal [both courses]

Traveling from Derry (Londonderry on some maps) the quickest route is to cross the Foyle Bridge then take A2 towards Moville, turning off for Carndonagh at Quigley's Point/Carrowkeel. Ballyliffin is 6 miles beyond the turn.
www.ballyliffingolfclub.com  (074) 937 8100
Links, 6600 yards, par 71, €110

**Amenities (for both courses):** The current clubhouse, built in 2000, has changing rooms and pro shop (very complete) downstairs. Upstairs is clubhouse lounge and Links Restaurant, both of which have fine views out over the courses and the Atlantic. Pub food served all day in the lounge, and a full restaurant menu in Links.

**Course Comments:** To play at Ballyliffin is to experience nature at its most majestic. As many clubs in Ireland, the Ballyliffin Golf Club has its roots in British soldiers stationed at the nearby Leenan Fort. Since before the 1920s golf of some sort has been played in this area, but it wasn't until 1947 that an official club was formed at Ballyliffin. The first 9-hole course was opened in 1948. When the lease on the land of the 9-hole course was up in in 1970, a new tract of almost 400 acres was found. By 1973, an 18-hole course, the Old Links, was completed. The most recent update to the Old Links was done by professional Nick Faldo, who wanted to bring the course up to today's standards without destroying any of its natural character. All who play now will say the task was superbly accomplished.

Though not long by today's standards for championship courses, the Old Links, the most northerly course in Ireland, will still be a stern test for even the best golfers. Moguled fairways, strategic bunkering, tricky greens, and always the wind will present plenty of challenge. The natural design in wonderful linksland will mean frustrating links bounces, but that's why you play links courses. The first hole, a 392-yard par 4, gives a good indication of what the rest of the round will be like. This dogleg right has a generous fairway between rough-covered dunes and typical rolling links fairway. Two bunkers and mounds left guard the moderate sized green. Another dogleg right is the 4th, a par 5 of 488 yards. It takes a drive of about 230 yards to reach the corner of the bend, but there are no bunkers to cause concern. You should be concerned though about the bumps and hollows of the fairway. The small raised green is nestled into the dunes. Next comes a great little par 3. The 162-yard 5th is a short, but challenging hole with no traps. You tee off uphill with a large dune on the left to a small, narrow, swaled green. The 13th is a straight par 4 of 414 yards with five bunkers, two in play on the drive, and two more fronting the green. The fifth bunker will give problems to those off line with their second shot. Number 16 is a 389-yard slight dogleg left par 4. Plenty of mounding in the fairways guarantees you won't have a flat lie for your second shot. The green is shaped like a double green and when the pin is on the left, your approach will be over rough-covered dunes. Stay to the right is good advice for your first shot. Holes 13, 14, 15, and 16 play along the water of Pollan Bay (not in play). Ballyliffin Old Links may be less than 40 years old, but the course feels like it's been here forever.

### Ballyliffin, Glashedy Links
Links, 7217 yard, par 72, €110

**Course Comments:** Some say that Ballyliffin Glashedy Links is the toughest links course in Ireland. Designed in 1995 by the team of Ruddy and Craddock, the course was first proposed as a relief course for the Old Links which was gaining a worldwide following. Instead, the course ended up being a second championship caliber course which plays alongside and inside the Old Links and makes dramatic use of some of the areas most massive dunes. All the same challenges of the Old Links are found at Glashedy, except they are ratcheted up a notch—the mounding and surrounding dunes are taller and steeper, the bunkers are bigger and deeper and more of them, and the fairways are firm and fast. Glashedy Links is not a course for the beginner, but it is playable by most decent golfers, if they will select the appropriate tees of the four provided. As always, I'll use the championship or back tee distances, but I played off the second tees with my 12 handicap and still found it tough going. The 2nd, *Creig na Caillighe,* is a 432-yard par 4 dogleg right. It takes a drive of about 230 yards to clear the two bunkers on the inside corner. Stay straight on this hole because it's hard to get out of the rough and dunes at the sides. Two more bunkers can be problems on your approach, especially the pot bunker at the right front of the green. *Loch na nDeor,* the 183-yard par 3 seventh has a downhill tee shot to a large tiered green fronted by two bunkers. A pond on the right waits for any off-line shots. The 10th is a 397-yard par 4 which doglegs right around a dune to a very ridged fairway. Traps left and right complicate the drive. The multilevel green is protected by dunes and one bunker right. At the 13th, *Bun a 'Chnoic,* it's about the bunkers; ten of them! Two on the right and one on the left will be in your thoughts as you drive on this

572-yard monster. Three more traps line the left of the hump and hollow fairway. Don't be long on your approach to the green, although only one bunker protects the left front of the green, three bunkers lurk in the dunes behind for those who are too strong. A long dogleg left (for a change) is the 440-yard par 4 fifteenth, *Tobar Mhuiris.* Bunkers sit on each side of the prime driving area, and mounds and hollows near the green, as well as four more traps, make the approach difficult. Whether you choose the Old Links or the Glashedy Links (or hopefully both), you will find stern, challenging golf in one of the most beautiful settings in the world.

**Comments from the Forward Tees:** A tough, tough course. I'm not sure if it was fun or not. I am sure it was beautiful.

### BOYLE GOLF CLUB, Knockadoobrusna, Boyle, Co. Roscommon

Off N61 just south of the village.
www.boylegolfclub.com  (079) 62 594
Parkland 9-hole, 4914 metres, par 64, €15/all day

**Amenities:** Changing rooms and a small lounge, only open 4:00 PM until late, make up the clubhouse. Honesty box for when nobody is around.

**Course Comments:** Boyle is like many of Ireland and Scotland's interesting village courses. It is built on land donated by a local farmer in 1971, and developed to meet the needs of local golfers and designed by Eddie Hackett. Sited in the Co. Roscommon hills, the short course has pleasant views of the farmland and surrounding hills, including Lough Key, Curlew Mountains, Sligo Mountain, and Mayo Mountains. The lush course can be soft when wet, but is well groomed with just a small staff. For the most part the course is straight forward golf with only a few bunkers, no water, and small to moderate sized greens. Boyle plays up, back, and across a fair sized hill (Knockadoobrusna) with plenty of trees to grab wayward shots. With three par 3s and six par 4s (one of which plays as a par 5 on the second nine), Boyle is not championship golf, nor might it be the equal of other village 9-hole courses such as Swinford or Lismore. What it is though, is a well maintained, easily accessible, stress-free layout with a 15 euro all-day price and a friendly staff. It also has a knoll just off the course (near the fifth tee) which is said to be an ancient child's burial ground. People who have gone up to the grave mound report a spooky feeling. Check ahead before venturing up as the ground is on private property.

### CASTLEBAR GOLF CLUB, Rocklands, Castlebar, Co. Mayo

Southeast of town off either N60 or N84, follow signs.
No functioning website (094) 902 1649
Parkland, 5907 metres, par 71, €25

**Amenities:** The club has a nice lounge which serves food all day. Lounge has views of the 16th and 18th greens. The small pro shop has all the essentials.

**Course Comments:** As we waited on the first tee for a group of men in front of us to clear, three ladies walked up and one said they were waiting for a fourth, but they wanted to go ahead of us because they were having a competition. We told them we were ready to go and this was our tee time. Two of the ladies backed off, but one insisted that competitions should have priority. Not wanting to cause a scene, Anne and I said go ahead, the tee is yours. The other ladies pointed out that their fourth had just pulled into the parking lot and that they weren't ready. They almost forcibly pulled the insistent one away. We asked the pro, Dave, about the situation after our round. He said that being a club's pro would be a great job if it weren't for some members. The Castlebar Golf Club is an excellent parkland course. It is well maintained and, except for 14 and 15, all the holes are distinct from every other hole. The course has a plethora of beautiful mature trees lining fairways, including several spinneys (plantings of a group of trees) separating fairways. Though most fairways are generous, plenty of trouble awaits at Castlebar. A mix of 47 fairway and greenside bunkers will direct shots. Some of the bunkers are large, a few penal, and most are in play. The greens tend to be average or large, but a couple are quite small. Subtle slopes and breaks to the greens means lots of interesting pin placements are possible. Ponds are in play on six holes, particularly 1, 3, 6, and 18. A commuter train passes the course and is visible from several holes. That's not particularly unusual, but we did take notice when a bread delivery truck drove past us on the first hole and drove behind the second green. We never did figure out where the truck ended up.

All the holes are interesting at Castlebar, even 14 and 15 which are mirror image par 4s. Several holes do stand out, though. The first, a 298-metre par 4 begins with a blind tee shot to the crest of a hill. Aim for the bunker at the top of the hill. The second shot slopes dramatically left toward a pond and bunker. The undulating green is challenging to putt. Another good short hole is the 291-metre par 4 fourth. The second shot must dogleg right around trees and group of four traps. The large green, shared with the seventh, is protected by three more bunkers. The 6th is a fine, challenging par 3 of 171 metres with OB, a pond, and a bunker on the right. Don't go there. Lots of bailout room exists on the left. Even though the green has a large mound in the middle, that's where locals say to hit no matter where the flag is. The 7th is a 361-metre par 4 dogleg right which can reward long hitters who cut the corner over the trees. The trees and OB will punish those who miss right. For we mortals, aiming to the left of the bunker visible from the tee makes good sense. The green, shared with the 4th, is severely undulating making three putts very easy. Trouble is everywhere on the short par 5 eleventh—eight bunkers, a pond, trees, a dogleg right second shot, and a multilevel green. Stay out of trouble, though, and the hole can reward you with an easy par or birdie. The par 3 sixteenth is the toughest shot on the course for visitors. You tee off straight towards the clubhouse lounge picture windows. It looks like a well struck shot past the pond, which misses the trees and two bunkers, could bounce or fly into the window. The reality is that more room exists between the green and clubhouse than it seems from the tee. Dave, the club pro, told us that about a month before a player pitched long and through the window which was luckily open. When he came to claim his ball, locals in the pub wanted him to play it where it lay, ala "Tin Cup." Truth or Irish blarney? The 18th is a tough finish, especially the first time you play it. The hole is a 467-metre par 5 with three traps on the left of the fairway to avoid on your tee shot. Your approach is between a stand of trees and a second set of bunkers. The raised, sloping green runs off left into a pond. Accuracy from tee to green is the key to scoring at this fine finish to a fine course.

**Comments from the Forward Tees:** Not a lot of difference exists between the men's and ladies' tees. Water will cause problems for ladies here, as well.

### CARNE GOLF LINKS (Belmullet), Carne, Belmullet, Co. Mayo

Coming through Belmullet take the 3rd exit at the Square (roundabout) and continue over the bridge. Take a left after Eurostar and continue for 3 km. Turn right at *Gailf Chaira* sign.

www.carnegolflinks.com (097) 82 292
Links, 6119 metres, par 72, €70

**Amenities:** The modern clubhouse has changing rooms downstairs and a new very complete pro shop. Upstairs is a small, but cozy lounge/bar serving food all day. In 2013 the club opened a new nine hole course, the Kilmore.

**Course Comments:** Call it Belmullet, Carne, *Cursa Galf an Chairn,* or golf Nirvana. The remote Eddie Hackett Carne Golf Links (Hackett's last project), nestled on a wild and natural thin strip of land between the Atlantic Ocean, Blacksod Bay, and Cross Lough, is drop dead spectacular. Built in 1993, this dramatic links course looks like it's been here forever. Regarded now as one of the finest links courses in the world, it is so far out-of-the-way that you can still just show up and get a game during the week (though, on weekends you'd better call ahead). The course is about two and a half miles from the village of Belmullet, which itself is thirty-five miles northwest of Westport and thirty miles east of Ballina. Hackett called the land Carne is built on perfect for great golf. All who play the 6119-metre, par 72 course will agree, regardless of what they score. The course can be brutal when the Atlantic gales blow, or only tough when the weather is pleasant, but it will never be a pushover. Even without the bashing impact of wind and rain, challenge aplenty awaits at Carne. The twenty or so bunkers on the course are not the most penal we've ever seen, but are definitely to be avoided. Though a couple of holes have small ponds, they're never much of a worry. The greens are fairly quick, even when wet, but play true and the slopes aren't too severe. What makes Carne the glorious test of golf it is are the dunes. Vast, towering, colossal are descriptors which have been applied to the dunes Carne plays over, around, and through. The views across Blacksod Bay and out to the islands of Inis Gloire and Inis Geidhwewild are almost as stunning as the dunes.

It wouldn't do justice to such a fine course to highlight just three or four holes. Instead, we picked several from each side to give a real feel for the easier front side and the more challenging second nine. The 1st hole is a medium length par 4 of 366 metres. *Croc na Ros* has a fairly narrow fairway which doglegs right about 240 metres off the tee. In the summer, a slice may end up in the Burnet Roses which sit to the side of the fairway. The narrow, but deep green has heavy rough all around, but no bunkers. The 4th, *Tober Ton* (The Reservoir) is a 473-metre par 5 with a large swale in the center of the fairway. With OB all along the left side and mounding on the right, the hole doesn't have to be long to play tough. A menacing pot bunker guards the right of the slightly elevated green. The 6th is the most difficult hole on the front. The troubles on *Staith na Sabhaircini,* a par 4 of 363 metres, are caused by an undulating fairway and tall dunes on both sides of a hole which turns sharply left about 60 metres from the green. The green is raised and surrounded by rough-covered dunes. The shortest par 4 on the front is the 327-

metre 9th. The drive uphill is between large dunes. The very elevated two-tiered green is fronted by a deep hollow.

After the 9th you come back to the clubhouse, which can be a welcome respite if the weather is nasty. A nip or two of Jameson or Bushmills might be in order to fortify you for the harder second nine at Carne. Whereas, the front nine led you out along Blacksod Bay and back, the finishing nine goes out to the stormy Atlantic before coming back to the comforting clubhouse. While playing the second nine, even in good weather, you'll earn a stop in the clubhouse lounge with its friendly staff. The 10th has an interesting story about its name, *Macalla,* which means "Echo." The name relates to a cow who could not find her lowing calf because of the confusing echoes in the tall dunes. Eleven is a short, but challenging par 4. This left to right dogleg has mounds and hollows waiting to grab your drive. The trap at the outer corner of the dogleg is a helpful aiming point 266 metres from the tee. The steeply lifted green has mounds and one small bunker behind. One of the most dramatic holes in the northwest of Ireland is the short, sharp dogleg 12th, which has a significantly raised green. The hill in front of the green on this 300-metre hole is so sloped that balls which don't reach the putting surface may roll back or to the right as much as 35 or 40 metres. The small green is tricky to putt. The longest par 4 on the course is *An Muirineach* (meaning maram or bent grass), the 399-metre 17th. The hole is rated the hardest at Carne because it climbs from tee to green on a narrow path of short grass. Hollows and mounds wait to grab any shot which doesn't stay in the middle. The long narrow green has plenty of tricky pin placements. The par 5 eighteenth at 495 metres isn't an easy finish. Drive through an avenue of dunes and then downhill toward the green. The deep hollow in front of the green, known as *The Bloody Hollow,* is the site where the lowly dead of *Ar Iorrais* are buried.

On your way around this world class track, be sure to notice the endangered cowslips and wild orchids on the course. Also, be thankful if larks flutter and sing above the rough—if it's raining, the larks stay on the ground. Carne Golf

Links, *Cursa Galf an Chairn,* or Belmullet Golf Course. By any name, this is one of the best links courses anywhere and well worth every effort to play. Absolutely my favorite course in Ireland!

**Comments from the Forward Tees:** Tee shots throughout are interesting and fair. The course has several spectacular views of the Atlantic, especially from the tee on 13. Several holes require very high approach shots which are difficult for me and might demand an extra shot to get close enough to pitch. Even when hitting down the middle, some holes have mounds and swells that will throw shots into trouble.

### CARRICK ON SHANNON GOLF CLUB, Woodbrook, Carrick-on-Shannon, Co. Roscommon
On N4 halfway between Boyle and Carrick-on-
Shannon.
www.carrickgolfclub.ie (071) 966 7015
Parkland, 5725 metres, par 70, €20

**Amenities:** In 1949 a clubhouse was built with two World War II Nissan huts used to billet US servicemen based in Enniskillen. A nice clubhouse opened in 1971 with a lounge serving food most usual hours. The club has one of the best stocked pro shops we've found outside of the "big name" or resort courses.

**Course Comments:** We first stopped on a pleasant spring day after a very unpleasant spring day which brought about 3 inches of rain. Most of the courses we visited that day were closed because of flooding. Hey, how do think Ireland stays so green. The course manager Lizze took me out to look at the course in the club's only buggy and left Anne alone in the pro shop and clubhouse. Lizze told Anne that if anyone came by to tell them we'd be back in a short while. So, for a half hour while I toured the course, Anne attended the pro shop. That kind of openness and trust on the part of people like Lizze is what we love so much about the Irish and the Scots. When we came back to play the next day, the course was well dried out and as enjoyable as it looked to be the day before.

Golf has been played in this area since 1910, but it took three moves to establish the Carrick on Shannon course on the Woodbrook Estate, the club's current location. The original 9-hole course here is the design work of famed architect J. McAllister. It wasn't until 2002 that the club could get enough land to expand to a full 18 holes. The present course was opened for play in August 2003. Built on the hills beside Lough Drumharlow (part of the Shannon River system), elevation changes are part of the course, but nothing too strenuous. The 48 bunkers, a good mix of fairway and greenside, will keep you thinking, but none of the bunkers are too penal. The greens are of moderate size with mild undulations. Streams and/or ponds are in play on three holes and you tee off over a corner of the lough on the 8th. The water hazard on the 10th is an environmentally sensitive area. The views of Lough Drumharlow, the Shannon River, and the Boyle River, as well as surrounding mountains and farmland are stunning. The best views are from the green at six and the tee at 14.

The holes at Carrick are interesting for a variety of reasons. The fairway of the 4th has a series of narrow ripples across it. It is said that these are left over from pre-famine potato farming. We saw these same type of ripples at Skerries GC, but got a couple of other possible explanations. Also part of the 4th hole is supposed to be the burial ground of Irish mythological folk hero *Diarmuid agus Grainne.* On the 5th, a 149-metre par 3, is the the remains of a fairy ring fort (another one is on the 9th). The tee shot on the 5th goes directly over bunkers guarding the 4th green to a small green with three fronting bunkers. A little help from the fairies wouldn't hurt. The 7th hole, a par 5 measuring 504 metres, begins with a drive over a creek and pond to a generous fairway. A large rock on the left indicates 200 metres to the green. Near the green the fairway twists to the left and two bunkers guard the right side of the green. The 8th must be considered the signature hole at Carrick. The 172-metre par 3 requires a shot straight over a corner of the lough to a green with bunkers on both sides. The left side trap is a saving bunker that can keep wayward shots from a watery grave. The 11th is a short par 4, only 305 metres, but is fraught with difficulties. Your drive is to a fairway bisected by a stream. The rock in the fairway is a good aiming point at only 90 metres from the green. The approach is again over the stream to a kidney shaped putting surface with traps on each side. A pretty hole is the 363-metre par 4 twelfth with its tee box set beside the lough (not really in play). The fairway is wide with forest on the left and only light rough to the right. The green is protected by two bunkers and mounding. Completing the Carrick  (Amen) Corner is the 13th, a 189-metre one-shot gem. With gorse left and a row of four bunkers right, accuracy is a must to score well on the two-tiered green. The 15th is a classic parkland hole with a generous fairway between stands of mature trees. A row of three fairway bunkers about 210 metres from the tee will encourage you to stay right. The long narrow green is fronted by two traps on the right and two on the left.  Carrick on Shannon Golf Club is being discovered and gets busy on the weekends. If you can, stop by on a weekday when its still possible to have a wonderful course practically to yourself.

**Comments from the Forward Tees:** Carrick on Shannon has lovely views over the Shannon River and nearby forests. It plays straight forward with no tricks. An enjoyable parkland course straight hitters should score well on.

### COUNTY SLIGO GOLF CLUB (Rosses Point), Rosses Point, Co. Sligo

From Sligo follow R291 (Rosses Point road) to the village of Rosses Point. The road deadends into the club.

www.countysligogolfclub.ie (071) 77 171
Links, 6136 yards, par 71, €125

**Amenities:** Pleasant modern clubhouse with restaurant/lounge above the changing rooms and pro shop. The lounge has an eating section which serves good pub fare all day and a bar section. Pro shop features a complete range of clubs and clothing. The Bomore Links 9-hole course is a good warmup for the championship course and provides its own challenges.

**Course Comments:** Golf has been played on Rosses Point since 1894 when the first 9-hole course was built under the direction of George Combe. In 1907 the course was expanded to 18 holes. The current out-and-back layout Co. Sligo Course, though, is the result of a major redesign by noted British architect Harry S. Colt (St. Andrews Eden, Royal Portrush, Royal Belfast) in 1928. Besides continually updating the course, Co. Sligo added a 9-hole track in 2000, the Bowmore Course. Well regarded as one of the finest links courses in the world, Rosses Point offers plenty of challenge for all levels of golfers. Sixty-nine bunkers, about half fairway, will demand accurate shots to avoid. And you will want to avoid them. Many of the traps are revetted and deep. The several fairway bunkers close to tees are particularly troublesome if you miss hit a drive. The greens come in two sizes—large and larger. Several are multilevel and four or five have false fronts. The greens play quick even when wet. On six holes a stream is in play, but often for only very wayward shots. As a links course, Rosses Point has all the typical links characteristics, including heavy fescue rough and links bounces caused by fairway mounding. The wind and weather will make a dramatic difference in how the course plays. On the day we played in May 2006, we started in light wind under cloudy skies. After six holes a light rain started to fall and the wind picked up to a decent breeze. The last three holes were played in driving rain and a howling gale. Such are the vagaries of an Irish spring. We were thankful that on the first few holes we got to enjoy the views Rosses Point is famous for, which include Sligo Bay, the Atlantic, Ox Mountains, Benbulben, and Knocknarea (where Queen Maeve is buried), beautiful dunes and shore, and Rosses Point village and harbour.

The course is composed of one quality golf hole after another. The 1st, *Greenlands,* is a 384-yard par 4, which plays gently uphill on a wide fairway with three bunkers. Another bunker protects the false-fronted green with OB behind right. The hole is a good warm-up for what's to come. Number three tee has the best views on the course. The 502-yard par 5 plays steeply down toward six bunkers which guard both sides of the fairway. A downhill drive of about 270 yards is needed to clear the traps on the most direct route toward the green. Three more bunkers make the approach to the green more difficult. The hole is definitely a birdie opportunity for long hitters. The hardest hole at Rosses Point is *Ewing's Profile,* the 432-yard par 4 seventh. On this hole you cross a creek twice (though just off the tee the crossing is not of much concern), but the the second crossing just before the green is a test. The hole is long with a rise in the middle of the fairway. The stream guards the right side of the green while two bunkers guard the left. For those of us who are modest hitters, a lay-up on the second shot may be the prudent choice. *Lighthouse,* the 12th, is a demanding par 5 of 534 yards which begins with a blind shot—aim to the right of the trap on the left (reachable at 234 yards). The rest of the hole plays down to a two-tiered green with several grass bunkers around it. Luckily, the hole usually plays downwind. As you come up the fairway, the lighthouse seems to float in the sea above the green. From the 13th to the 18th, the course hugs the shore. The 14th, *Mahon's Burn,* is almost a double dogleg (left then right) with bunkers to aim over (a carry of about 220 yards). This 433-yard par 4 has a stream (the burn) across the fairway about a 100 yards from the green which is tucked right behind heavy rough. The green is another of the false-fronted greens and falls off behind. *Knocknarea* is the fine 213-yard par 3 sixteenth separated from the sea by a rough covered berm. Two bunkers, front and left, guard the green, which seems a mile away when the wind blows against you. The downhill 17th, called *The Gallery,* is indexed as the second hardest hole at Rosses Point. The fairway on this long par 4 of 455 yards runs out at 275 yards, but into the wind only Tiger Woods or John Daly need to worry. Your second shot is over heavy rough to a fantastically swaled fairway rising up to the green.

Co. Sligo or Rosses Point stands proudly with some of the finest links courses in the world. Although the course fits well with other quality links courses on Ireland's west coast (Tralee, Dooks, Enniscrone, Carne, Murvagh), it reminded Anne and myself of either Royal Dornoch in the north of Scotland or North Berwick West in East Lothian, Scotland.

**Comments from the Forward Tees:** Not a beginner's course because it requires so many precision shots to stay out of trouble. The elevation changes play tough and a lofted uphill power shot is needed. The ladies' tees make the holes play fairly without changing the character of the hole.

### CRUIT ISLAND GOLF CLUB, Kincasslagh, Co. Donegal

From Dunglow (Dungloe on some maps) on N56 turn left onto R259 to near Kincasslagh village where you follow signs out to the end of the Cruit Island (*an Chruit*) peninsula.
www.cruitislandgolfclub.com (074) 954 3296
Links 9-hole, 5141 metres, par 68, €22/18 holes

**Amenities:** Cruit Island GC has a pleasant, modern clubhouse which serves meals and checks in golfers (no pro shop). An Honesty Box is provided; if nobody happens to be around, drop your money in and head out.

**Course Comments:** What course could elicit players to say it was the "most unfair golf course" they'd ever played, and that they didn't care because "it was such a glorious place?" It's a course called "magical" and "impossible to find." The magnificently wild and windswept 9-hole links layout (5141 metres, par 68) plays over *Cionn Caslack* (Head of the Sea Inlet). The views of Rosses Bay, Inishfree Bay, the Atlantic Ocean, Aran Island, and Owey Island (with its abandoned village visible from the course) are stunning. Cruit Island Golf Club (pronounced "krit") will challenge you with numerous blind shots, seaside links bunkers (many of which are hidden until you're in them), small fast greens, the Atlantic in play on a couple of holes, and the persistent wind. It's easy to get on at Cruit Island because it's so out-of-the-way, but on the weekends and in high season the course can be busy. Two items you should be required to carry here are camera and binoculars—you'll be thankful if you have both. The views are especially spectacular from the 3rd and 7th tees and the 3rd green. But you've come this far for golf, and the course is as spectacular as the views. The 302-metre par 4 third begins with a blind tee shot—it's about 160 metres to crest the hill. From the top it is all downhill to a green stuck out into the Atlantic. Be careful on your approach shot because three bunkers front the entire green, and, if you're very far back, they're hidden from view. Behind the green is a few feet of rough and Inishfree Bay—you don't want to go there. The 5th is a unique hole; a par 4 of only 256 metres, but a strong dogleg right (almost an acute angle). If you choose to follow the fairway, take a medium iron and shoot away from the green. Your second shot is another mid-iron to a green protected by several bunkers. If you dare (maybe on your second time around), aim at the white marker in the rough on the hill to the right of the fairway. A shot of about 160 metres should land in the fairway about 25 to 30 metres short of the green. Have your playing partners help track your ball because, if you miss the cut grass, the rough short or long is thick. The tee shot on the next hole, the 137-metre par 3 sixth, is dramatic, to say the least. You drive across a sea chasm, with the crashing Atlantic below, to a green with OB behind (actually, it's a cliff, and your ball drops down to the sea, but it's marked OB). Wind direction and strength or lack of wind complicates the shot. The 7th completes a trifecta of exciting holes. The tee shot on this 293-metre par 4 makes or breaks the hole. To the right of the landing area is a dune with heavy rough. A roomy bailout area is left, but it lengthens the hole. The second shot is blind to a green hidden by the hummocked fairway.

Anne and I planned to play nine here and head on to another course. With a bright May sun and only light winds, we came off our first nine so enamored by Cruit Island, we had to play again. After a stop at the clubhouse for a quick bite, a call to cancel our second course, and a trip to the car for our binoculars and a second camera, we headed back into the golf heaven of Cruit Island Golf Club. We have no question as to why some call this course the best 9-hole golf course in the world.

**Comments from the Forward Tees:** Water is never easy; now add very difficult rough, the need for precise shots, and distracting views. Together it means you have a difficult course. But I enjoyed every minute of it and eagerly agreed to a second nine. Six is a real test because if you can't carry to the green, your ball is lost and you have to try the same shot again.

**DONEGAL GOLF CLUB (Murvaugh), Murvaugh, Laghey, Ballintra, Co. Donegal**
From N15 (Donegl to Sligo road), the turn off is signed from N15, 10 minutes from Donegal Town or 15 minutes from the Ballyshannon bypass.
**www.donegalgolfclub.ie** (074) 9734054
Links, 6249 metres, par 73, €70

**Amenities:** In addition to the very comfortable clubhouse facilities including a complete pro shop, and upstairs lounge which serves tasty food all day and wonderful views, the course has some other attractions. Harebells and cowslips decorate the course while larks float high overhead singing. Donegal GC provided three toilets strategically dotted around the course, and placed ball-getters near the streams (a common practice in Scotland, but something we haven't seen much in Ireland).

**Course Comments:** Donegal is a prime tourist destination in the northwest corner of Ireland. People are drawn by the castle, the tweed, and the beautiful scenery of this region. Outstanding golf ought to be another reason to visit Donegal County. Courses like Donegal, Narin and Portnoo, and Cruit Island should be enough draw to call any golfers to the area. A 9-hole course was laid out near the Donegal Town in 1960, but the course proved to be a poor venue for winter golf. Finally, in 1974, designer Eddie Hackett was engaged to create a new course on the Murvagh Peninsula next to the Blue Stack Mountains about six miles south of Donegal Town. Hackett observed about the linksland around Moyne Hill that he could "only dress up what the Good Lord provides." His creation, the 6468-yard par 73 Donegal Golf Club, known to locals as Murvagh, has been recognized as one of the top ten courses in Ireland (Golf *World,* November, 2004) and has hosted both the men's and women's Irish Amateur Close Championships. The course, playable by all levels of golfers, will challenge play with 69 bunkers (most in play and always in your mind), small to moderate greens which can be quick, and a creek which will affect shots on several holes. The views at Donegal GC can be a distraction, albeit pleasant, as well. Vistas include the surrounding hills, Donegal Bay, and the islands of St. Ernan and Belle's famous as staging areas for emigrants.

Weak holes don't exist on the Murvagh course, and though some may have a similar look, they all play quite differently. The middle holes on the front (three through eight) receive much deserved praise. The two which we liked the best were the 5th and 8th. Number five, *Valley of Tears* (after playing it, you'll know where the name comes from), is a brutal 179-yard par 3. Your semi-blind tee shot needs to reach a narrow, raised green over the valley which contains a large bunker. If you avoid that bunker and the four others around the green, putting will still be a challenge on this large sloping green. A hint to playing the second shot on the par 4 seventh is to look for the target behind the green as an aiming point. We also liked *Moyne Hill,* the 502-yard 8th. A drive needs to carry 200 yards of rough to find the narrow fairway. Because the fairway slopes left, the second shot should stay as far right as possible without getting hung up in the hillside rough. Don't be fooled—the green you see on the left as you approach your third shot is the 10th; your green is tucked to the right and protected by a particularly nasty looking pot bunker. The hole is demanding from first shot to last. We thought that the final three holes at Donegal made a fine end to the round. Sixteen, *Big Dunt,* is a long par 3 of 228 yards. Besides the length of the hole, five bunkers (to the right and behind) guard this elevated green. From the great view on the tee at the 17th, the hole plays as a 325-yard par 4 which gently doglegs right to left. The fairway is generous and only one bunker fronts the right side of the green. The green has two levels, but a precise second shot can leave you a good birdie opportunity. *Bolgie Hill* isn't as frightening a hole as the name implies. At 399 yards this par 4 has four bunkers dotting the landing area for your drive and the green has four more bunkers surrounding it. I know Tiger Woods did it for four rounds at St. Andrews in the 2000 Open, but I think anyone who can get around Murvagh without ending up in the sand ought to receive some kind of award. Great links golf is found all along the west coast of Ireland. Be sure to include the excellent Murvagh (Donegal) Golf Club in your itinerary.

**Comments from the Forward Tees:** This course is long from the forward tees at 5971 total yards with all par 5s well over 400 yards. Par 3s aren't short, but are more reasonable at from 173 to 199 yards. Water can be a factor for ladies, especially on 2, 4, 12 and 14. The course is well worth the challenge.

**ENNISCRONE GOLF CLUB, Enniscrone, Co. Sligo**
From N59 out of Ballina take R297. The course is just before you get to the village of Enniscrone.
**www.enniscronegolf.com** (096) 36 297
Links, 6776 yards, par 73, €110

**Amenities:** The modern clubhouse has a nice lounge and more formal dining area, both of which get high marks from locals. A small pro shop completes the facility. Enniscrone also has a nine hole course, The Scurmore.

**Course Comments:** One player called Enniscrone Golf Club, "links golf with a vengeance." Another said it's "links from which no player comes away disappointed no matter how badly they may have played." This is truly one of the great links courses of Ireland (if not the world), and certainly ranks well with Tralee, Ballybunnion, and Waterville. Enniscrone is relatively undiscovered, but destined not to remain that way for long. The course, a par 73 with five par 5s, plays in stunningly dramatic dunes set beside Killala Bay. Holes twelve through seventeen play beside the beach, while the rest of the holes play into and through the dunes. A second course, the 9-hole Scurmore course, is set inside the 18-hole Enniscrone on fine linksland. While Scurmore can provide a fine practice round, it is Enniscrone you must play. Impressive even in 40 mile per hour winds and horizontal rain, Enniscrone has much to test your game. The winds on this seaside gem can add hundreds of yards to the layout and add degrees of toughness to the play. But even without wind Enniscrone will challenge you with blind shots, almost impossible rough, pot bunkers, and large, quick, undulating greens. In other words, Enniscrone has everything you seek in links golf.

Great variety in the holes is a signature of golf at Enniscrone—every hole is different and each is excellent. When forced to pick favorite holes, I have to start with the 1st, *Barta,* a 373-yard par 4. Even though the first drive of the round is rather innocuous, a straight drive of 220 to 240 yards to the corner of a dogleg right, the second shot, to a tiny elevated green wedged into narrowing dunes, lets you know what to expect from the rest of your round. The 2nd, *Killcummin,* at 556 yards, is a long difficult par 5. The drive is to a generous fairway, but your second shot must thread its way down a narrow avenue between dunes about 200 yards out from the green. Length and the wind are the problems this hole throws at you. The 8th, *Scurmore,* is a classic links par 3. The 170-yard hole plays from an elevated tee to a gently sloping green guarded by three bunkers. The wind can play havoc with club selection on what looks to be a simple hole. Four holes on the back deserve special note, starting with *Cnoc na gCorp,* the par 4 twelfth. This 345-yard dunes hole begins with a blind tee shot where it takes an almost 200-yard carry to clear the rough. The fairway is made of large hummocks (almost 40 feet tall), and a deep swale fronts the green. Your approach shot needs to be precise to avoid the heavy rough at the sides and behind the green. *The Burrows,* the 350-yard par 4 thirteenth, is a little easier, but no less fun. Aim over the white marker stone on another blind drive. It only takes a tee shot of 200 yards to be in good position for your approach to a very large, well-protected (two pot bunkers) green. The 15th, *The Strand,* is a quite challenging par 4, the number one handicap hole on the course. Your drive needs to be long and down the right side to have a good look at the green on your second. The 39-yard long green is tucked left into the dunes. No bunkers are needed to protect the difficult to putt three-level green. If that weren't enough challenge, the hole is situated right along the bay where the winds can be especially strong. Also playing along the bay is *The Long Bank,* the 514-yard par 5 sixteenth. It's a straightforward long hole where you will want to stay on the right side to have a good approach to the green for your third shot (for we mortals). The green isn't huge, but its two levels can allow some tricky pin placements.

Not only does Enniscrone GC come with great views of Killala Bay and the Atlantic, it comes with a great pedigree, as well. What began as a 9-hole course in 1918, was extended in 1974 to 18-holes by one of Ireland's greatest golf architects, Eddie Hackett. The course was further refined by renown Scottish designer Donald Steel in 1990, who worked hard to retain the Hackett character. Were Enniscrone Golf Club in the Dublin, Cork, or Galway regions, you'd have to book months in advance. But located as it is, in the isolated beauty of Ireland's west coast, it's still possible to drop in and get a game on one of the best links courses in the world.

**Comments from the Forward Tees:** The tees for ladies are fair, yet still challenging. The par 5s are long for women, especially considering the tough rough. On several holes the second shot was so difficult that a lay-up was the best play. Enniscrone is a beautiful course with pleasant visual variety with the ocean, bay, and high dunes.

## MULRANNY GOLF CLUB, Mulranny, Westport, Co. Mayo

16 miles northwest of Westport on N59, just before you cross over to Achill Island.

www.mulrannygolfclub.com  (098) 36 262

Links 9-hole, 6143 metres, par 73, €15

**Amenities:** Small clubhouse, open limited hours in summer. No concession for 9 holes, must pay for 18.

**Course Comments:** One of the oldest courses on Connacht, Mulranny Golf Club sits by the shore of the Atlantic and faces powerful sea breezes. Among the hazards are cows and sheep that roam the course—greens used to have electric fences around them. All the bunkers on the course are greenside, and a stream is in play on eight and nine. The two sets of tees for playing 18 do not make much difference in length of holes or angles of drives. The lovely scenery and tranquil setting, though, makes up for some of the courses shortcomings. Number one, a 426-metre par 5 (the 10th plays at 455 metres), begins with a blind uphill tee shot. The second shot is steeply down towards a narrow green set diagonally to the fairway. The second hole is a par 4 of 358 metres (11th at 346 metres) where you want to work at staying in the middle. A wild shot left off the tee brings the stream into play, but too far right means you'll have to contend with a greenside bunker on your approach to a fairly large green. The 9th is a 275-metre par 4 (312 metres as the 18th). The green can't be seen from the tee box on this, the shortest par 4. The green is set between two sand hills and is severely sloped.  Not a bad course for a rustic round, but Achill Island GC (a few miles west) is even more rustic and a great deal more accommodating for those wishing to just play nine.

## NARIN & PORTNOO GOLF CLUB, Portnoo, Co. Donegal

From Donegal Town take N56 west to Killybegs and then north to Ardara. Then take R261 to Narin

(Naran on some maps) and follow signs to the course.
**www.narinportnoogolfclub.ie**  (074) 954 5107
Links, 5930 yards, par 69, €80

**Amenities:** The first thing you will notice about the course is the comfortable clubhouse with a pleasant lounge. That's where you check in for golf—the club has no pro shop, but a few essentials are available at the bar. The second thing you'll notice is the warm Irish welcome you'll receive from whomever is in the lounge. The greeting is typical Irish: friendly and welcoming, but with an Irish sense of humor. A sign over the bar reads, "Everyone brings joy to this clubhouse; some when they enter, some when they leave." The lounge offers tasty soups and toasties and has a full bar. One of the other local options, Lakehouse Hotel, isn't as reliable.

**Course Comments:** The northwest coast of Ireland is rich with great undiscovered links golf courses. Along with the well-known Lahinch and Ballybunnion further south are finds such as Carne, Enniscrone, and Murvagh. Even further north up the coast is a gem called Narin and Portnoo Golf Club, named for the two nearby hamlets. Twenty-five miles northwest of Donegal, set on two small peninsulas jutting into Gweebarra Bay, Portnoo is a picturesque 18-hole links course of 5396 metres and a par of 69. The club was formed in 1930 by five locals who had the help of famed British champion Harry Vardon in designing a 9-hole layout. A couple of the original holes were redone in 1959. In 1980 the course was expanded to the present 18-holes. Narin and Portnoo GC fits J. Michael Vernon's description of "Scarborough Fair Golf," played out of parsley, sage, rosemary, and thyme (The *Greatest Player Who Never Lived,* Gale Group, 2000). Off the fairways, the rough is thick with clumps of wild flowers and heavy dune grasses. A plethora of bunkers line the fairways and surround the greens at Portnoo; some deep, and a few vicious (almost too small for a swing). The greens are varied with some flat, while others have wild slopes. Thankfully, none are monsters and most are moderate speed even in the dry of summer. One stream is in play on a few holes, but it won't be a major concern. Neither will be the ocean, which is in play on a couple of holes. Besides the bunkers, the wind is the biggest defense the course has. Oh yes, in the spring the flowers can cause no end of trouble even for the straight hitter. At that time of year the fairways seem to disappear under a blanket of small white daisies. The course will be especially beautiful, but it can be frustratingly difficult to find your white ball in sea of white. This might be a course on which to use those orange balls you've been saving and never knew why. The first time we played Portnoo, in the spring of 2002, the greens on one, two, and eighteen were encircled by low electric fencing to keep the cows off the greens. The arrangement with a local farmer was to let the livestock have access to this part of the course for winter and early spring grazing. This gave rise to the local nickname for the club: Port-Moo. Sadly, by the time we returned in fall of 2004, the cows were gone for good and so was the fencing. In the lake to the right of one and two, though, twenty-five pairs of swans winter over.

From start to finish, Portnoo provides a quality golf experience and gorgeous vistas. Though the ocean isn't in view until the 6th, the views of the bay, Croghy Head, and Aranmore Isle from the 9th and 12th are breathtaking. It's the middle and later holes that we find most interesting. For instance, nine and ten are an absolutely wild combination. The 9th, a par 4 of 294 metres, begins from an elevated tee and plays down to a fairway set between tall dunes. The second shot is to a green backed by Gweebarra Bay. Long hitters will be tempted to drive the green, but heavy rough and deep swales protect the putting surface. At ten you tee off from a small peninsula stuck out in the bay, and you actually drive over a corner of the 9th green, blindly uphill. Over the crest, the green is protected by unforgiving rough and severe mounding. The 13th is a 170-metre par 3 which starts from an elevated tee. Watch out for the tiny pot bunker just in front of the green, it's not visible as you tee off. The longest hole on Portnoo is the 476- metre par 5 fourteenth. The hole is a double dogleg, left to right off the tee, then the fairways makes another right turn near the green, which is tucked behind a dune. The fairway bunker is a good aiming point for your second shot (just don't go in). On one of our visits it started to rain as we walked toward our drives on the 14th. I quickly put up my umbrella, and Anne put up hers and started searching in her bag for her rain hat. She had to take almost everything out of her bag before she found the hat. By that time, it had stopped raining. [I don't know what message there is in that story, but I get to tell so few on Anne, I just had to tell this one.] The 15th is another par 5. This 454-metre hole begins with a drive from an elevated tee to an undulating fairway. The green is hidden from any approach, except the extreme left, by a knoll jutting into the fairway. The green is guarded by a fore-bunker and another greenside. The par 3 sixteenth is known locally as "High Alter" because of all the scores sacrificed there. In the late afternoon sunshine, the shadows the dips and hummocks of the 17th fairway create are spectacular. This 377-metre par 4 will never play the same twice because of the linksland bounces off the moguled fairway. The small green needs no additional protection. Narin and Portnoo Golf Club is definitely worth listing on your golfing agenda for the quality golf, the beautiful scenery, and the welcoming Irish hospitality.

**Comments from the Forward Tees:** Every hole is unique and the linksland adds extra unpredictability to each shot. A good score here is probably a few shots higher than normal. Overall, the course isn't too long, the par 3s range from 104 to 179 yards (94 to 162 metres), and the longest par 5 is 449 yards (405 metres). The course is a delight and I always want to go back and play it again.

**STRANDHILL GOLF CLUB, Strandhill, Co. Sligo**
Right on the beach at Strandhill about 5 miles out of Sligo on R292.
www.strandhillgolfclub.com (071) 916 8188
Links, 5675 metres, par 68, €35

**Amenities:** The modern welcoming clubhouse has changing rooms and a small pro shop below the upstairs lounge with nice views over the course. The lounge is a good meal option (food served until half eight) and won a Best Clubhouse Award in 2004.

**Course Comments:** Near Sligo are two great links courses, County Sligo GC and the less well known, but no less fun to play, Strandhill Golf Club. Strandhill began as a 9-hole course in 1931, and was expanded to 18 holes in 1973 by designer Eddie Hackett. The course has a lovely setting with holes actually coming down to the beachside parking area. Views of the Atlantic to the west and Ballysadare Bay to the south contrast with the famous Benbulben and Knocknarea Mountains with the massive Queen Maeve's Grave Cairn. The combination of fantastic scenery and great layout caused professional Christy O'Connor Snr to call Strandhill GC "the jewel of the northwest." With fifty bunkers, numerous blind shots, sea breezes, and tough linksland grasses, this jewel has some sharp edges.

When we played on a fine spring morning, the chorus of larks flittering above and the cinnamon butterflies fluttering about, didn't lessen the challenge of Strandhill and the wind. All the holes here are interesting, but several are standouts. *Bone Bawn,* the 352-metre par 4 fourth starts with a blind tee shot over rough-covered dunes. Stay straight because bunkers left and right are ready to grab stray shots. Another bunker fronts the left side of a slightly elevated green. The great view from the tee is only part of the charm of the 7th, *The Cannon.* This 391-metre par 4 runs along the strand (beach) with a fairway which narrows in the landing area. Heavy rough frames the fairway, but the most intriguing feature of the hole is the location of the green. The green, with its three surrounding bunkers, sits adjacent to the beach parking area. A big audience can watch you play the green. Strandhill's "Amen Corner," 13, 14, and 15, make a fantastic and difficult stretch of holes. Beginning at the 13th, which presents the best vistas on the course, you face a wonderful golfing test. *The Valley,* a 376-metre par 4 is a dogleg right with a carry of 140 metres to reach the nearest part of the fairway; 200 metres to be in prime position. The tee shot is blind over the thick rough. To find the green, you must shoot through a ten metre gap between two large sand-hills. No other defense is needed. In fact, so many balls can be lost on the drive on this hole that in competitions there will be a backup two or three groups deep. It is often best to send a spotter or fore-caddy 50 metres ahead to try to spot balls as they land. Next comes *The Short Pack,* a 160-metre par 3 which plays through a gap in the dunes to a green fronted by a large bunker. The natural bailout area puts golfers on the 15th tee in the line of fire. Finally, in this set is *Misgaun Maeve,* a par 4 of 336 metres. The second most challenging par 4 on the course, the 15th begins with a blind drive from an elevated tee to a right to left dogleg. The fairway runs out about 200 metres from the tee, so either play short or play a slight draw. The approach is to a steeply elevated green with two bunkers behind. Saving the toughest for last, *Buster's Lodge* is a 444-metre par 4 and the number one stroke index hole. Play to the left of the equipment shed (which is OB) with your drive to be in good position to approach the long sloping green. No bunkers, no ponds, no hidden hazards; the finish at Strandhill GC is just long tough frills-free golfing fun!

The one complaint we've heard about Strandhill GC (from more than one source) is that the course design is sometimes so tight that you must beware of hitting at players on other holes or being hit at by them. I'd have to agree that several times shots came uncomfortably close, especially on the tee at fifteen. After your round drop into the clubhouse or venture into one of the pleasant eateries along the beach.

**Comments from the Forward Tees:** The many challenges on this course include choosing a proper landing spot, long par 5s, avoiding rough, gorse, sand, water, and even people. There are lots of up and downs as you walk through the dunes. I enjoyed the challenges and loved the views.

### SWINFORD GOLF CLUB, Barbazon Park, Swinford, Co. Mayo

The course is a little southeast of the village. Exit off N5 onto R375 north. Turn left on Park Ave and follow it around to the course.

www.swinfordgolf.com  (094) 925 1378

Parkland 9-hole, 5542 metres, par 70, Inexpensive

**Amenities:** The small clubhouse has changing rooms and lounge (only open limited hours), but no pro shop. An honesty box is in the clubhouse, if nobody is about.

**Course Comments:** Swinford Golf Club is an interesting 9-hole track and worth a visit if you are in the area. The problem on this 9-hole course, like many others in Ireland, is that it only has an 18-hole price. If you only have time for nine, try to negotiate. We haven't been very successful at doing that (except at *Cill Dara,* Kildare GC), but otherwise it's a very expensive nine holes. At Swinford we put our money in the honesty box for one full 18-hole round. Anne, then, played the first nine, and I played the second nine. We just played them at the same time. I don't truly believe Swinford, or any other course, intends a round that way, but it's a way for us to justify paying for just nine holes. Whether playing 9 or 18, the Swinford course is a fair challenge. Bunkers (15 of them) are on all holes except the 3rd and 6th. The bunkers are a mixed lot of greenside and fairway, steep-sided and flat enough to putt out of. A stream is in play on four holes—3, 6, 8, and 9. The greens are small with some slope or undulations, but nothing severe. Numerous blind shots (drives and approaches) add to the difficulty. Swinford GC is decorated by some of the most beautiful mature trees. Besides the trees, the views of farmland and mountains (including Croagh Patrick) are attractive.

The course makes good use of available land by having a couple of holes cross others, and by tucking a few tee boxes back from the fairways; thus, extending the hole without needing a lot of land. It does mean a couple of long walks from one green to the next tee. For those playing 18 holes there are two greens at 8/17. Play the yellow flag on the second nine. The first hole is typical of a round at Swinford. It's a 271-metre par 4 which begins with a blind drive where you can see the green, but not the landing area. The hole plays over a hill and then back up to a green protected by three bunkers. The 6th, a 342-metre par 4, is a dogleg right beginning with a drive downhill over a creek and around a stand of trees. The approach is up hill with only the top of the flag visible. The short 304-metre par 4 seventh is another dogleg (right to left) where you drive down hill between two stands of trees to a generous fairway. Your second shot will be completely blind over a knoll to a green with bunkers on both sides. Look at the 7th green from the 6th to get an idea for your second shot on the next hole. This is a hole at which you'll probably want a second chance. The finish at Swinford is a 314-metre par 4. Your first shot needs to clear a creek cutting across the fairway, which is a serious visual challenge for many ladies. The second shot is blind over a hill to a green surrounded by three bunkers. Swinford Golf Club will keep your attention from first to last. On the Saturday we played, several groups of children were getting lessons on the course from local adults. It is nice to see such strong community support for golf.

**Comments from the Forward Tees:** You need precision, distance, and height to get up and over trees, creeks, and hills.

**TUBBERCURRY GOLF CLUB, Tobercurry, Co. Sligo**
Off N17, Sligo-Galway road, on R294 on the east side of the village.
www.tubbercurrygolfclub.ie (071) 9185849
Parkland 9-hole, 5490 metres, par 69, €15

**Amenities:** The course has a pleasant clubhouse, but no pro shop. An honesty box is provided for times when nobody is in the Secretary's Office. Food is available in the clubhouse lounge most usual hours, and the lounge is even a music venue some evenings.

**Course Comments:** If you are a fan of designer Eddie Hackett, as we've become, you should seek out the little known Tubbercurry Golf Club. The course, opened in 1991 and set between town and the rolling farmlands, is well bunkered, particularly with fairway hazards, most of which aren't very difficult. With no water in play, it's the bunkers and small greens which will demand your attention. Though two sets of tees are provided for those playing 18 holes, on only three holes will they make any real difference. What small elevation changes there are at Tubbercurry are used to add interest. The 5th, a 374-metre par 4, is an interesting challenge. From a slightly elevated tee this two-shotter plays as a long dogleg left with heavy rough on the inside corner. A large tree makes it necessary to approach the green from the right. The small green has bunkers on both sides. We also liked the 321-metre par 4 seventh. This hole, too, is a dogleg left and has a large bunker halfway across the hole about 110 metres from the green. Your approach shot is half-blind with only the top of the flag visible and bunkers left and right. The 8th plays longer than its 168-metre distance. A bunker in the center of the fairway about 10 metres before the green encourages players to take more club. Tubbercurry Golf Club is enough fun that, though we had only planned to play nine, it wasn't difficult to talk ourselves into going around again.

**Comments from the Forward Tees:** This course looked easy, but I found my shots often aimed at trouble (sand, rough, trees). It takes good course management to be in the right place for approaching the greens, especially on 3/12, 5/14, and 9/18.

### WESTPORT GOLF CLUB, Carrowholly, Westport, Co. Mayo
2.5 km west of the town on the Newport road (N59), turn left at the sign.
www.westportgolfclub.ie  (098) 28 262
Parkland, 6417 yards, par 72, €60

**Amenities:** The large modern clubhouse on the bottom floor has changing rooms and a very complete pro shop, with a particularly knowledgeable and friendly staff. The busy upstairs lounge serves tasty meals from lunch until early evening hours. The bar is an ebullient meeting place for all the local players. We played with Pat and Pam McIntyre, members from Dublin, and were treated royally when the clubhouse gang found out we were visiting Americans. Everyone was eager to find out how we liked their course.

**Course Comments:** In an area of wonderful links courses like Lahinch, Ballybunion, Connemara, Carne, Enniscrone, and Murvaugh, the Westport Golf Club, a parkland oasis in a sea of links, can easily be overlooked. It shouldn't be! Westport is certainly the best parkland course on the west and one of the best in Ireland. As fun as links golf can be, fine parkland challenges like Westport can be equally entertaining. With views of Clew Bay and Croagh Patrick (Ireland's famous holy mountain from which St. Patrick banished all snakes), the vistas here play second fiddle to no other course. Speaking of playing the fiddle, the town itself is a great draw for the traditional music in the pubs—book well ahead if you plan to visit Westport on a Bank Holiday; Dubliners love to spend their long weekends in Westport's music pubs [see Pubs and Attractions]. Though the golf club began in 1908, the present course on the Westport House Estate wasn't laid out until 1973. Architect Fred Hawtree, who was responsible for the latest work on St. Andrew's New Course, designed the current 18-hole layout set in 260 acres of rolling parkland. Though the course begins relatively benign, once past the first six "warm up" holes, Westport shows its teeth. The course is well bunkered with both fairway sand and greenside hazards. The sand is excellent (I would have preferred to stay out of it) and easy to play from. The few pot bunkers on the course are hazards you really want to avoid. Ponds and streams are in play on several holes, but are only a major concern on the last hole. The sea is indeed a condition of play on one hole, but more about that later. Greens are, for the most part, large and flat, but have subtle borrows which will challenge your short game. A couple of holes have greens with interesting undulations, but the moderate speed keeps them playable. Since the course is at the head of Clew and Westport Bays, the wind can be fierce, particularly on the more difficult back nine.

Once you get past the easier first six holes, you find out what a challenge Westport GC is. The 8th hole is a 436-yard par 4, which plays as a downhill dogleg left to right. With out-of-bounds on the left and trees on the right, the hole is tough enough without the pond that encroaches on your approach (whether your second of third). Bunkers on the left further protect the green. The run from the 12th through the 15th is a fine stretch of holes. Playing from an elevated tee, the par 3 twelfth is a beauty, with Croagh Patrick looming in the distance behind the green. The 14th, a par 3 of 180 yards, is both stunning and daunting, with two bunkers in front and the bay behind the green. It is the 15th, though, that will hold your attention. A par 5 of 495 yards from the members tees, the hole begins with a drive against the prevailing wind and over an inlet of the bay. At low tide you can see the rocks and sand strewn with the golf balls of those who failed. From the championship tees, it's a 200-yard carry to reach the other side. From the member's tees, the carry is only 140 yards, but as one player commented, the drive is "as intimidating as any you will get." I felt it was a good rival for the first at Machrihanish in Scotland. The rest of the hole doglegs left around the bay with saving bunkers on the left to catch the errant shots of those who try to shorten the hole. Croagh Patrick is a magnificent sight directly behind the green. The final hole is a long par 5 of 550 yards. It plays downhill and around a large lough on the right. Fairway bunkers on the left catch shots trying to stay too far away from the water. The green has a large hump in the middle which makes a three-putt a distinct possibility. Though not a links legend, Westport Golf Club is a course which should take a back seat to no other course.

**Comments from the Forward Tees:** The course is quite scenic with bays, loughs, and the mountain. It seemed to play longer than others at the time, possibly because it was wet, but it wasn't overly long. Trouble in the form of sand and water comes into play often. The longest par 3, number 12, plays from an elevated tee and was fun.

**Other courses in the region:**

Ballybofey & Stranolar GC (18), Ballybofey, Co. Donegal
        (074) 913 1093
Ballyhaunis GC (9), Coolnacha, Co. Mayo (094) 963 0014
Bundoran GC (18), Bundoran, Co. Donegal (072) 41 302
Castlerea GC (9), Castlerea, Co. Roscommon (090) 20 072
Claremorris GC (18), Claremorris, Co. Mayo (094) 937 1527
Dunfanaghy GC (18) Dunfanaghy, Co. Donegal
        (074) 913 6335
Letterkenny GC (18), Letterkenny, Co. Donegal
        (074) 912 1175
Portsalon GC (18), Portsalon, Co. Donegal (074) 915 9459
Rosapenna Old & Sandy Hills (2 x 18), Downings, Co.
        Donegal (074) 9155 5128

## *PUBS AND EATERIES*

**The Annora** in Portnoo, Co. Donegal, just before you get to the Nairn & Portnoo GC. Annora, named for owners Ann and Nora Toner, receives rave reviews from locals (at least the ones we've met on the golf course) for both its pub food and atmosphere. It has also received awards as Best Pub for Traditional Music.

**Asgard Pub & Restaurant** on The Quay in Westport, Co. Mayo, overlooking Clew Bay. Good choice for fish lovers, serving in both the pub and more formal restaurant. Owner Peter Kelly has created an establishment where you can find both casual fine dining and the Irish pub experience. Winner of Dining Pub of the Year.

**The Beehive Craft & Coffee Shop** at Keel on the main road (R319) through Achill Island, Co. Mayo. Cafeteria coffee shop with three rooms with tables and various island and Ireland crafts for sale. What do you expect, it's a cafeteria with a nice location. The craft shop is also interesting with some unusual products and quality jewelry.

**Blueberry Tea Room** just off the diamond (town Square) in Donegal Town. Donegal Town's only internet cafe (at the time), the Blueberry is a great place for the traveler to grab a bite and go upstairs to check e-mails or e-mail home. Service is warm and friendly. The food is top quality. In fact, the Blueberry Tea Room Pasta Salad recipe was featured on Tracy Gallagher's Travel Channel report.

**The Brewery** on the main town square in Letterkenny, Co. Donegal. Typical brew pub with a pub menu plus a few Mexican items. Nothing remarkable about the pub or the food, except that the building dates to 1815.

**The Bridge Bar** on the main street through Bundoran. The Bridge Bar is a warm, friendly, lively pub in the heart of the holiday town of Bundoran. It's becoming a haven for local and guest surfers discovering the good breaks nearby. With many rooms having views out to the Atlantic, Madden's Bridge Bar is a comfortable place for a drink or a meal. This family run business in the seaside resort of Bundoran offers pleasant pub atmosphere and casual dining in true Irish pub character.

**Broadhaven Bay Hotel, Kilmore Bar** in Belmullet on the main road from Ballina (R313). Kilmore Bar has pleasant seating with a view out onto Broadhaven Bay. Food was good tasting pub grub. The wait staff leaves something to be desired: service, but the hotel was still quite new.

**Campbell's Pub** on R335 eight miles west of Westport, 50 yards down from the beginning of the ascent path of Croagh Patrick (St Patrick's mountain). A local's drinking pub which has a couple of small tables, and lots of stools and kitchen chairs. Owen Campbell's Pub is famous as a stop after climbing Croagh Patrick, the mountain from which Saint Patrick supposedly cast all serpents out of Ireland. Patrons are a mix of young and old, locals, climbers, and tourists. On the last Sunday of July each year the mountain will have as many as 30,000 pilgrims climbing the rocky path to the top of the 2200 foot peak. Many will make the climb barefoot. Most will stop (or try to stop) at Campbell's Pub when they get down. Must stop to visit the pub, whether you climb or not.

**The Countess Lounge Bar and Restaurant** on shore Road in Strandhill, Co. Sligo. The food is excellent at The Countess and the prices are reasonable for beach resort area. The establishment is dedicated to the memory of Constance Markievicz who was born in Strandhill and was involved in the Easter Rising of 1916. Although sentenced to death by the English, she escaped the firing squad and was even elected to the English House of Commons.

**Crockett's on the Quay** along the River Moy about a mile north of Ballina, Co. Mayo. Modern, upscale riverside pub and restaurant. Awards, including Black and White Pub of the Year (2002) and Best Connaught Pub (2003), are well deserved. Service was very friendly and efficient. We especially appreciated that the owner/ manager worked the room, helping and checking. The meal we had could only be called superior! Seared Spiced Salmon with Haddock Mash and Cauliflower Mornay was tasty and tastefully presented. The Baked Cod, Clam, and Cockle Linguini was heavy on the fish and light on the sauce; a nice balance and delicious. The spicy tomato soup was lovely, even to those of us who don't usually appreciate tomato soup. The location, the atmosphere, the quality, and the service combine to make Crocket's on the Quay a delightful stop.

**Dunning's Cybepub** on the Octagon in the heart of Westport. Mix of locals and tourists in pleasant, old surroundings (the building was built in the early 1800s), but the food was only mediocre. The internet resources are a major draw.

**The *Grainne Uaille* Pub** on N59 just before coming into Newport, before you cross the bridge. The *Grainne Uaille* Pub, named after Grace O'Malley, Ireland's famous pirate Queen, is a local pub with a tourist location. The Irish Stew and Lamb Cutlets were excellent. Service was exceptionally friendly from a young lady from New York City newly transplanted to Newport. Talk about culture shock! But she said she was enjoying the change.

**The Harbour Restaurant** on Quay Street in Donegal across from the harbour and Tourist Office. We've eaten here several times and enjoyed it each time. Can be very crowded on weekends and during high season. Busy all the time. One weekend we had an hour wait for a table and spent it sharing a table in the bar with a young couple from Belfast. Good craic.

**The Harp Tavern** on Quay Street in Sligo overlooking Garavogue River and near Town Hall. A drinking and music pub in traditional style; a tradition that says there's been a licensed tavern at this location since 1791. The bar does serve a selection of sandwiches at lunchtime and teas, coffees, and snacks all day. Great music venue with traditional Irish sessions on Monday (and sometimes Wednesday), and a Jazz/Blues session on Sunday afternoons. One of Sligo's most popular pubs, The Harp Tavern is a relaxed, comfortable place renowned for its "craic" and music.

**The Loft** on Lord Edward Street in Sligo above the M.J. Carr Pub. This was one time we ate in the restaurant and by-passed the pub. It was the recommendation of our B&B hosts Freddie and Carolyn Jones, and I'm certainly not one to dispute the recommendation of one of the Jones boys. Our dinners were an excellent Gaelic steak and lamb cutlets. We then enjoyed one of the Loft's special delicious chocolate cake desserts.

**Matt Molloy's** on Bridge Street in Westport. Owner Matt Molloy is the flutist with the famous traditional Irish group, The Chieftains. A social gathering, drinking, and music pub. Three rooms with the front two along the bar with stools and booths. The back room is for music with booths, tables, and stools. Decor is irrelevant because you're here to visit, drink, or listen. This is the place to be to hear music in Westport, a town with numerous musical venues. We visited once in the middle of a week in September and thought the place was crowded. We visited a second time at the end of a holiday weekend and we now understand what crowded is. One night we watched a player try to join a session. The group was kind, but after two numbers even he could see he couldn't keep up.

**Murphey Brothers Pub and Restaurant** on Sligo Road (R59) just before the bridge over the Moy River on the outskirts of Ballina. Busy pub/restaurant in an old Irish pub style. Murphy Brothers is very lively (Friday night), but not overcrowded. Established as a tea, wine, and spirit merchant shop in 1901, it was converted later to a restaurant. The staff hustles, the food is good, and the pub prices are reasonable.

**Pier 1, Dom Breslin's Bar and Restaurant** on Quay Street in Donegal. Great food, wonderful service, and spectacular location (especially if you get an upstairs window table) make Dom Breslin's the pick of Donegal Town. We've eaten here three different years and never been disappointed. On our last visit we had lamb cutlets (4) and prime roast beef. Both entrees came with generous portions of garlic potatoes and steamed (crisp, not mushy) vegetables. When we ordered a coffee after dinner, we got a small pot with more than one cup's worth— unheard of in Scotland, and unusual in Ireland. We learned a nice trick on our last visit. Our B&B host at Arches [see Accommodations] called for our reservation. When we arrived, our table was a window table with a special table setting. A nice touch, and the view of the harbour, the Franciscan friary, and the Hassans (islands in Donegal Bay where famine refugees were brought) was gorgeous at sunset. Combine the quality with reasonable prices and it's easy to see why Pier 1 has won numerous Pub of the Year and Pub of Distinction awards.

**Quay Cottage Restaurant** on the harbour at Westport just before the entrance to Westport House. A nautical themed cottage restaurant with seating for about ten groups. Small, but strong, menu specializing in seafood. Quay Cottage is winner of many awards, as well it should be. The food was beautifully prepared, service was efficient and friendly, and the prices were closer to pub than restaurant prices. The setting, directly across from the harbour, is fantastic as well.

**The Strand Bar & Restaurant** on main street in Strandhill about five miles west of Sligo. Old oceanside resort-style pub which serves good, simple food. We've visited twice, early in spring and late in fall, and the Strand Bar is always packed. I imagine summers here would be wild fun. Locals and tourists come here for the drinks and the quick food which is well prepared and inexpensive. It's fun, too, to read the poster/sayings around the pub, including: "There's nothing so bad it couldn't get worse," and "Never kiss a fool or be kissed by a fool."

**Torrino's** at 10 Market Lane, Middle Bridge Street in Westport, a little off the main shopping street. Torrino's offers a very complete Italian menu with pages of pasta dishes, gourmet and regular pizzas, starters, and specials. Get your reservations early at Torrino's if you want to visit during high season or on weekends. The restaurant was turning away people by the droves. When we got there, our reserved table was not ready (people were lingering over their meal). The manager handled the problem professionally and we got special service. Food is outstanding.

**Vitto's Restaurant and Bar** on Market Yard off the main street in Carrick-on-Shannon, Co. Roscommon. Lunch menu specializes in pizza, pasta, sandwiches, and wraps. Dinner menu is more complete. Vitto's offers six varieties of value meal combinations. Many downtown locals stop for lunch at Vitto's, as did we. Food was good and plentiful. Nice open feel to the eating area with lots of windows.

**Weaver's Bar and Bistro** in Nesbitt's Hotel on the main street of Ardara, Co. Donegal. The name is a reference to the area's main industry, wool and tweed production. Friendly staff recognized us as visitors and asked about our travels. We've eaten twice at Weaver's and both lunch and dinner were high quality food well prepared. The fish chowder with real crab, shrimp, and white fish was particularly tasty.

**Yeats' Tavern** in Drumcliff four miles north of Sligo on N15 just before you get to the Drumcliff Church where famous Irish poet W.B. Yeats is buried. This cross between a traditional Irish pub/restaurant and an American-style family restaurant serves excellent meals and has a friendly, efficient staff. It's worth driving out of Sligo for. It was good enough that we went back a second night.

## *ATTRACTIONS*

Ireland's northwest is a land filled with archeological and historical treasures. In the Carrowmore region near Sligo more than 60 megalithic monuments have been identified. This is but one tiny section of the northwest. As you explore the golf courses of the region, you will find that many have connection to ancient or historic sites.

We start our tour of northwest attractions in **Westport**, whose focal point of the Georgian town is the Octagon (rather than town square). The town itself is a good shopping area with two main streets leading to the Octagon. On one of the streets is **Matt Molloy's Pub** which ought to be noted as musical attraction in this section as well as in the pubs section.

A stop to listen to a late night session is almost mandatory. Down along the quay or harbour at the west end of town the visitor will find **Westport House,** a Georgian country house from the 1730s. The former residence of the Browne family, Westport House has much to offer: fine art and furnishings of the period, horse and buggy rides of the grounds, a small zoo, and even a games arcade for the kids (which seems to fit more a theme park rather than a stately mansion). Despite the arcade, a tour of the house is interesting and informative. To the southwest of Westport along R335 is the geological dominating feature of the area, 2509 foot **Croagh Patrick** (The Hill of St. Patrick). Known locally as "The Reek," Croagh Patrick is the mountain where the patron saint of Ireland fasted for 40 days and 40 nights. It is from the summit that St. Patrick cleared Ireland of all venomous beasts (although he missed the midges), and secured from God the pledge that the Irish would never lose their faith. The last Sunday of July, "Reek Sunday," is the official day of pilgrimage to the top of the mountain, about a 5 mile scramble from the saint's statue to the top and back. As many as 30,000 faithful will make the trip on that one day, many barefoot, to attend a continuous mass at the small summit church. The remains of the original dry stone corbelled oratory (430 AD) sits next to the church. Whether you intend to hike to the summit or not, the view from St. Patrick's statue (about 150 yards above the parking area) of Clew Bay is a fantastic sight. Across the highway from the parking area and Campbell's Pub are two additional worthwhile sites. First, you will come to the poignant, but slightly gruesome, **National Famine Memorial.** The sculpture of a "coffin ship" of skeletons by John Behan is dedicated to the million lives claimed by the potato blight famine in the 1800s. Further down the same side road is the ruined **Murrisk Abbey,** a 15C Augustinian abbey which looks out over Clew Bay.

As you head east toward Carrick-on-Shannon, a lovely riverside resort village, the one stop we'd suggest is at Boyle to visit one of Ireland's loveliest ruined abbeys. **Boyle Abbey,** in town beside N4, was built by Cistercian monks in 1146.

What remains has some fine detailed carvings along the pillars and walls. Another major Irish attraction to the east of Westport is in the town of **Knock,** 21 miles southeast of Castlebar. In 1879 two village women reported seeing the figures of Mary, Joseph, and St. John against the south gable of the town church. Others also claimed to have seen the blessed apparitions. Two church commissions confirm the accounts, and the precession of pilgrims began. Pope John Paul II visited Knock on the first-ever papal visit to Ireland in 1929. The huge hexagonal Basilica of Our Lady, Queen of Ireland, containing the glassed-in south gable of the old church, was consecrated in 1976 and can hold 12,000 worshippers.

Heading north and west from Westport along N59, just past Newport, you will see to the left **Burrishoole Abbey** on the north shore of Clew Bay. The Dominican friary here was formed by Pirate Queen Grace O'Mally's second husband "Iron Dick" Burke (it's a name I didn't ask about) in the 15C. The site of the abbey overlooking a bay inlet and the graveyard surrounding the ruins are worth a look. The true jewel on this route is **Achill Island,** Ireland's largest at 12 by 14 miles. At Mulranny leave N59 and turn onto R319. About 9 miles from Mulranny you will cross the Achill Sound (the Atlantic ocean) over a 300 yard bridge. Shortly onto the island look for the sign to the small tourist office and stop in for information. Pick up handouts and brochures about things to do and see on the island, but also ask for advice from the tourist office steward. When we asked, she told us about several things that didn't appear in the printed materials. The best feature of the island is **Atlantic Drive,** the signed route that takes you along the sea (part of it is also the main road of the island). The view from the narrow road along sea cliffs is stunning, and good pullouts are provided so the driver can enjoy the view as well. At the west end of the island, past the small hamlet of Dooagh, the road climbs up and over a headland while hugging the cliff side. The road is wide enough for two small vehicles to pass, but the Irish haven't heard of an American convenience called the guard rail. The views at the parking area at the end of the road (about 4 miles from Dooagh) are magnificent, but the road is definitely not for the even mildly squeamish. Besides the villages and the views, two other sites are worthy of the visitor's time. On an unnamed road by the village of Keel climb up toward Slievemore Mountain (2204 feet). At the end of the road is a small parking area, cemetery, and footpaths that lead up to an **abandoned village** of booley houses or summer pasture dwellings. This mini-village was depopulated during the 19C famine years. Without too much effort, you can wander through the roofless dwellings and get an idea of living conditions in those trying times. About a quarter of a mile away along the road is the head of the footpath (sheep path?) which leads up and up and up to two **burial dolmens.** It's a strenuous walk that took about a half hour, but the view from the dolmens, seemingly half way up Slievemore, is grand. From Westport you could make the trip out to Achill Island, take in the sights, play nine at Achill GC or Mulranny GC (or play nine at both), have a nice dinner at The *Grainne Uille* Pub in Newport, enjoy a session at Matt Malloy's, and die in bed at your B&B—happy!

One route from Westport north takes the traveler through Castlebar and Foxford to Ballina. Before venturing to Foxford, swing toward Swinford to find two well preserved and picturesque **round towers** at Turlough (visible from the main road) and Meelick (signed from the highway). Foxford is home to the **Foxford Woolen Mills,** set up in 1890 by Irish Sisters of Charity nuns to help the impoverished of the area. The audiovisual tour explains both the history and the workings of the still operating tweeds and plaids mill. The gift shop contains local products as well as the usual tourist trinkets. The other route from Westport goes northwest to Bangor and Ballina, or the more fascinating coastal path around Carrowmore Lake and east to the unique **Ceide Fields (KAY-dgah) Visitor Centre.** The astonishing Neolithic farming settlement was discovered in the 1930s by a local school teacher when he recognized the significance of the buried stone walls being found by turf cutters in the bog fields. Archeologists have now found a farming landscape 5000 years old buried four metres deep in blanket bog. "A bog contains over 90% water and creates a closed ecosystem suitable for mosses, heathers, purple moor grass, a range of bog plants, and little else." [Ancient *Ireland,* Meager and Neave, Arris Books, 2004] Through films and displays, the Visitor Centre tells about the geology and archeology of the several square mile system of fields. A tour takes visitors out into the field to view some of the excavations. Our guide even explained that Bog Butter, containers of butter buried in the peat to preserve it, has been found that is over a hundred years old as fresh as the day it was churned. To anyone with an interest in ancient people, the Ceide Fields is one of the most interesting attractions in Ireland. Across the road for Ceide is a view point to Downpatrick Head. From here continue east and south on R314 to the port village of Killala which has a hard to visit round tower. A better choice would be to stop at the 15C **Rosserk Abbey** along the banks of the River Moy (well signed). Rosserk, the first Franciscan abbey in Ireland, is small, but well preserved.

Sligo is the next major stop on our northward journey. The 13C **Sligo Abbey** on the south bank of the Garavogue River is the main historic attraction in town. The ruins of this Dominican abbey, rebuilt after a fire in 1414, contain some beautiful carvings on the stone arches and cloisters. It is around Sligo where you will find the main areas of archeological interest. Overlooking Sligo's seaside suburb of Strandhill is **Queen Medb's Cairn** or Queen Maeve's Grave atop Knocknarea mountain. The immense pile of stone, visible from the Strandhill GC far below, is said to be the grave of the Celtic queen of Connacht, *Miosgan Meadhbha*. From the visitor's centre with archeologist in attendance it's only a short walk to the cairn with a panoramic view of the whole Sligo coast. East of Queen Maeve's Grave is Ireland's largest Stone Age cemetery, the **Carrowmore Megalithic Cemetery.** From the visitor's centre, whose attendant really loved his job, you can walk out into the fields of dolmen, stone circles, and burial cairns, or you can take a free one hour guided tour. At least 30 tombs are scattered over a large field, some having been radiocarbon dated to before 4000 BC. A more modern structure to visit is **Parke's Castle,** an extensively restored manor house of the 1600s, located on the shores of Lough Gill (take R286 out of Sligo, the castle is well signed). The family home of the O'Rorkes is a large tower house inside a complete curtain wall or bawn. The more than an hour long guided tour gives a good history to the castle and nice views onto the lough.

The route north from Sligo to Donegal Town (N15) passes through Drumcliff, a small village with a powerful presence. At the Church of St. Columba, most often referred to as the **Drumcliff Church,** you'll see a nice example of a high cross and the remains of a round tower. But it is one stone in the church graveyard that draws the most attention. Here is buried one of Ireland's premier poets, William Butler Yeats (1865-1939). Yeats, poet and dramatist, won the Nobel Prize for Literature in 1923 for his writing as the "soul of a nation." His tombstone with his self-written epitaph draws many visitors:

*Cast a cold eye On life, on death. Horseman, passby!*
And if you're not of a literary bent, you too can cast a cold eye, and pass by on to the next attraction, the **Creevykeel Court Tombs,** located on N15 between Drumcliff and Bundoran, a little north of Cliffony. These very accessible tombs are from the Late Stone Age (c2500 BC). In 1935 excavators discovered cremated human remains, Neolithic pottery, arrowheads, scrappers, and axes at the site which is easy to find and explore. Be sure to mind your head as you pass under the capstone. Anne didn't and had a headache the rest of the day.

**Donegal** (Dun *na nGall,* the Fort of the Foreigners) is the main town in the county and is a pleasant tourist town built around the Town Diamond (instead of square). We found a good example of Irish Time at the Tourist Information office. The clerk gave all her attention helping a couple find a B&B for the evening, while the line waiting for help grew longer and longer. Anne finally put the book she wanted to buy back on the shelf and we walked away, not mad, but just not in the same time zone as the clerk. In town are two historic buildings, the castle and an abbey. **Donegal Castle** is the preserved impressive tower house of the O'Donnell family which sits on the bank of the River Eske. The self-guided tour and a series of models gives a good history to the castle. The much ruined Franciscan **Donegal Abbey** (1474) on the banks of Eske estuary by Donegal Harbour was destroyed by explosion in 1601, when the British army was using it as an arsenal. The views and interesting gravestones make the abbey worth a visit.

West from Donegal Town will take travelers on an exciting day journey to some of Ireland's most impressive scenery. Head out of town on N56 to the fishing town of Killybegs. Turn off onto R263 and then take the marked turn off to the village of Kilcar. At the west edge of town is **Donegal Studios,** a great tweed factory and shop. You can browse in the showroom and visit the working factory. We've yet to get out of the Studio without some gift for ourselves or others. Return back to the main road (actually it's fairly minor, but there is room for two cars to pass) and continue west. On the other side of the Glen River inlet is a road leading to the view point for **Slieve League,** the largest sea cliffs in Ireland at over 700 feet tall. Back on the road west is **Glencolumbkille Folk Village** with a short guided tour of cottages depicting village life in 1720, 1820, and 1920. The road ends at Malin Beg and views from the other end of Slieve League. The whole peninsula is a *Gaeltach* or Gaelic speaking area where signs are almost all in native Irish. We stopped for lunch at a charming little tea room, *An Cistin,* in *Gleann Cholm Cille* (it's not on a map). Next door to the tea room was a Gaelic bookstore and behind that a Gaelic college.

# Chapter Six:
# Northern Ireland — Golf, Pubs, and Attractions

Bushfoot GC, Co. Antrim

## GOLF

### GENERAL INFORMATION ABOUT NORTHERN IRELAND

Northern Ireland may be a separate country, a part of Great Britain, but don't make the mistake of calling it that to an Irishman. Most will say that there is only one Ireland, and all in it are Irish. The reality is, though, when you travel from the Republic of Ireland into Northern Ireland, say from Donegal to Enniskillen, you do cross a border and there will be differences. The roads will change (better in the North), road markings will change from Ns and Rs to As and Bs, the money will be pounds instead of euros, but the Guinness will be the same and the golf just as good.

### BALLYCASTLE GOLF CLUB, 2 Cushindall Rd., Ballycastle, BT54 6QP, Co. Antrim

West of the village off A2 (Mary Street) overlooking Ballycastle Bay and adjacent to Bonamargy Friary.

www.ballycastlegolfclub.com  (028) 2076 2536
Seaside links/parkland, 5812 yards, par 71, £70

**Amenities:** Clubhouse extensively modernized in 2003. Pro shop with full rentals including buggies.

**Course Comments:** Ballycastle Golf Club is located less than 20 miles east of the Royal Portrush and Portstewart golfing meccas, yet doesn't receive the publicity or recognition of its western brethren. Ballycastle, though, has as much history as any course in the area, and more than most. The first 9-hole course was founded here in 1891, extended to 18 in 1925, and the club was one of the nine clubs who formed the Golfing Union of Ireland. Sited along Ballycastle Bay and the Rathlin Sound, the course affords visitors great vistas out to the North Channel and Scotland beyond, Ballycastle harbour, and Rathlin Island. Rathlin Island (along with Scotland's Arran Island in the Kilbrannan Sound between Ayr and Kintyre) claims to be where Scotland's Robert the Bruce hid from the British and penned the phrase "try, try, again" as he watched a spider struggle to construct a web.

The golf at Ballycastle is as good as its history and its views. While the first five holes play in a parkland setting, the rest occupy links and clifftop. Number one, *The Margy,* is a par 5 of 456 yards, where the River Margy runs the entire length on the left. Three bunkers, also on the left, will cause additional concern on the drive. The gently swaled green is protected by more traps. On the tee of the third we had to wait for traffic on the road next to the hole to clear before we could hit. *Hog's Back*, the 310-yard par 4 sixth, may be drivable by big hitters, but plenty of trouble awaits. OB from tee to green on the left is a strong incentive not to pull your tee shot. The approach from the undulated fairway is to a sloping green with a bunker on the right. The 9th, *Dooans,* is a 359-yard par 4 with a tee shot over the corner of the 17th green. The fairway goes steeply uphill to a green with heavy rough behind. *The Chasm,* the 10th, is a 115-yard uphill par 3. The tee shot is relatively easy, but the green is very swaled. There are great views along the coast and to Rathlin Island from the clifftop green. The 15th and 16th fairways cross, so be aware of golf balls and other players. The 17th is a visual delight and slightly reminiscent of the 12th at Royal Tarlair on the Moray Firth in Scotland. This 180-yard one-shotter, named *The Pitch,* has a 150 foot drop from tee to green. Take two clubs less, unless the wind is strong into you. If the wind's up, have a guess, and go for the small two-tiered green with six bunkers around it. The Ballycastle course has much going for it: wonderful links golf, grand vistas of villages, headlands, and islands, the 16C Bonamargy Abbey beside the course, and a pleasant modern clubhouse.

**Comments from the Forward Tees:** The course didn't have a lot of difference between ladies' and men's tees on several holes. Whatever difficulties on the course are made up for by the splendid panoramas.

### BUSHFOOT GOLF CLUB, 50 Bushfoot Road, Portballintrae BT57 8RR, Co. Antrim

At the end of Bushfoot Road on the northwest side of
town.
www.bushfootgolfclub.co.uk (028) 2073 1317
9-hole links/parkland, 6075 yards, par 70, £10/9 or
£18/16 holes

**Amenities:** The course has a pleasant modern clubhouse with starter's office, changing rooms, lounge which serves pub meals all usual hours, but no pro shop. We played on a Sunday morning early and the club restaurant was already filling up with locals coming in for a before church meal.

**Course Comments:** The attractions on Co. Antrim's north coast are literally world class. The Giant's Causeway is a World Heritage site. Not far away are Dunluce Castle, Carrick-a-Rede Rope Bridge, and Bushmills Distillery, all exceptional tourist draws. The golf in this area is world class, as well. Portrush and Portstewart golf courses are only a few miles apart. Don't stick only to the known facilities for some hidden gems lurk not far away. Bushfoot Golf Club, at Portballintrae a couple of miles north of Bushsmills village, is a real find. The 9-hole links/parkland course is relatively easy to get on; they raise a special flag when the course is closed for a competition. The first three holes and the last three all play across linksland, while the middle three are parkland. The course makes constructive use of some gentle elevation changes with some elevated tees and a few blind shots. We only had time for a 9-hole round, but would have liked to play 18. Alternate tees are available on 1, 2, 6, and 8, and an alternate green is used for your second round on three. We hit to the wrong green when we played, and some locals pointed out the correct green and we hit again. The course map is clear if you know to expect a second green. The bunkers aren't many nor are they severe. You can expect most of the challenge to your score to come from the wind and the Bush River which crosses one hole and plays along three others. Another quaint feature of the course is that the Giant's Causeway and Bushmills Tourist Railroad cuts through the course. The chugging, whistling steam train may be a slight distraction, but otherwise doesn't affect play.

The 2nd hole is the most picturesque on the course and it's one of the most difficult as well. A par 3 of 169 yards, your tee shot needs to carry a corner of the Bush River (about 140 yards). Good bail out area is to the right, but there is very little room to miss left. Across the river to the left (but not in play) is a lovely set of dunes. The beach and the Atlantic aren't visible from the second, but the best views are from the 1st and the last two holes. The 4th is a tough straight hole, a par 4 of 355 yards, with the green blind from your second shot and the fairway slopes to the left up to the green. Your natural desire is to hit to the right of the green and let the slope carry the ball down, but a bunker on the right of the green adds to the challenge. Another hole with a blind approach is the 335-yard par 4 eighth. From the elevated tee you can get a long drive if you avoid the rough left and right on this generous fairway. The flag, but not the putting surface, can be seen on your second shot. As wonderful as the well-known courses in the area are, some interesting and stress free golf is available for those willing to look.

**Comments from the Forward Tees:** A fun course to play, but does not have separate tee boxes for ladies so it plays long.

### CASTLE HUME GOLF CLUB, Enniskillen, Co. Fermanagh, Northern Ireland

On the shores of Lower Lough Eske 4 miles from Enniskillen on the Balleek Road. Take A46 northwest out of Enniskillen.

www.castlehumegolf.com (028) 6632 7077

Parkland, 6800 yards, par 72, £25, subscribes to numerous 2 for 1 deals

**Amenities:** The modern clubhouse houses a fully stocked pro shop and the Dove Cote Restaurant and Bar. Pub meals are served all day until 6 PM, and the full restaurant menu is available at lunch and Friday, Saturday, and Sunday at dinner. Changing rooms and pro shop are on the lower level.

**Course Comments:** This beautiful parkland golfing haven is four miles northwest of Enniskillen in Northern Ireland. With more than 7000 trees, the 1992 designed Castle Hume Golf Club offers a wonderful challenge to golfers of all skill abilities with five tee boxes on each hole. The mostly flat course is an easy walk with views of pleasant farmland, forests, Lough Castle Hume, and Lower Lough Erne. One of the great features of Castle Hume is its playability. The course, situated within the grounds of the Old Ely Estate, drains particularly well, and thus retains its playability when wet.

Thirty bunkers, mostly quite large, will test your shot making skills, as will numerous ponds and streams. To the plus side, Castle Hume doesn't hide its hazards. Most are easily visible, except the pond on 18. A prime feature of the course is its quality greens. They roll consistent and play quick, even in wet conditions. Several of the greens are sloped back to front, but the roll is so true that the slopes don't create major problems. One interesting item which might have changed since we played is that the score card indicates hole length in metres, while the course signage is in yards. Since the course is out-and-back, it was nice to see toilets near the 10th tee.

From the 1st hole on, Castle Hume has many quality golf holes. *Banagher,* a 340-metre par 4, is a good beginning to the round. Two bunkers frame the drive with a stream crossing the hole before the fairway begins. Staying to the right side makes the second shot, which must avoid a pond left and traps on the sides of the green, easier. The green, like many on the course, has a false front, but otherwise is fairly flat. The driving range practice bays are next to the first tees and could be a distraction on a busy day. The 5th, *The Coagh,* is a 387-metre par 4 which doglegs left to right around trees. Big hitters can try to cut the corner over the trees, but a controlled fade is a safer shot. A pond and bunker are in play on your approach to a smallish green, justifying the hole's stroke index of 1. *Little Paris* is an enjoyable finish to the front nine. Not a long hole at only 351 metres, this par 4's drive needs to stay to the left while avoiding the bunker 200 metres from the tee. A good first shot sets up an easier approach to a green with many subtle breaks. The next hole of note is *Ballyhose,* the 327-metre par 4 twelfth. Long players can cut the corner of this dogleg left. For those of who don't hit 230-metre drives, a shot of 190 to 200 metres can give us a look at the green if we are on the right. Be careful, a bunker 200 metres from the tee will be in play on the right. A creek 40 metres in front of the green will affect your approach decisions, especially if you are well back off the tee. The green again has a false front, so be sure to take enough club. The signature hole at Castle Hume, the 16th named *Ely Island,* is a

139-metre one-shotter playing downhill from an elevated tee (take about half a club less with no wind). The green is backed beautifully by the lough. A creek is in play on the left, while trees encroach on the right. The 18th is a hole you need to see once to get an idea of how to play. If nobody is close behind you, a lucky occurrence on a course which can be busy, take the time to walk out to the middle of the fairway to see the full layout. The *Dove Cote* is a 293-metre par 4 double-dogleg right around two significant ponds. Besides the ponds, three traps and OB on the right protect the green. From the member's tees, I had a par by hitting a 9-iron lay up (100 metres) to the first pond, a six-iron (140 metres) directly across the lake, and finally, two putting for my par. It was pure luck, and I probably wouldn't play that way next time. That's the quality of Castle Hume's last hole; it can be played many ways. The quality of the course and facilities at Castle Hume Golf Club is acknowledged by the fact that the course has hosted the Ulster PGA Championships several different years.

**Comments from the Forward Tees:** Castle Hume is a nice parkland course with trees, bunkers, and lots of water to hold your attention. Four of the par 5s are over 445 yards long, but the par 3s are more reasonable. Water is definitely in play on ten holes, but can be avoided with good shot management.

### CASTLEROCK GOLF CLUB, Mussenden Course, 65 Circular Rd., Castlerock, Co. Londonderry, Northern Ireland

In the village of Castlerock off Sea Road, 5 miles west of Coleraine.

www.castlerockgc.co.uk  (028) 7084 8314

Links, 6687 yards, par 73, £75

**Amenities:** Modern clubhouse with lounge and changing rooms. Fully stocked pro shop with trolleys, buggies and club rentals. A 9-hole course is also part of the facility.

**Course Comments:** Less known than Royal Portrush or Portstewart, but deserving of wider recognition is

Castlerock Golf Club's Mussenden Course. The course has a prestigious heritage, starting in 1901 as a 9-hole track. Ben Sayers was responsible for the extension to 18 holes in 1908. The course has been redesigned twice since. First, Harry Colt worked on the course in 1925, and then the latest design work was by Eddie Hackett in 1960. With spectacular views including Scotland, the Insihowen Peninsula, the River Bann estuary, and the North Atlantic, Castlerock is playable by all levels of golfer, but will challenge your game at every hole. Elevated greens, fast putting surfaces, an abundance of typical linksland bunkers, and a river in play on five holes are made more difficult by the ever-present sea breezes.

Castlerock has many memorable holes. *Knocklayde,* a 367-yard par 4 begins your round. From the tee on this dogleg left to right, you need to avoid the OB right and the mounds lining the left. A slight fade on your first shot can set up an easier approach to the sloped green with bunkers on both sides. The 3rd, where you tee off surrounded on three sides by gorse, is aptly named *Whins.* The 523-yard par 5 has a generous fairway, but two fairway traps and a large swale provide some challenge on your way to a green protected by three more traps. *Leg O'Mutton,* the 200-yard 4th, is the first of Castlerock's fine one-shotters. A rail line runs down the right, but should be in play only on a really wild shot. Two bunkers are on the left, one right and one behind the green. If you miss the green and the bunkers, don't be surprised to find your ball in unforgiving rough. The 6th hole, *Burn,* a 347-yard par 4 has a wide fairway with a small bunker on the right. The big trouble is, of course, the burn or stream in front of the tiered green. That, and the three bunkers around the green. The 9th, 14th, and the 16th are all challenging par 3s. *Quarry,* the 9th, is another 200-yarder with an old quarry left. It's now filled with water and easy to avoid. The amoeba-shaped green, with subtle borrows, will still be difficult to putt. *Corner,* at 192 yards isn't much shorter than the previous par 3s. Two bunkers and a ditch which crosses the line of ball flight about two-thirds of the way to the green are ready to catch any miss-hit shots. Three more bunkers (both sides and back) protect a large green. It's bunkers and more bunkers at Castlerock. *The Summit,* the 157-yard 16th, has five bunkers guarding a narrow green. The final hole, *Mussenden,* is a challenging dogleg right which starts with a nice village view. The fairway on this 357-yard par 4 is narrow with tall dunes on the right and a deep swale to be crossed on your approach to a sloped putting surface. The three bunkers around the green aren't nearly the problem as the bunkers on other holes. The best views are from the tee box at 17 and from the clubhouse lounge. Don't pass up a quick round on the Bann Nine which is short, but still a shot-maker's delight.

### PORTSTEWART GOLF CLUB, Strand Course, 117 Strand Road, Portstewart, Co. Londonderry BT55 7PG

On the west edge of the village.
www.portstewartgc.co.uk  (028) 7083 2015
Links, 6895 yards, par 72 (74 for ladies), £130

**Amenities:** Modern welcoming clubhouse is a good stop for a bite, a pint, or a dram, and some enticing views of the linksland and the sea. Changing rooms and fully stocked pro shop complete the facilities shared with the Old Course and Riverside Course.

**Course Comments:** Along with Portrush, the Portstewart golf complex is the premier facility in the north. The Portstewart Strand Course, designed in 1894 by Willie Park Jnr and redesigned in 1992, is a magnificent links challenge. The area is steeped in World War II history. The region was a staging area for US troops for D-Day, while German submarines often hid off shore waiting to sink allied warships. Be prepared to battle the elements at this breezy venue right from the start. And it's a wonderful start. Some say the first hole at the Strand Course rivals the famous first shot at Scotland's Machrihanish. I won't go that far, but it is a daunting shot from high on the dune above the fairway with the ocean right, the River Bann left, and a fairway which doglegs right. From that start, the front nine plays around and through tall dunes covered in thick grass and thistle. *Devil's Hill,* the 2nd is a 366-yard par 4, which has an elevated tee shot which must fit between two sand hills and then plays up to a raised green. Portstewart has its share of blind shots and penal bunkers, as well as a river in play on several holes. The 5th, a 456-yard par 4, has the River Bann running its full length. The finish is testing as well with final par 4s of 422 yards, 434 yards, and 464 yards. Besides the Strand Course, Portstewart GC provides two other 18- hole courses to test visitors and members. The Old Course is 4730 yards with a par of 64 and some dramatic ocean views. The Riverside Course has recently been expanded to 18 holes (5725 yards, par 68) with plentiful bunkers and river in play.

**Comments from the Forward Tees:** Even though the par was extended to 74 from the forward tees, the course is still long and challenging. A difficult links course.

### ROYAL BELFAST GOLF CLUB, Station Road, Craigavad, Holywood, Co. Down BT18 0BP

Off A2 northwest of Belfast and Holywood village.
www.royalbelfast.com   (028) 9042 8586
Parkland, 6185 yards, par 70, £97

**AMENITIES:** The Craigavad House, a refurbished Victorian clubhouse, has four different drinking and eating areas. High class food and service throughout the day with reasonable prices. There is also a very complete profession shop with everything for the golfer and the golf tourist. Buggies and electric trolleys are available, but must be pre-booked.

**COURSE COMMENTS:** The oldest club in Ireland, the original course opened in 1881 as a six-hole course. In 1892 the course was relocated as a nine-hole course. The course played today is a Harry S. Colt design from 1926 which has continually been upgraded and modernized without losing the Colt character. As a tough world class tract it was good to see the course rule which says that 3 1/2 hour rounds are expected of four-balls. The venerable tree-lined course has views of the Belfast Lough across to Carrickfergus. The course will challenge golfers on practically every shot with more than 120 bunkers in sight, although about a third of them aren't really in play. The bunkers are a mix of fairway and greenside and many are quite penal. Only the 11th has no bunkers. There's no real water hazards on the course, except that three holes play on the shore of the lough. The moderate size greens look flat, but some will have definite slopes and all have subtle breaks. Add to these challenges the wind that will be with you most rounds and you have a demanding golf test, indeed.

The opening hole at Royal Belfast is a good opener to get your golf mojo going. This 411-yard par 4 is a slight dogleg left bending around a nest of three bunkers 225 yards from the tee—stay to the right. Your approach is to a sloped green with traps front, right, and left. The shortest par 3 on the course is the 4th at 137 yards. Just because it's the shortest doesn't necessarily mean it's the easiest. Four bunkers trouble the front and sides of the green—only the back is bunkerless and there the trees come right up to the green. The 9th is a par 4 of 405 yards. With the Belfast Lough (the sea) down the left you'll want to stay right with your drive [Thank you, Mr. Obvious!]. The aiming post right is a good guide as the fairway slopes left. Second shots (or thirds) are bothered by fore-bunkers on each side and two more traps at the green. A nice par 3 on the back is the 11th at 170 yards. It's a blind one-shotter with trees all around and a narrow chute to the green, which means the mid-length hole is not easy even though it's the only hole with no bunkers. On the 13th, a 361-yard par 4, a set of four fairway bunkers about 250 yards out from the tee make it prudent for big hitters to scale back. The green has two more traps guarding it. It's all about the bunkers—as many as 14, although not all will be in play unless you're really wild—on the 16th, a 476-yard par 5. Even straight players will find the fairway traps bothersome. The green is a small target with three more guarding bunkers. At Royal Belfast the descriptors "extremely hard," "challenging," and "fantastic" are often put into the same sentence.

**Other Courses in the Region (near courses in the chapter):**

Brown Trout GC (9), Aghadowey, Co. Londonderry
(028) 7086 8209
City of Derry GC (18), Londonderry, Co. Londonderry (
028) 7134 6369
Cushendall GC (9), Cushendall, Co. Antrim (028) 2177 1318
Enniskillen GC (18), Enniskillen, Co. Fermanagh
(028) 6632 5250
Foyle GC (18), Londonderry, Co. Londonderry
(028) 7135 2222
Gracehill GC (18), Ballymoney, Co. Antrim (028) 2075 1209
Roe Park GC (18), Limavady, Co. Londonderry
(028) 7772 2222
Royal Portrush GC, Dunluce & Valley, Portrush, Co. Antrim
(028) 7082 2311

### *PUBS AND EATERIES*

With only limited travel in Northern Ireland we've had little opportunity to sample the fine dining and pub life available. The places we have been have all been worth a stop and some we'd count among the finest finds.

**Bushmills Inn** on Dunce Road in the center of Bushmills, Co. Antrim. A 19C coaching inn where the building could date back to 1608. Warm, cozy feel with rich wood trim and open peat fires in the the Hall and Gas Bar. Bushmills Inn takes pride in using Irish ingredients in both the pub and restaurant menu. Restaurant dishes are traditional with a modern twist. One of the specials was called Dalraida Cullen Skink, this meal in a bowl was smoked haddock topped with a poached egg. The Bushmills Inn has received high praise since reopening in 1987, after years as various residences. Has received numerous awards, including British Airways Travel Award.

**The Distillers Arms Restaurant** on Main Street in Bushmills, Co. Antrim just down from the distillery. After major renovation in 2001, Simon Clarke's Distillers Arms has received the prestigious Michelin "Bib Gourmand" and is listed in the Jameson Good Food awards. Distillers Arms is a listed building in the designated conservation village of Bushmills. Originally it was home to the owners of the local distillery. Broad pub lunch and early evening menus available. A very complete dinner menu is offered starting at 6:30.

**Fitzroy's Bistro** on Bridge Street in Limavady (between Derry/Londonderry and Coleraine on A2) just outside city walls. Modern European-style lunch and dinner restaurant. Great service and top quality food.

**The Jamaica Inn** on the coast road near Bangor (Northern Ireland). It's not the Inn of du Maurier's 1936 novel—that's in Cornwall on Bodmin Moor—but it is in a nice setting. Serves typical pub food for decent prices. Live music most evenings.

**Oscar's Restaurant** at 29 Belmore St. (A32), Enniskillen, just coming into town from Omagh and the airport. Eclectic style restaurant, a cross or combination of Art Nouveau and Beatnik. Housed in an old downtown building, there is an upstairs restaurant and downstairs themed Irish writer's room and a Dorian Grey Room. The bar dates from the early 1800s. Named for famed Irish writer Oscar Wilde who went to school in Enniskillen. Busy on a mid-September Friday night with a few tourists and lots of locals. Service and the food were excellent. Ask your server about the history of the restaurant and for an explanation of the rooms; you might get a personal tour. Very deserving of its numerous awards and won't damage your wallet too badly.

**Pat's Bar and Restaurant** at 5 Downhill St., Enniskillen, Co. Fermanagh, on the main street about a third of the way through town. A modern restaurant and pub with an old look (building is old). Wide range of lunch items and a full evening menu. A mix of clientele on a weekday mid-afternoon; young, business, shoppers, tourists, and elderly in for low-priced specials. Friendly and helpful wait staff.

**The Ramore Restaurant and Wine Bar** at the corner of the harbour in Portrush, Co. Antrim. Wine bar is an upscale fast food restaurant serving a wide range of pub type meals at good prices. We stopped after golf for a late lunch. The atmosphere is nonexistent, but the burger was one of the best I've had in Ireland. Owners George and Jane McAlpin have done a good job with the new restaurant which has already received several awards.

**The Smugglers Inn** halfway between Bushmills and the Giant's Causeway on A2. Upscale establishment with bar and restaurant. The food and the surroundings are wonderful. The service we had the night we visited was poor at best (wrong order, forgotten items, incorrect bill). The problems could have been with wait staff, but the manager messed up the bill. For the setting and the quality of the food, we'd give it another chance.

### *ATTRACTIONS*

Northern Ireland is a rich historical area to explore. We've seen only a tiny sampling of its offerings in our brief visits. One excursion took us through the southwest corner of Northern Ireland as we traveled from Donegal to Dublin, and our other trips gave us a quick look at the geological wonders of north Antrim county. We know that we want to go back to delve more deeply into the political history seen in Londonderry (Derry, to those in the Republic) and Belfast, but that will wait for future trips.

Anne has a couple pieces of Belleek Pottery in our display cabinet at home. It was natural for us to want to visit the factory on our way to play golf at Castle Hume near Enniskillen, Co. Fermanagh. That particular day we needed petrol, so we figured to stop just before we crossed the border in order to pay in euros (cheaper then) than in pounds. When we pulled into the station in Belleek we knew we'd missed our chance. There is no major sign on the road that you are leaving one country and entering another; the transition is now seamless. It wasn't that way several years ago, and Jimmy Kinsella, the pro at Skerries, regaled us with stories of sneaking items through or around the border guards when crossing between the two. We paid the pounds for petrol and drove on to the **Belleek Pottery Factory** well signed in the village. The guided tour of the Parian ware factory, which begun in 1857, explains in detail the process of making the delicate pottery. The Visitor Centre has a showroom and shop, and they will mail your purchases directly to your home. That's great for packing, but can be damaging to your pocket book because it's so easy to buy.

From Belleek two routes lead to Enniskillen. The northern path from Belleek takes A47 across Boa Island and connects to A35 and into Enniskillen (40 miles). The small island has some interesting archeological figures, but they are on private property and not accessible. By cutting off just after leaving the island on a minor road (a longer route stays more on major roads) you can reach the **Drumskinny stone circle,** a small but attractive circle in a very out-of-the-way location. The circle has an alignment of 24 stones running tangentially from the circle. On the road to the circle we found an interesting old church and some unmarked standing stones. The southern route on A46 to Enniskillen stays closer to Lower Lough Erne and is shorter, only 31 miles. Along this path is a view point at the **Cliffs of Magho** which allows views of the broad expanse of the north of Lower Lough Erne and Boa Island. About half way to Enniskillen is the marked turnoff to **Tully Castle and Gardens.** We visited the castle on a rainy afternoon which was fitting for this brooding 17C fortification and its stark gardens. In the lough closer to Enniskillen is **Devenish Island** (accessible by passenger ferry from the town or a terminal 3 miles north) which hosts several religious antiquities, including Lower Church, St. Mary's Priory, a 6C monastery, a 12C round tower, and high crosses.

Enniskillen holds two real prizes. The first is the 15C **Enniskillen Castle** (Main Street), the family home of the Maguires who were rulers of Fermanagh. A good audiovisual program explains the history and importance of the castle strategically located by the river channels connecting Lower and Upper Lough Erne. The self-guided tour has exhibits which included the Regimental Museum of Royal Inniskillin Fusiliers, a prestigious military corps. It's easy to spend an hour or two in the castle. The second prize is about a mile southeast of town on A4. **Castle Coole,** a 1798 Neoclassical mansion of the Corrys of Coole, was restored to its former grandeur in the 1980s. The guided tour takes visitors through several rooms and the grounds beside Lake Coole are an enjoyable stroll.

Another of our ventures into Northern Ireland was across the north from Co. Donegal and down to Dublin. Here we got a chance to play several of the great courses in the area before heading for our flight home. From Ballyliffin on the Inishowen Peninsula you can go through Londonderry or cross on a small ferry at Greencastle to get to Northern Island. We took the small ferry and stayed on the A2 to our base in a nice farmhouse B&B near Bushmills. From here we had quick access to several fine golf courses and a number of unique attractions. The closest attraction to our B&B was not the most unique, but a visit was certainly enjoyable. The **Bushmills Distillery,** the oldest licensed distillery in the world (1608), was a pleasurable stop. The tour explained the process of making Irish whiskey and how that differs from Scotch whiskey or American bourbon. The dram at the end of the tour (we volunteered again to be special tasters) let us taste the differences. The distillery also has a good cafe for a spot of lunch.

The most impressive geological site in Northern Ireland is the World Heritage **Giant's Causeway.** Slightly northeast of Bushmills off A2, take B146 to the visitor's Centre. The Giant's Causeway is a mass of approximately 40,000 hexagonal basalt columns in interesting arrangements with names like Wishing Well, Wishing Chair, Giant's Gate and Tilted Columns.

You can walk from the centre down about a half mile to the beginning of the trail around the features, or you can pay for a shuttle down. We walked down and then paid for the shuttle to come back up. This site is connected geologically to the Isle of Staffa near Mull in Scotland, which has Fingal's Cave which Mendelssohn made famous in his *Hebrides Overture.* The hexagonal columns in both are part of the same ancient lava flow. Plan to spend half a day exploring the Causeway, but leave time in your schedule for two man-made attractions. West on A2 from Giant's Causeway is the evocative **Dunluce Castle** sited 100 feet above the crashing waves. In fact, part of the castle is now in the crashing waves. Home to the Scottish MacDonnell clan, "Lords of the Isles," the late 13C castle is the most spectacularly sited castle in Northern Ireland (some say in all the British Isles, but then I'm not sure those people have seen Dunnottar in Scotland). Most of what remains of the castle is from the 16C and there is a cave underneath for secret boat landings. The castle does afford great views up and down the coast. North of the Giant's Causeway on B15 watch for signs to **Carrick-a-Rede Rope Bridge.** A 30 minute round trip walk along the cliff edge (good path) to the bridge and back is well worth the time, whether you cross the bridge or not. The bridge was installed about 250 years ago by fishermen who use it to cross over to their salmon fishing area off the little island. The bridge bounces and sways about 80 feet above the ocean and is only passable with little or no wind. There's not much to see on the island, but it is great sport for the daring to get their picture taken crossing the bridge.

# Chapter Seven:
# East Coast — Golf, Pubs, and Attractions

Layton & Bettystown GC, Co. Meath

## GOLF

This section covers two distinct areas, the heartland from west to east and down the east coast to Dublin. In the first are some of the best playable parkland courses in Ireland, and in the latter are some true Links gems (plus a few parkland courses).

## ATHLONE GOLF CLUB, Hodson's Bay, Athlone, Co. Roscommon

Northeast of town a couple of miles off N61. Follow signs.

www.athlonegolfclub.ie (090) 649 2073

Parkland, 6194 metres, par 71, €40/18 holes, €30/15 holes

**Amenities:** Large clubhouse with great views over the course and Lough Ree from the lounge upstairs where food is served all day (7:30 AM - 11:30 PM). Fully stocked pro shop and changing rooms downstairs.

**Course Comments:** The first course in Athlone was laid out in 1892 and the present course at Hodson's Bay was designed by Mr. J. McAllister in 1938. Development of the course has continued through 2005 with greens brought up to USGA standards. Because of recent upgrades, the course drains well and is playable when others in the area are too wet for good play. While much of the course is flat, noticeable elevation changes affect several holes, especially 12 and 13. Thirty-eight bunkers, mostly greenside, add challenge to holes whose most prominent protections are the numerous mature trees. The quick greens have pronounced slopes and swales, but all are fair and playable. Water is in play on six holes, and on 4, 5, 6, and 11 ponds are a major factor of play. The ponds, Lough Ree, and surrounding hills add visual interest to the alluring holes at Athlone.

The course starts out tight, widens out in the middle holes, and narrows down again for the last few holes. Within this general pattern are many diverse and intriguing holes. The 2nd, a 140-metre par 3, plays from an elevated tee down to a green protected by two bunkers on each side and one behind. Short is safer than long. The 389-metre par 4 third is a slight dogleg left with trees on the inside and two traps on the outside of the turn. The second shot is uphill to a raised green with one bunker left. The first par 5 is the 532-metre 5th which doglegs right around one of the many ponds on the course. The second and third shots need to contend with the pond and/or three fairway bunkers. Two more bunkers defend the small green. A dogleg right where a good shot can cut the corner begins the 429-metre par 4 seventh. If you try to shorten the hole, be careful of the OB all along the right. One fairway bunker left will cause problems on the approach, but more problems will be caused by large trees and three bunkers around the green. The 13th is a funky, fun hole even the first time you play. Your drive is a blind shot over a large mound or hill where the short grass is a very narrow chute. Drive straight over the left side of the fairway. Your second shot is also blind over another mound, but the landing area is much more open. This 396-metre par 4 certainly plays more like a par 5 until you know where to aim. The green has only one bunker and a small stand of trees as protection. Indexed as the fourth hardest hole, 13 is a good example of using the natural contours of the land. The 14th, a two-shotter of 313 metres, begins with a tee shot over a small pond. The fairway doglegs left around an oak and your approach is uphill to a raised green with four bunkers around it. Sidehill lies for your second shot (the fairway slopes left) will complicate your approach. After the 15th, you can shorten your round (the 15-hole price), but to continue cross over Roscommon Road, the road into the course, to play the par 4, 421-metre 16th by the lough. The hole is a dogleg left with mature trees all down the left side. The green is partially hidden by trees and has a large trap on the right. After your round be sure to stop in at the fine clubhouse lounge for a relaxing pint.

**Comments from the Forward Tees:** I very much liked this visually appealing course. I hit "down the middle" which is a great advantage at Athlone with all the trees, sand, and water about. The variety in the holes held my attention throughout the round.

### COLD WINTERS GOLF CLUB, Newtown House, St Margarets, Co. Dublin
Off R122 south of town.
No web site   (018) 640 324

Parkland, Yellow 9, 2943 yards; Red 9, 3030 yards; Blue 9, 2163 yards, Yellow and Red par 71, €inexpensive

**Amenities:** The course boasts a fully stocked large pro shop with small snack bar (serves food all day), and a 16 covered bay driving range.

**Course Comments:** The Open Golf Centre is the home for Coldwinters Golf Club and the 27 hole facility is a good stop for 9-holes (or 18) on your way away from or to the Dublin Airport. The golf is not championship caliber, but that doesn't mean it can't be fun. We found good bunkering on most holes, several holes with ponds in play, quality greens of moderate speed, and bunnies everywhere. As near as the course is to the Dublin Airport, jet noise was only a minor distraction. Two holes on the Yellow 9 and one on the Red caught our attention. The longest hole on the Yellow is the 467-metre par 5 third. The drive on this hole needs to thread between stands of mature trees. Your approach shot, second or third, must avoid a pond on the left and a large bunker on the right of the green. The 7th is a 337-metre par 4 dogleg left. Trees on the inside corner of the dogleg are flyable with a good shot of about 175 metres. Lots of room on the right allows a safe shot. A small lake fronts the green to the left, so play to stay right. On the Red, we liked the 2nd hole. This 362-metre par 4 has trouble all along the left side with four fairway bunkers. Two more bunkers near the green add to the challenge. Either as a first round after landing in Dublin or as a last round before flying out, The Cold Winters GC can provide an enjoyable round. And if you didn't bring clubs, the course has a full range of good rental equipment.

**Comments from the Forward Tees:** A very open new course where many of the trees were young. Water on several holes added difficulty. Though not a championship course, it was an enjoyable round.

**COUNTY LOUTH GOLF CLUB (aka Baltry), Baltry,
Drogheda, A92 HK03 Co. Louth**
East of Drogheda off R167 at the mouth of the river
    Boyne.
**www.countylouthgolfclub.com**  (041) 988 1530
Links 6936 yards, par 72, €140

**Amenities:** Lovely formal clubhouse with changing rooms and lounge serving food usual hours. Nice views onto the course.   Very complete professional shop also in the clubhouse.

**Course Comments:** The first course for the club opened in 1892 with just a few holes near the present Laytown and Bettystown course. The first course at Baltry was laid out by a Scottish professional and then redesigned in 1914 by architect Cecil Barcraft. The final redesign was by Open Champion James Bruen in 1938. A program of modernization was completed so the course could host the 2004 Nissan Irish Open. The course was a relaxed country course where members could walk on anytime. Although the course still has a country feel, the course needs time sheets now.  Baltry is a true championship links with all the challenge of a great links course. Sixty greenside and fairway bunkers will challenge players' accuracy. Bunkers are medium to large and none are easy; at Baltry in a bunker is a penalty. The greens are medium to large with some severe slopes and interesting borrows. As with most links greens, they play fast. The greatest difficulties at the course come from the strong sea breezes, the heavy links rough, and the hard to avoid fairway bunkers. For all its challenge, Baltry is a beautiful course with grand vistas of the sea and the Mountains of Mourne in Northern Ireland.

Number three, *Punch Bowl,* is a classic seaside par 5 of 544 yards, and one without bunkers (one of only three holes with no bunkers at Baltry). A good drive to a fairly generous landing area will still leave a blind second (or third) shot to a long, narrow, elevated green which slopes right to left. The best approach is from the left because the right is blocked by dunes, but avoid the drop-off left of the fairway. *Heaven* is the 158-yard par 3 fifth. The hole is a short one-shotter, but don't miss the green to the right where two traps and sand hills await. A miss to the left leaves a reasonable chip to the green. The 9th, *Cloc Stuca,* is a 419-yard par 4. The hardest hole on the course (according to the stroke index) begins with a drive to a fairway guarded by six bunkers, four left and two right, with most in play on a good shot from any tee. Your second shot, assuming you avoid the bunkers, is to a green with an approach made narrow by a fore bunker. Two more bunkers wait for balls which roll off the sides of the green. On the back side, *Long Bank,* the 481-yard par 5 eleventh, is a birdie opportunity if you stay clear of the two fairway bunkers to the right in the driving area and four more around the green. The narrow green is angled so that an approach from the left is best. The 12th is named *The Crater,* after the large depression off the right of the fairway. The 410-yard two-shotter offers plenty of trouble. Off the tee two bunkers right, a large mound left, and a steep swale which can push balls toward the bunkers or the crater will demand the best shot-making. You come into the green over a mound between dunes. The green doesn't need any more protection. Another testing short par 3 is 15 at 152 yards. *Jubilee Bank* demands an accurate shot to find the elevated green with a pot bunker in front and two more bunkers on the right.   County Louth Golf Club has recently emerged from relative obscurity onto the stage of world class links courses, yet the people are friendly and eager to share their lovely course.

**EDMONDSTOWN GOLF CLUB, Edmondstown**
     **Road, Rathfarnham, D16 N5 Y8, Dublin, Co.**
     **Dublin**
From the M50, take R116 towards Rathfarnham and the
     course.
**www.edmondstowngolfclub.ie** (014) 931 082
Parkland, 6011 metres, par 71, €35

**Amenities:** Well appointed clubhouse with a reputation for good food served usual hours. Small, but well stocked pro shop.

**Course Comments:** The Edmondstown Golf Club, situated in the suburbs of Dublin, was recently (2002) upgraded to championship condition. Sand based greens roll well all year because of good drainage. The greens are also tricky to putt because of some significant undulations. Many of the holes are tree lined with lots of bunkers in play. The course plays in the Dublin foothills, but is not difficult to walk. Elevation changes create challenge, but are never unfair.

Edmondstown has its share of intriguing holes. The 4th, a 494-metre par 5, sweeps right slightly downhill with two bunkers on the outside corner, about 185 metres from the tee. From there two more bunkers on the left of the fairway can catch missed shots, but the biggest problems come from a ditch fronting the rolling green with five bunkers around it. A good par 4 is the 382-metre 6th. You drive to a generous fairway, but two bunkers left at about 215 metres mean stay to the right. A stream in front and a pond left protect a raised, mounded green which slopes back to front. Try not to be behind the pin. The 9th, a 355-metre two-shotter, is a strong dogleg left with a tree hedge right and three traps backed by forest on the left. It would take a drive of 250 metres to clear the last bunker. An aiming post on the right side of the fairway helps direct you where to hit. The tricky to putt green is surrounded by three bunkers. A fun short hole is the 13th, a 140-metre par 3. Tee off from an elevated tee with great views of the Dublin Hills to a miniature, undulating green with two bunkers fronting the left and two behind. A gentle dogleg right with trees on the inside corner is where you drive on the short 15th, a par 4 of 275 metres. A straight drive of 210 metres can find the two bunkers on the left of the fairway. The slightly raised green has one bunker on the right. At only seven miles from the city center, Edmondstown Golf Club can get busy. Be sure to call ahead.

## GLASSON COUNTRY HOUSE HOTEL & GOLF
### CLUB, Glasson, Athlone, Co. Westmeath

On the Athlone bypass (off N6 or N7) take Exit 9 (N55 Cavan/Longofrd). At top of Exit 9 reach Glasson village.  At end of village, after the petrol station take a left. Go approximately 1.5 miles, course is on the right.

www.glassongolf.ie  (090) 648 5120
Parkland, 7120 yards, par 72, €40

**Amenities:** More than a fine golf course awaits the visitor to Glasson Country House Hotel and Golf Club. When they built the course, the Reid's converted the family farmhouse into a clubhouse and then added a 29-room 4 Star hotel to complete the complex. The hotel also has conference facilities to cater to up to 100 participants. In the clubhouse, visitors will find a small pro shop with a golfer's essentials and full equipment rental. The clubhouse also boasts four pub areas and a more formal restaurant. Quality pub fare is served all day and the dinner menu is complemented by an extensive wine list.

**Course Comments:** In the early 1990s, turnip farmer Tom Reid (the first Irish farmer to export turnips) and his family made a fateful decision. They called famed Irish golf architect and Ryder Cupper Christy O'Connor Jnr to look over the 200 acres of family farmland by Lough Ree. O'Connor pronounced the site "one of the most scenic pieces of land" he'd ever seen. By 1993, the spectacular Glasson Golf and Country Club was open for play.  While Ireland has become known for its great links golf courses, such as Lahinch, Ballybunion, Waterville, and Tralee, Glasson Golf Club proves that wonderful parkland golf is equally a reason to visit the Emerald Isle. Glasson, set in the rolling countryside of Westmeath in central Ireland, plays with views of sparkling Lough Ree, part of the Shannon River system, on almost all holes. Twelve through 18 play off beautiful Killinure Bay. While being distracted by one picture-postcard view after another, enjoy the wonderful mix of fairway and greenside bunkers—

more than 100 in all, with some quite penal. Small lakes and ponds will affect shots on five holes. You will also appreciate the immaculately groomed greens which are quick enough to keep your attention, while still being quite playable even on the greens with slopes. O'Connor needs to be complimented for the whole design, but most particularly for the use of natural elevation changes which adds both length and interest to the course. Lastly, but never least in Ireland, the wind can be a condition of play at Glasson. Play in the light breeze of a spring afternoon like we did and the course can be nicely benign; a challenge, but not as difficult as it could be. Play on a day when the wind is whipping across the lough, and Glasson will definitely show its teeth. In whatever conditions you play, Glasson GC is a joy to play.

Full of great holes, it's difficult to pick favorites at Glasson, but several of the holes are standouts. The 5th, a 199-yard par 3, is one of those holes. After the 3rd, a nice par 3 with a drive towards the lough, players face another drive towards the water on the 5th. This time, though, four bunkers guard the green. The biggest and meanest of the traps fronts the green about 20 yards short of the putting surface. The 6th is a hole which receives universal praise. It's a long, 559-yard downhill par 5 with OB (a hedge fence) running the length of the hole on the left side. A pond and several bunkers affect your second and third shots. The dogleg right to left 8th is another hole with water in play. Bunkers and gorse guard the inside corner on this 432-yard par 4. Your second shot is downhill with a bunker crossing the fairway about 40 yards from the green and a large pond wraps around the green from the left. This hole requires both length and accuracy. Playing uphill the double-dogleg right 13th offers plenty of challenges. Fairway bunkers on both sides remind you to keep your ball in the cut grass. The real trouble, though, is on the approach with three traps guarding a narrow green. If there is one hole on the course I would pick to play again it would be the 566-yard par 5 fourteenth. It's a spectacular hole and I didn't play it well. I believe this is a hole you need to play several times in order to learn to score. From the members' tee, your drive needs only to be about 200 yards to reach the corner of a sharp dogleg right. Although steeply downhill, the second shot is not a go-for-it, green light even for big hitters. On the left approaching the green are two bunkers, one very large, and on the right are two ponds. The green is two-tiered and three-putts are a distinct possibility. One of the great things about 14 is that once you are safely in the hole, you get to move to 15, the ultimate signature hole on a course with many signature holes. No island green here. Instead, the 185-yard one-shotter begins from an island tee. On this hole, it's all about the water. Your tee shot must carry 160 yards of the lough to reach a two-tiered green with bunkers right and back. Since the green sticks out into the lough, right becomes the miss of choice. It's very reasonable to call Glasson's 15th one of the best par 3s in the world. The round doesn't end there, though, and the final three holes are as good as the rest of the course.

Beyond great golf, lodging, and eating facilities, Glasson offers something more important: the personal touch. Everyone we met at Glasson, including those who had no idea we might write about our experience, from the grounds crew to the receptionist to the barkeep was courteous, eager to serve, and happy. We've never been treated better at a golf course anywhere in the world. As we were surveying a particular hole with a stokesaver in hand, a grounds worker told us to avoid hitting too close to a bunker because the grass was particularly sticky there. After our round, when I ordered a Guinness the barkeeper asked what I thought about the 15th. The friendly Irish hospitality has definitely found a home at the fantastic Glasson Country House Hotel and Golf Club. A must play destination.

**Comments from the Forward Tees:** This was a wonderful day of and for golf. The weather was perfect and the course is varied enough from hole to hole to be extremely interesting. The course isn't easy with many strategically placed bunkers and so much water. For me, it was a fun and successful challenge.

## HEADFORT GOLF CLUB, Old Course, Navan Road, Kells, Co. Meath [both courses]

A short mile southeast of Kells, off R147, the Navan Road.

www.headfortgolfclub.ie  (046) 924 0146

Parkland, 5973 metre, par 72, €50

**Amenities (for both courses):** Modern clubhouse with changing rooms below and lounge upstairs. A two million euro expansion and remodel was done in 2007. A separate building houses club offices and a very complete pro shop with club fitting facilities.

**Course Comments:** Headfort Golf Club is a 36-hole facility with two championship 18-hole courses of very different design. The original 9-hole course was designed in 1928 and extended to 18-holes in 1958. The New Course is a 2000 Christy O'Connor Jnr design. The Old Course is noted for over 500 varieties of trees on the course, and especially its large and impressive chestnuts. Even though the course isn't particularly long, some of the holes play longer than the card with fairways lined with mature trees. Forty-six bunkers, mostly greenside, add difficulty, especially because many are large and steep-sided. Greens are small to moderate in size with subtle slopes and undulations. Even on the wet spring day that we played, the greens were speedy. Water comes into play on two holes where streams cross fairways. Though the Old Course is relatively flat, slight elevation changes are used well to add to the holes.

The holes at Headfort Old are classic parkland holes and are all interesting. Particularly noteworthy is the 369-metre par 4 third. The hole opens with a downhill tee shot to a generous fairway with stands of trees right and left. The approach to the slightly elevated green is over a small ridge. Three bunkers, two left and one right, guard a large green with mounding behind. The most difficult hole on the course according to the stroke index, the 394-metre par 4 fifth, begins with a drive into a hill (it's about 250 metres to the top). The second shot comes off the hill to a green surrounded by mounds with two fronting bunkers. The 9th, a 318-metre par 4, is a gentle right to left dogleg with plenty of trap trouble. Only strong drivers need to worry about a bunker on the right hidden by the down slope (270 metres), but the left fairway bunker at 220 metres is reachable by most. Your next shot will have to negotiate an undulating fairway while avoiding the five bunkers guarding the raised green. The 13th is a 351-metre two-shotter which is a slight dogleg left over a hill with many large trees to grab wayward balls. The green, fronted by a large bunker and a second one on the right, has serious left to right slope. The 15th starts with an intimidating drive if you don't draw the ball. This short par 4, only 301 metres, doglegs left around a dense forest; big hitters can cut the corner, if you know the angle. A stream 150 metres out is more a visual challenge, but the bunker on the right at about 190 metres is in play for those who bail right. The green has a large trap on the right and the stream (OB) behind. The same stream comes into play on 16 as well. You drive over a mound on this 372-metre par 4 towards the stream. At 320 metres from the tee, it's not in play until the next shot. Short hitters will contend with the stream on their approach to the left-to-right sloping green. The Old Course is a traditional, fair but challenging test of your golfing skills. In many ways, it's more enjoyable than the tougher youngster across the road, Headfort New Course.

**Comments from the Forward Tees:** A long course for ladies which makes scoring well difficult, but it's a beautiful walk through the forest.

### HEADFORT GOLF CLUB, New Course
Parkland, 6524 metres, par 72, €50

**Course Comments:** Designed by Irish architect Christy O'Connor Jnr and opened in 2000, the New Course shares little with the Old Course, except the clubhouse and the trees. This is a parkland course designed around water features that would make the Ground Force crew (British TV garden makeover show) proud. More than 70 bunkers, some very large, dot the course and water (lake or stream) is in play on

12 holes and is present on a couple others. The moderate to large greens, flat or gently undulating, will be quick. With over 500 varieties of trees on the course, including two islands in the River Blackwater which contain an impressive Asiatic tree collection of the former estate, the New Course would be a pleasant forest walk if it weren't for water, water everywhere! To put the water features of this course into perspective, you will cross over bridges 13 times in a normal round.

The combination of trees, water, and O'Connor's design skills make Headfort New a pleasure to play, though it is a testing pleasure. All the par 3s are spectacular. The 4th at 157 metres is the shortest and boasts a tee shot over water (140 metres from the back tee) to a green with two bunkers on the left. Bailout room is left of the bunkers and long, but not right where there's nothing but water. The carry across water isn't shorter at the 170-metre seventh, but more room to miss is available, except short left. A bunker short right can save balls from rolling back into a watery grave. The 11th is the only one-shotter with no water to cross, but water is behind the green on the 163-metre hole. Here you hit through an avenue of trees and over a yawning trap to a very undulating green. The last of the par 3s, the 180-metre 17th needs a carry of 150 metres to barely clear the water. The hole is as close to an island green as you can get. Imagine the 17th at Sawgrass in Florida, except longer with a bigger island and trees. Two bunkers protect the right side of the green and a stand of trees the left. The quality par 3s doesn't exhaust the intriguing holes at Headfort New. The 2nd, a fine 480-metre par 5, is a dogleg left with water encroaching at the outside of the turn (reachable by long hitters). Water crosses the fairway about 70 metres in front of the green protected by a bunker and stream on the left. The 9th is a demanding layout with a drive over the river (about 180 metres) to a landing area with a bunker left and the next water reachable with a strong drive off any of the tees (270, 230, 220, and 185 metres). The approach is to a narrow two-tiered green surrounded by four large bunkers. You'd best be thinking well on this hole. The 15th is a quality par 4 of 398 metres with no water trouble. The drive is downhill to a narrow twisting fairway. The next shot is still down to a good sized green with large bunkers on either side. It's a straight ahead golf hole that's a pleasure to play.

The Headfort New Course has been voted in the top 25 of Ireland's most popular courses (*Irish Golf Digest* reader's survey). The course tends to get the most play from individuals and societies. That makes the Old Course easier to get on, which is fine because I think it's more fun to play.

### HOLLYWOOD LAKES GOLF CLUB, Ballyboughal, Co. Dublin

On R108 about 1-1/2 miles north of Ballyboughal.
**www.hollywoodlakesgolfclub.com** (018) 433 406
Parkland, 6088 metres, par 72, €40

**Amenities:** A modern clubhouse has a lounge which serves bar meals all day, and a more formal restaurant with separate menu. The club also has changing rooms, but no pro shop.

**Course Comments:** Designed in 1988 by Mel Flanagan, Hollywood Lakes Golf Club is an engaging course not far from the Dublin Airport. The undulating course has elevation changes which affect play on several holes. About half the holes have bunkers, but the water on the course, lakes and streams, is more of a problem. On four holes water becomes a serious hazard, but the course is fair and the hazards are clearly visible. While Hollywood Lakes boasts the longest hole in Ireland (at least at the time we played) at 605 metres from the championship tee, 14 is not our pick for the best on the course. That distinction goes to the 1st hole, a 321-metre par 4. You need a 180-metre drive to reach the corner of this dogleg right. Big hitters can have a real advantage with a drive cutting the corner. Your second shot is over a large pond to a green with more water left and another pond behind; it's almost an island green. Trees and a bunker on the right further protect the green, but right is preferable to short, left, or long. It's a good hole to get the adrenaline flowing. The flow of the course is very natural and trouble can be avoided with wise decisions. The highest point on the course, from which you can see the Irish Sea, Howth, and the Eye of Ireland (island), is at the 12th tee. The downhill 325-metre par 4 with a creek down the right is as good as the view. The par 4 thirteenth, at 324 metres, has a large lake in play on the left and the fairway bends around the lake. The right side affords plenty of room, but makes the second shot quite a bit longer if you play too safe. Big bombers need to be aware of a couple of tough fairway bunkers which could be within reach. Hitting short is no disadvantage on this hole. The course saves the most difficult hole for last. The 403-metre 18th is a demanding finish which begins with a blind shot up the middle (use the hawthorne tree on the horizon as an aiming point). If you're following anyone, listen for the bell telling you the landing area is clear. The bell is about a 100 metres from the green.    Since we last played, Hollywood Lakes GC has undergone some major reconstruction to add challenge to the course with increased length, additional bunkers, and even more water features.

**Comments from the Forward Tees:** The course has several surprises— views across a corner of Ireland, ponds, creeks, and lots of trees. It is also a bit hilly. I thought play here was challenging because of the water, hills, and long par 5s.

### THE ISLAND GOLF CLUB, Corballis, Donabate, Co. Dublin

Leave the M1 at the Donate exit. At the next two roundabouts take exits to Donabate (thrid and second respectively).  You are now on R126. Pass Newbridge House and take second right, just before the hump back  bridge. Follow the road to the clubhouse.

**www.theislandgolfclub.com**  (018) 436 205

Links, 6206 metres, par 71, €150

**Amenities:** The modern clubhouse, completed in 1997, has a lounge and dining room and serves food all day. Below the lounge is a complete pro shop with a full range of clubs and clothes.

**Course Comments:** When world player Darren Clarke calls the course "a fantastic links which tests every club in the bag," why does Island Golf Club remain unknown? Island, which isn't on an island at all, but is surrounded by water on three sides, must be regarded as one of the finest links courses anywhere, full of challenges and wondrous vistas. The Irish 1999 PGA was held there, and it's a qualifying course of the British Open from 2004 to 2010. Yet, in mid-May we called up in the morning and were playing before noon. Perhaps it's because the club is so close to Dublin, and yet not easy to reach. After our round, Past Captain Frank Walsh told us that the club was created by a group of Dublin businessmen who rebelled when Royal Dublin wouldn't allow Sunday play. To reach the course originally, players had to row across the Broadmeadow estuary, the inlet between Malahide, a Dublin suburb, and the spit of land called "the island." The boat access from the Malahide marina was kept until the 1970s when the course went through major changes. Because golfers were dependent upon the boat to both get them across the bay to the course and bring them home, there are many tales of golfers "stuck" on the island by deteriorating weather. Actually, they would have to return to Dublin via Swords (our normal route, today). In the early part of last century, though, it was a huge journey. The course had remained private until after World War II, when cash flow troubles forced it to open to the public. Fred Hawtree, renowned Irish golf architect, redesigned the layout in the 1970s, and respected designer Eddie Hackett completed more work while retaining the Hawtree greens. Final revisions were completed in time for the Irish PGA in 1999. Island GC has all the troubles you'd expect from a links course: wind, sand, dunes, heavy rough, gorse. It's how these typical links features are laid out that give Island its character and its quality. Only 25 bunkers dot the course, but all of them are in play and some of them are hidden. The greens range in size from fairly large to downright tiny with lots of undulations. The greens were in great condition when we played, even though they had been recently plugged and sanded. Though the course would be considered flat, the Hackett design makes great use of what elevation changes there are. As you play, look for wild orchids which dot the course.

The holes at Island GC are interesting from start to finish. The 4th, *Pot,* a 318-metre par 4, is a short dogleg left where the green is tucked behind a dune on the left. Your drive must avoid the pot bunker on the inside corner. The 4th's amoeba-like green has some very tricky pin placements. Do not take a driver on the 278-metre par 4 eighth. A couple of easy iron shots are all that's needed on this short tester. The fairway runs out about 170 metres from the tee and drops off into the *Well,* a depression covered in tall grass. The undulating green means that a three-jack is possible. *Bowl,* the 153-metre par 3 ninth, has a green which peeks out from behind a tall dune on the left. Two bunkers on the right are visible from the tee, but two dangerous pot bunkers are hidden behind the dune. It is nice that the 9th comes back to the clubhouse, so facilities are available at the turn. Another exciting par 3 is *Broadmeadow,* the 13th. This 192-metre hole is more difficult than it looks. As the most exposed hole on the course, the wind will challenge your club selection. Your swing must be good as well because OB runs the length of the hole on the right and a deep rough-covered area fronts the green. If anything, miss left. My favorite hole at Island is the 14th, called *Old Clubhouse.* In the original configuration this was the first hole, and the dock area can still be seen. Although the hole is only 316 metres long, this two-shotter has plenty of bite. A very narrow fairway (later I found out it is considered the narrowest fairway in Ireland), with dunes left and the estuary right, leads to a tiny, narrow green. It took a lucky putt to par after puting my drive in the dunes. Aim at the last of the three traps on the left side on the par 5, 507-metre 15th. *Prairie* is a long hole with a fairway of humps and hollows. The equally swaled green is protected by a single pot bunker. On your approach look for the white round target on the hill behind the green. It's hard to say that a hundred year old club less than 12 miles from Dublin is a hidden gem, but if any club could fit that description The Island Golf Club could.

**Comments from the Forward Tees:** I enjoyed golf at The Island GC, but I had to work hard. The course has so many great views it's hard to concentrate on golf. Also, a player here has much to consider: water, wind, bunkers, gorse, and especially Out of Bounds. Scoring well wasn't easy because of too much trouble around, but it was still great fun.

### LAYTOWN & BETTYSTOWN GOLF CLUB, Mornington, Bettystown, Co. Meath

Twenty minutes from the Dublin airport. Take the M1 to junction 7, the Julianstown exit to R132. In Julianstown take the first right to R150 which takes you through Laytown and right to the course.

**www.landb.ie** (041) 982 7170

Links, 5862 metres, par 71, €30

**Amenities:** A modern clubhouse with changing rooms downstairs and lounge upstairs with full dining facilities. A small, but complete pro shop is downstairs near the changing rooms. Pro Bobby Browne (R.J.), designer of numerous golf courses including Bearna GC in Galway, is enjoyable to talk to before or after your round.

**Course Comments:** Laytown & Bettystown Golf Club is a true links gem set alongside the Irish Sea, but it's also set beside Mornington Village. While six or seven holes play next to the beach, an almost equal number are across a road from the village homes. The original 1909 nine-hole course was extended to 18-holes in 1913, with major upgrades in the late 1990s. The course isn't long, but plenty of challenge awaits at Laytown. Many of the courses 42 traps are pot bunkers and tough to get out of. Several revetted fairway bunkers need steps to climb out of; you only need bad luck to get into them. The greens are flat, quick, and roll true. The water, which is in play on a couple of holes, is never a major concern. Of more concern are the narrow fairways and typical links rough where it's easy to lose a ball.

As tight as the course is, snuggled between the village and the Irish Sea, it is still an engrossing track. The 2nd, a 309-metre par 4, starts from an elevated tee with a drive over a small hill between dunes. Your second shot is to a raised, right sloping green protected on the right by a pot bunker. The 5th, named *The Mournes* for the view over to the mountains of Northern Ireland, is a 333-metre two-shotter whose wide fairway narrows dramatically at 240 metres. Watch out for the two pot bunkers on the left edge of the fairway. The approach shot is steeply uphill to a long, narrow green. Playing into the wind, it is better for most players to lay back of the hill. *The Quarry* is the 163-metre par 3 ninth. Drive over heavy rough to an elevated green partially hidden by dunes. Take enough club and look out for the unseen traps in the dunes to the right and short of the green. On 14, *The Reservoir,* stay left with your first shot on this 312-metre par 4 to have an easier shot to the green. Avoid the bunkers on either side of the sloped green and a birdie is a good possibility. The two finishing holes at Laytown are both fun. The 17th, *Barnanna,* is a short 278-metre par 4. With wind behind you, distance isn't a problem, so play for position. A bunker on the right is the green's only defense. *The Road Home,* a par 5 of 432 metres, ends your round at Laytown. The hole is short, especially downwind, but tricky. Drive towards the two small traps on the right side of the slight right to left dogleg. At 230 metres from the tee, with wind, the bunkers are reachable. The second shot, even for big hitters, should be a lay-up to the right of the dune on the left. This leaves a pitch over a small hill between two dunes to a large green. Laytown & Bettystown Golf Club has a long tradition of welcoming visitors. It's also justly proud of it reputation as a breeding ground for top quality players, such as Ryder Cuppers Des Smith and Philip Walton.

**Comments from the Forward Tees:** This is a long course for ladies. Even though longer and links, it was very playable. A visually attractive course.

## MULLINGAR GOLF CLUB, Belvedere, Mullingar, Co. Westmeath

From Mullingar town centre follow the signs to Belvedere (R400, the old N52). The course is four miles out on the right.

www.mullingargolfclub.com (044) 48 366
Parkland, 6466 yards, par 72, €40

**Amenities:** Beautiful clubhouse serves meals all day and has good views out to the course. No pro shop, check in at the Secretary's office.

**Course Comments:** The original 9-hole Mullingar course was built in 1894 near the race course. The club made three moves (1903, 1909, and 1919) before settling at the present Belvedere location. The present course was designed by James Braid, and has been recently updated (2005) to include USGA standard greens. With generous, rolling fairways which wind their way through stands of mature trees, Mullingar has a tranquil beauty that belies its teeth. More than 50 bunkers are in play, a trademark of a Braid design. The mix of strategic fairway and greenside hazards range in size from penal pot bunkers to huge, yawning traps, all with good sand. Water is in play on four holes, most dramatically on 18 where a pond fronts the green. Most of the greens are quick and moderate in size, except the wide green at six, which is only 19 yards deep. Several of the greens have entertaining slopes, and all have subtle borrows, And if the course needs any more defense, on eight holes you contend with OB.

One and two make a good starting pair, they are not difficult, but get you thinking. The 1st is a 343-yard par 4 with a long carry over mild rough to reach the short grass. The second shot to an elevated, back to front sloped green, must contend with a fronting bunker 50 yards from the green protected by three more bunkers. The par 3 second, at 209 yards, plays from a slightly raised tee down over a stream to a mildly elevated green. A large bunker fronts the green on the right with smaller bunkers on either side. Middle of the green is a good shot regardless of pin placement. The 6th is not long at 332 yards, but there's plenty to hold your interest on this two-shotter. The gentle curve left has a mound on the left and a reachable bunker right to challenge your drive. The green, protected in front by a pot bunker, is more than twice as wide as it is deep, which makes it a hard target to hold. A mound behind can save a shot long, but can also make for a difficult chip. Another short testing hole, the 9th (345-yard par 4) begins with a drive uphill towards a series of bunkers reachable from any tee box. The approach is uphill to a green surrounded by three more bunkers. The first hole on the back is the 474-yard par 4 tenth. The longest par 4 on the course (Thank heavens!) is a dogleg right gently downhill. Stay to the inside of the curve because it's easy to drive into trees and rough left. A large bunker about 75 yards from the green will be in play for many on their second shots, as will the three small bunkers around the narrow green. A straight ahead par 5 is the 498-yard 14th with a bunker on the left in play on your drive. The second shot is complicated by a large hill across the middle of the fairway making the shot blind. The good sized, raised green is guarded by two large bunkers. The 17th is a 406-yard par 4 with trouble everywhere on this sharp dogleg right to left. With OB left and right and two bunkers on the inside corner, it's a dangerous drive. If you find the fairway with your first, your approach to a small green only protected by one bunker on the left is much easier. The crowd in the lounge on the day we played were eager to show off their fine course and clubhouse. Very welcoming to visitors.

**ROYAL DUBLIN GOLF CLUB, North Bull Island Nature Reserve, Dublin 3, Co. Dublin**
Seven km from Dublin city centre on Bull Island, follow signs.
www.theroyaldublingolfclub.com   (018) 336 346
Links, 6462 yards, par 72, €150

**AMENITIES:** The original clubhouse was destroyed by fire in 1943 and the new one opened in 1954.  The current clubhouse has informal dining (Lumsden Room) and lounge (Moran Room), both with views out to the links. There is a more formal (coat and tie required) member's area named for Christy O'Conner, former club pro. There is also a fully supplied professional shop under the direction of PGA pro Leonard Owens.

**COURSE COMMENTS:** Royal Dublin opened in 1885 and moved to the Bull Island location in 1889. In 1920 Harry S. Colt did some redesign work or repair work after damage done during the Great War. Martin Hawtree has made upgrades to the course in the late 1990s. The location of the course on a nature reserve is fairly unique. The Bull Island site is a bird sanctuary and Area of Special Scientific interest for some rare orchids and the Brent Geese among others. The course is characterized by narrow holes and long stretches of OB. Golfers will pay attention to the more than 60 mixed fairway and greenside bunkers in play. Like the flocks of geese, the often penal bunkers come in groups. Water is a major concern at Royal Dublin with hazards in play on all but five holes. Sometimes the water is fairly innocuous, but other times it's quite bothersome. Water is in the form mostly of creeks or drainage ditches, but there are some ponds as well. The moderate to large greens all have significant swales. The greens have a deserved reputation for always being in good nick, but I found them tricky to putt the first time around. The lovely island can lull you to sleep a bit, but the challenges at Royal Dublin will wake you up.

The challenges start on the 3rd, *Alps*, a 405-yard par 4. This is a slight dogleg right over a mound to a narrow fairway. Second shots need to contend with Curley's Yard (stone enclosure) on the left and five bunkers guarding the green. *Ireland's Eye* is the long (445-yard), narrow between dunes, straight par 4 fifth with OB on the right. Dunes are enough trouble that you won't find fairway bunkers until your second shot—then there is a trap on each side of the fairway about 60 yards from the green. A nice long par 5 is *Valley*, the 570-yard 6th. Bunkers left and right will bother your drive. The rest of the way there are dunes left and OB right. A fore-bunker right at 75 yards out and a couple closer to the green complicate the approach to the narrow green. Reasonable hole if you can play straight; and I can tell you it's a scoring disaster if you can't. The back starts with *Marne*, the 436-yard par 4 tenth. Listed as Index #1, the long, tough hole is made tougher off the tee by two bunkers right and small burn down the left. The water crosses in front of the green—average players will have to lay back and wedge to the raised green. Bogey can be a good score. Finally, a reasonable birdie chance—*Dolly*, the 282-yard par 4 fifteenth—that is if you can avoid the nest of seven bunkers filling the last 65 yards to the green. The prudent play is a 200 yard tee shot and pitch to one of the largest greens on the course. The course saves the most dramatic hole for the last. The 18th, *Garden*, is a par 4 of 470 yards. The hole is an impressive sharp dogleg right at about 100 yards from the green. The tee shot must negotiate past a pond left (shouldn't be a concern, but it's water and it's there), three bunkers at the left edge of the fairway (will be a concern), and a burn all down the right (OB). Second shots are either layups to the corner of the dogleg or a dangerous shot towards the green over the OB right. Two greenside traps side the large green in case you think the hole is too easy. This hole would be testing in the middle of the round— at the end it's dramatically testing. Royal Dublin is a great challenging course in an outstanding location near a world class city. What more could you ask for?

**ROYAL TARA GOLF CLUB, Bellinter, Navan, Co. Meath C15 CFP3**
Just east of the village of Bellinter and west of N3 (take junction 7).
www.royaltaragolfclub.com  (046) 902 5508
Parkland, 5988 metres, par 72, €25

**AMENITIES:** The new (2000) clubhouse has views of 9th and 18th greens and surrounding countryside. Clubhouse has a lounge and restaurant open to the public with a reputation for good food well priced. PGA professional John

Byrne runs a well-stocked shop at the clubhouse. Course, even with three nines, is busy, so be sure to book ahead.

**COURSE COMMENTS:** In 1906 the club built its first course at Navan and then moved to the Bellinter Estate in 1923. Irish architect Des Smyth designed a new course in 1995 and that's the course we play today. There are three nines at Tara: Cluide (Blue), Tara (Red), and Bellinter (Yellow) which is the back nine of the original course. Normal routing today is to play the Cluide and the Tara as an 18-hole course. Playing only a short ways from the historic Hill of Tara, Royal Tara is a course which offers enough challenge for any handicap player. Each of the main nines (Blue and Red) has more than a dozen mixed fairway and greenside bunkers— none are too penal, but all are in play. There are fewer traps on the third nine. There is no water trouble on the course, but the river is left of the 4th. Greens here are excellent—all sand-based and built to USGA standards. Greens are moderately sized, but most have interesting slopes and are always in good condition. Royal Tara is a lovely course, but mostly you'll see trees.

On the first nine, Cluire (Blue), I liked the 2nd, *Lia Fail*, a 369-yard par 4. You must be accurate with your tee shot on this tight hole in order to have a decent approach opportunity. A large oak about 90 yards out blocks shots from the right and the green has traps on both sides. *Cuchulain's Grave* (I didn't ask), is a nice short par 4 of 257 meters. Be careful with your tee shot because the tee box lines you up toward the river on the left. A fairway trap on the right adds trouble as do the bunkers around the green. The 6th, *Royal Seat*, a 291 metre par 4, is a dogleg right around a stand of trees with a bunker on the outside of the turn. Big hitters can try to cut the corner (over the trees), but the green does have bunkers on each side of the entrance. On the back (Red) two holes caught my attention. The 1st (10th for 18) is a 368-metre par 4. *Rath Maeve* is a slight dogleg right and is listed as the hardest hole on this nine, mostly because of OB all down the left. The raised green is guarded by two traps on the right. I also noted the 5th (14th for 18), *Sloping Trenches*. On this 457-metre par

5 you hit towards the narrow avenue between the trees.  On your approach be aware of the large bunker on the right of the large raised green.  The hole is an opportunity to score well if you manage your shots.  The course is popular with golfing societies and is used often for tournaments.  A good course and good value.

**RUSH GOLF CLUB, Sandyhills, Rush, Co. Dublin**
From R18 take Healy's Road then turn left on Sunriver Road, then right on Golf Road which deadends at the course.
www.rushgolfclub.com (018) 438 177
9-hole links, 6158 yards, par 70, €25/18, €15/9

**Amenities:** The new clubhouse (2003) has changing rooms on the lower floor and a lounge and dining room upstairs. The lounge affords a wonderful view over the ninth green, and serves tasty meals. It's one of the most popular dining spots in the village. No pro shop.

**Course Comments:** Described by some as "quaint and quirky," Rush Golf Club should be considered one of the true 9-hole gems of Ireland. Spanish Point and Connemara Isles might come close to Rush, but of the courses we've played, only Cruit Island is a match for Rush GC. Separate tees exist for a second nine, with tees at 17 and 18 dramatically changing the holes. A good mix of 16 fairway and greenside bunkers can be deadly, at least to your score. The greens are moderately sized with subtle borrows. Christy O'Connor commented that when he played, he never had a straight putt. Great vistas of Lambay Island, Dublin Bay, and the Irish Sea is the limit of water on the course, with the best views from the first and second tees.

The course record, set in 1984, is 68 off par of 70. Obviously, the course is no pushover. The 1st is a short, but testing par 4 of 238 metres, especially into the prevailing wind. More landing area exists on the left than it seems from the elevated tee. The green is protected by mounding and two fronting bunkers. The only par 5 on the course is the 535-

metre 3rd. A long hole, the 3rd starts with a drive from a raised tee down to a broad fairway. The dune ahead looks like your target for your second shot, but it's really at the right of the left dogleg. The large green has one bunker on the right side. The 8th is an impressive par 3. From an elevated tee you hit down to a gigantic green with three bunkers around it and heavy rough behind. Though it's only 141 metres, it's still a tricky shot because the ever-present wind is a crosswind. Even though the shot is downhill, take more club because of the wind. On the 9th, drive from a raised tee over the eighth green (be sure it's clear) down to a narrow fairway. Find the fairway because it's difficult to get out of the heavy rough. Accuracy is far more important than distance on the drive. Accuracy is also needed on your approach because the large green is surrounded by six pot bunkers. For those playing a second round, 17 and 18 have dramatically different tee shots from the first round. The 17th plays 20 metres shorter from a lower tee and the shot will not be as affected by the wind. The 18th plays only 20 metres longer than the 9th, but from a spot which turns the hole into a dogleg right. Where you should aim is over a dune which is at the right edge of the fairway for nine.

Rush Golf Club is Irish links golf at its low-key best. Even though the course is only a half hour's drive from Dublin, the number of members remains low, so you can usually get on easily. The members are friendly to visitors and love to share their hidden gem.

**Comments from the Forward Tees:** The rough is hard to deal with, especially on two. Number four (the #1 handicap hole) is very long and it's easy to get into trouble on the links. Visually Rush is a wonderfully inviting course.

### SKERRIES GOLF CLUB, Hacketstown, Skerries, Co. Dublin

Take Skerries Road (R127) to Millers Lane, then turn right onto Golf Links Road. Course is1/4 mile on left.

**[www.skerriesgolfclub.ie](www.skerriesgolfclub.ie)** (018) 491 567
Parkland, 6107 metres, par 73, €40

**Amenities:** Very nice new clubhouse built in 1996. Changing rooms downstairs and lounge upstairs. Lounge serves good meals all day and affords a good view of the 18th green. By the first tee is a well stocked pro shop run when we played by Jimmy Kinsella, a former Irish Open Champion. He is now retired and the pro is his son, Bobby. It makes the third generation of Kinsellas to be the club pro at Skerries. Bill was club pro from 1930 until 1976 when Jimmy took over. With Bobby taking over it means that a Kinsella has been the club professional at Skerries GC for the past 80 plus years. An arrangement very agreeable to the club. The original Skerries clubhouse was burnt to the ground in 1920 under suspicious circumstances, but there was no proof of IRA involvement.

**Course Comments:** The Skerries Golf Club is an old respected club with a lovely course not far from Dublin. Today's 18-hole parkland track occupies the same ground as the original 1905 nine-hole layout. Architect Eddie Hackett was responsible for the extension of the course to its present configuration in 1971. One of the unusual design features at Skerries is found on both the first and 18th fairways, holes which are mirror images. Both fairways have regular ridges about two feet apart running across them (we saw similar ridges across a fairway on Carrick-on-Shannon GC). The ridges are either left from grain plantings, from famine potato planting, or from a system of potato storage used in war years. Everybody has a different opinion, but the club has no intention of leveling those fairways. Besides the mysterious ridges, plenty of challenging golf exists at Skerries. Sixty-five bunkers, a good mix of fairway and greenside, will test your accuracy. Many of the bunkers are large and penal. Several holes have fore bunkers which seem closer to the green than they are. One pond and a stream in play on a few holes add difficulty. The greens at Skerries are moderate in size, a couple are sloped, and a couple are tiered, but all are tricky to putt. The Hackett course design makes effective use of elevation changes and mild fairway undulations.

The quality golf at Skerries begins at the par 4, 370-metre 1st. The hole starts with a slightly downhill drive to a wide fairway with a bunker on the left and the ridges across the fairway in the landing area. The second shot continues downhill to a raised green with a bunker on the right. Trees on both sides of the fairway will cause trouble if you stray. Keep it in the middle and you can be off to a flying start. A pond awaits wayward drives from big hitters on the 479-metre par 5 eighth. The hole plays longer than the yardage because its uphill. Trees will encroach on your approach which should stay to the right to avoid the two left traps. The view coming up nine, with the green, two large traps, and tall beech trees behind is a classic. One of Jimmy Kinsella's favorite holes on the course is the 133-metre par 3 twelfth. This short one-shotter to a small green is a good test of shot-making. Four bunkers (one fore, two left, and one right) guard the green which is above the tee. Par is a decent score here. The mirror hole to the first is the 371-metre par 4 eighteenth. The hole plays over a hill where a good drive will put you at the top. You then hit down to a sloping left to right green protected by four bunkers. A stern test as a finish to your round.

One of the best stories we heard while at Skerries Golf Club was about the time several ladies encountered a "flasher" on the 11th while playing in a competition. Word got around quickly, and at the end of the competition the flasher was all the talk. According to one of the male club members, the ladies were able to confirm that the flasher was not a member as "they'd all had a good look."

**Comments from the Forward Tees:** This is a pleasant, mature parkland course with many tree lined fairways. The holes are interesting and include several uphill and downhill shots. The club members were very friendly to visitors.

## St MARGARET'S GOLF & COUNTRY CLUB, St Margarets, Co. Dublin

Off R122 a little north of St Margaret's Village and 5 minutes northwest of the Dublin airport.

www.stmargaretsgolf.com (018) 640 400

Parkland, 6917 yards, par 73 (Ladies 5770 yards, par 75), €25

**Amenities:** The modern clubhouse has a reputation for quality food from an extensive menu, with Sunday lunch being the specialty. The lounge has a magnificent oak bar and panoramic views. In the summer there is a patio behind the ninth green. New locker rooms have been added, and the pro shop is fully stocked for all your needs, including full rental equipment. Nice driving range with covered bays.

**Course Comments:** St Margaret's Golf & Country Club is a championship facility just minutes from Dublin Airport. The course sits in rolling east Ireland farmland and makes use of water, gentle slopes, trees, and whins to challenge players of every level. More than 50 bunkers, a mix of fairway and greenside, make accuracy a premium; doubly so because of water, streams, lakes, and ponds, in play on more than half the holes. The quality golf starts at the 358-yard par 4 first, playing downhill from the tee to a tree lined fairway. The second shot on this slight dogleg left is up to a green with one bunker in front of the left side of the green. That pleasant start is followed by a challenging short par 3. The second hole is only 149 yards from the back, but you have to thread your way through trees to the gently undulating green with a bunker on the right and rough and water behind. The second nine begins with a 395-yard par 4 with water left and right off the tee (shouldn't be in play), but three fairway bunkers (two on the right and a large one left) might be. The approach from an undulating fairway is to a green with a bunker left. Water is the main trouble at the 13th, a par 3 of almost 200 yards. It's almost all water from the tee to the large kidney shaped green with one bunker left and trees right. The finishing hole at St. Margaret's is a tough par 4 of 458 yards. Tee off downhill on this double-dogleg left then right. A huge bunker is sited on the left side in the driving area and two smaller bunkers are on the right. The approach to the plateau green is guarded by bunkers and a pond. Many say the 18th is one of the best finishing par 4s in Ireland.

Players call St. Margaret's Golf & Country Club a "magnificent track" with "friendly and helpful staff." With its prime location, the course would be a smart way to begin or end an Irish golfing holiday.

### SUTTON GOLF CLUB, Cush Point, Barrow Rd., Sutton, Co. Dublin
On Burrow Road off R106, near Howth.
www.suttongolfclub.org (018) 323 013
9-hole links, 5778 yards, par 70, €15/9, €25/18

**Amenities:** Clubhouse is new in 2001 with changing rooms, and a restaurant serving up good food and nice views all day. Ireland's Eye (island) and Howth Head are visible from the lounge. Locals say the views at night are stunning. The lounge, Dr. Joe Carr Room, is dedicated to a leading amateur and club member who was Ireland's first president of the R & A in St. Andrews.

**Course Comments:** The Sutton Golf Club has a long history beginning in 1890. The original nine holes became six in 1971 and three new holes were added. The next remodel was in 1993 by Patrick Merrigan. The course, set on a neck of land connecting Howth with Dublin proper, has narrow fairways which require serious course management. A saying at the course is "Never mind the length, but feel the width." Besides the tight fairways, bunkers and water make this a testing small course. The challenges start at the 310 yard par 4 first. Drive down to a wide fairway that constricts at about 250 yards with bunkers pinching in. The sea is OB on the right and mounds and rough are left. The sloped green is defended by three bunkers. The 2nd, a 346-yard par 4, starts with a tee shot over the first fairway and past the first green. Proceed with caution. The fairway has mounds and rough on the left with a lake on the right. Five traps protect the green. Tee off over a small creek (not really a concern) on the par 4, 320-yard fourth. The fairway doglegs right around a large pond. The green is raised and is protected by the pond on the right and two bunkers left. The shortest hole on the course is the 107-yard 6th; in fact, I think it's the shortest hole we played in Ireland. Tee off over rough and a lake with an island in it to a three-tiered green. Bunkers on both side complicate what has to be a precise shot. A last note about the course layout is that the 9th tees off almost over the 8th green. It is indeed a tight course, but fun to play and well situated.

**Comments from the Forward Tees:** Not as difficult or impressive as Rush, Sutton is still a fun course in a great location. It was nice to play nine, then be able to go to the Abbey Tavern in Howth for lunch, and visit ruined St. Mary's Church after.

### SWORDS OPEN GOLF CLUB, Balheary Avenue, Swords, Co. Dublin
Northwest out of Swords on R125 then turn right on R108 to the course.
**www.swordsopengolfcourse.com** (018) 409 819
Parkland, 5631 metres, par 69, €20

**Amenities:** The clubhouse is an Irish Log Cabin with changing rooms and snack shop. The club has no pro shop, but golfing essentials, and club and trolley hires are available in the snack shop. A problem is the lack of a licensed lounge for a pint or two after your round.

**Course Comments:** The first nine was built in 1991 and the second nine added in 1995. Both nines, with the Broadmeadow River meandering through, are the design work of Tommy Halpin. The course is not overly busy and is very accommodating to visitors. Built on typical east Ireland farmland, the river is in play on four holes and small stream on three others. Fairways and greens are mostly flat, but there are more undulations on the newer back nine. The river and OB on several holes will be the biggest challenges on the course. It's a fairly simple track, but so close to Dublin airport that Swords is a good stop for a jet-lagged traveler.  The 8th hole, a 255-metre par 4, is one that Anne really liked. It plays with an open fairway, but OB left and trees right mean you can't take this short hole too lightly. A sharp dogleg left to right is the 350-metre par 4 fourteenth. When we played, it was possible for a long driver to cut the inside corner, but by now the young trees might have grown into a problem for those who try. The hole reminds me of a story about one of the world's great golfers. Sam Snead was playing on a course with a young macho golfer. They came to a dogleg hole where his companion asked Snead how he played the hole. Snead said that when he was the lad's age, he'd take his drive right over the trees on the inside corner. The young player teed it up and ripped a monster drive which rattled around in the tops of the trees before dropping into trouble. The young golfer looks incredulously at Snead, who said with his rye humor, "Of course, the trees were much smaller then." The green on this one is well protected by bunkers. I particularly like the 17th at Swords. It is a 170-metre par 3, but large trees near the green make the shot more challenging than the length. The trees aren't in play as much from the front tees.

Swords Open Golf Course is not a championship track, but neither is it what we'd call "Cow Pasture Golf." The course was well kept and enjoyable, with enough challenge to keep our attention. A good place for a relaxed, stress-free round.

**Comments from the Forward Tees:** First appearances aren't always good indicators of what's to come. The course was like that. It seemed to be very easy straight ahead golf in a big meadow. But just when you least expected it, there would be a tree in the way, or a small creek would cross. At one point you cross over into a hilly section almost in a forest. I liked the course.

## TULLAMORE GOLF CLUB, Brookfield, Tullamore, Co. Offaly

Just south of town off N52 take R421, the course is one mile on the right.

www.tullamoregolfclub.ie  (057) 932 1439

Parkland, 6428 yards, par 70, €38

**Amenities:** Clubhouse has changing rooms for members and guests. There is a nice bar and the restaurant serves breakfast, lunch, and dinner. Pro shop is stocked with all your golfing needs.

**Course Comments:** The present challenging parkland track set amongst mature trees with lakes and streams wasn't the original course. Begun in 1886, Tullamore Golf Club has had several homes, which is not unusual for Ireland's older clubs. For a while, the course was located at the Ballykilmurray Race Track. The final move to the Brookfield location in 1926 was precipitated by the destruction of the former clubhouse by arson during Ireland's civil war. Today's club crest shows a Phoenix rising out of the ashes. Today's course has an impressive pedigree listing Captain Hewson and Scotland's James Braid as designers. Recent work to the course by Patrick Merrigan to upgrade to modern standards has remained true to Braid's 1938 ideas. Trees and water hazards will continually challenge all levels of players at Tullamore, yet the course is very playable by all levels as well.

As many other Irish courses, Tullamore has a gentle start on the front side. Once you get warmed up, the finishing holes demand more from your game. The 359-yard par 4 first hole will get your round off to a good start with just enough test to hold your attention. The slight dogleg left to right climbs slightly uphill and leaves a moderate length second shot to an elevated green. Long hitters need to be mindful of the fairway bunker on the right, and everyone needs to be aware of the four bunkers siding the green. Speaking of bunkers, the 177-yard 2nd has five protecting the two-tiered green. The 5th is a demanding hole, especially for anyone who has a tendency to slice (for a right-hander). This par 5 is a big dogleg right with a lake on the inside of the turn. If you can avoid the lake, the hole's only other defense is a small fairway bunker and another greenside. Even though the hole is only 439 yards from the tips, it deserves its stroke index as the second hardest hole on the course. Eleven is a classic, simple golf hole that is fun to play. The relatively easy two-shotter is only 325 yards long, but there are some challenges. A fairway bunker left sits exactly where it can collect any drives that come its way (about 210 yards out). The green also has four small bunkers fronting it and gorse behind. A birdie hole for the shot-maker. A long par 5 is the 548-yard 15th, a dogleg right with a creek about half way to the green. Fairway bunkers and three bunkers by the green add difficulty to your approach. The finish is a long par 4 of 452 yards. A drive to a wide landing area, which narrows for long drivers, sets up a long second to a green with large bunkers on each side. For we mortals, the hole is really a par 5. This is where it's best to play to your personal par, rather than struggle with what the card says. Tullamore is not a demanding walk being relatively flat, and can be enjoyed by all levels of golfers.

## Other Courses in the Region:

Ashbourne GC (18), Ashbourne, Co. Meath (018) 352 005
Corballis GC (18), Donabate, Co. Dublin (018) 436 583
Donabate GC (27), Donabate, Co. Dublin (018) 436 346
Howth GC (18) Sutton, Co, Dublin (018) 323 055
Moate GC (18) Moate, Co. Westmeath (090) 648 1271
Mount Temple GC (18), Moate, Co. Westmeath
        (090) 648 1957
Portmarnock GC (18) Portmarnock, Co. Dublin (018) 462 968
Roscommon GC (18), Roscommon, Co. Roscommon
        (090) 662 6382
Seapoint GC (18), Termonfeckin, Co. Meath (041) 982 2331

## PUBS AND EATERIES

One of the problems we have with recommending eateries in this region is that we discovered a fantastic B&B in Skerries from where we can reach most of the courses in this chapter. That in itself isn't a problem, but when you add a great pub in the same village, one that we go back to over and over, it leaves limited eating opportunities. It may be our loss, but when you walk on the beach from White Cottages B&B to Stoop Your Head pub and back on a moonlit night, you'll understand why we don't mind the loss. We have, though, found some other good eating locations in the area, just not a lot of them.

**Druid's Chair** on Pearse Street in the heart of Mullingar, Co. Westmeath. Druid's Chair is a classy pub, well decorated, and with a hard working staff. Fairly complete pub menu including fish, grill, vegetarian, house specials, salads, and chicken. The pub has received several "Pub of the Year" awards.

**Fiddler's Elbow** on Main Street (N2) in Carrickmacross, Co. Monaghan. Castle-theme pub and restaurant with high-backed chairs, red carpets, and dark wood. Very nice place. Pleasant surroundings, friendly staff, quality food. When we visited a large family was gathered in one area having dinner. The adults let their children run wild in the restaurant. We've seen that more in Ireland and Scotland than in the US. Must be a cultural thing.

**The Olde Abbey Tavern** one block up from the waterfront marina in Howth, Co. Dublin. Really old pub, one of the interior walls is part of a 14C Augustinian abbey. Old wood and stone walls throughout. On one wall was a beautiful stone fireplace. Busy in the middle of a weekday afternoon. Mostly college age crowd and a smattering of tourists. Excellent quality food—brisket-style corned beef on the sandwich and a brothy, rather than creamy, fish chowder.

**The Old Post Office Restaurant** on N51 in Slane, Co. Meath, down from the main intersection. The tea room food was well prepared and of ample portions. Mix of locals and tourists on Sunday afternoon. Very pleasant lunch stop. I believe the owner was male, but it's obvious from the signs around the dining area that ladies run the place: "PMS: Putting Up with Men's Stupidity," "Coffee, Chocolate, Men—Some Things Are Better Rich," and "Give a Man an Inch and He'll Take a Ruler." On the day we visited, I parked a couple of blocks away from the cafe and we had to cross the N2 during busy Sunday traffic. We stood at the corner trying to find a break in the steady stream of traffic. Two elderly (well, older than us) ladies approached the corner and said, "Follow us." They both then stepped into the traffic which came to a screeching halt. We all crossed easily. Alone, we weren't as gutsy as we went back to the car.

**R.M. Taylor's The Star** at the north end of the main street in Swords, Co. Dublin. Very busy bar on a weeknight, two deep in many spots at the bar. Looked like young, business crowd at the bar and families eating. Mostly locals. Food was good with generous portions. Moderate prices.

**Sean's Bar** in Athlone, Co. Westmeath, at the end of the street down from the castle. Recognized as the oldest pub in Ireland (Guinness *Book of Records* plaque on the wall) and maybe the oldest anywhere. Part of the pub wall is on display at the National Museum in Dublin. The Saturday night crowd was mostly locals and a few tourists. You could tell who was a tourist because they were the ones not shouting at each other over the music, but were gawking at everyone else. Pub has a heated smoker's area out back with a retractable roof. There might be food available, but nobody is here to eat. Traditional music every night.

**Stoop Your Head** on the harbour facing the bay in Skerries, Co. Dublin. The name is derived from the need to duck when coming through the low doorway between rooms. Stoop Your

Head is a busy, bustling, crowded place. We couldn't get a seat on Sunday (they stop serving at 8:00), and we had to wait a half-hour on Monday. It's worth the wait. Wait-staff is busy and friendly; quick with conversation, but had to keep moving. The seafood chowder has a great variety including crab and mussels. The specialty of the house, prawns in garlic butter, is light on the garlic and heavy on the prawns. Big portions of outstanding food. Other interesting eateries are in the area, but we keep going back to Stoop Your Head; it's that good.

## *ATTRACTIONS*

Though the central and eastern part of Ireland covered in this chapter does not contain dramatic geological features such as the Giant's Causeway, The Burren, Cliffs of Moher, or the peninsulas, it does have some of Ireland's most important anthropological and religious sites. Along the Shannon River signposted on R444 south of Athlone is **Clonmacnoise** in Co. Offaly. Founded 545 by St. Kieran, Clonmacnoise is one of the foremost monastic sites in Ireland. It sits on the border between two of the great Kingdoms of Ireland—Connacht and Meath. It is the burial place of the kings of Connacht and Tara. Today, Clonmacnoise has a fine visitor centre with audiovisual presentations and ancient stones on display. The site itself consists of churches, a 10C cathedral, 9C and 10C high crosses, ancient grave slabs, and round towers. The Temple of Doolin, pre-12C and restored in 1689, is one of five temples on the property. You can easily spend a couple of hours wandering through Clonmacnoise, but avoid September 9, which is a day of pilgrimage and draws thousands of visitors. Just outside the Clonmacnoise parking lot is well stocked Ireland Tourist Information Centre with a good bookstore and some unusual tourist items.

The best route from Athlone's great golf courses to Mullingar GC is the N6 through Kilbeggan. It's worth it to stop in the quiet village of Kilbeggan to visit **Locke's Distillery.** Unlike Midleton or Bushmills, the distillery here is "still" or closed. A self-guided tour allows you to explore at your leisure the distilling process. Of course, a complimentary dram is provided after your tour. Continue to Mullingar via N52 and there visit **Belvedere House and Gardens** next to the fine golf course south of town on N52. The 1740 mansion was used as a fishing lodge for Robert Rochfort, called the Wicked Earl for his manner of treating people. The house has been restored to its original elegance and is open for touring. The grounds contain a Walled Garden and woodland walk. Northeast of Mullingar on N52 the next stop we'd recommend is in little market town of **Kells** to visit St. Columba's Anglican Church. The monastery at Kells is famous as Irish home of the Book of Kells, probably written at St. Columba's monastery at Iona in Scotland, and transported to Kells to safeguard the illuminated manuscript of the Gospels from raiding Vikings. The Book of Kells now resides in the Library at Trinity College in Dublin. The church grounds display a splendid 100 foot tall round tower from the 11C and four 9C high crosses.

At this point we are close enough to Dublin to describe the next attractions as if they were trips out of the city, rather than along the route into the city. The **Hill of Tara,** 5 miles south of Navan off N3 offers splendid views of surrounding countryside. It is also the symbolic heart of Ireland. The hill has been an important religious and political location since Neolithic times. An audiovisual presentation of the history of the Hill of Tara (aka Tara of the Kings) is presented in St. Patrick's church (early 19C), but we've never seen it. Instead, we've wandered the hillside visiting Iron Age ring forts, the Mound of Hostages (a small passage grave from about 1800 BC), and standing stones (Lia *Fail).* North of Tara near the intersection of N51 and N2 is the **Hill of Slane,** a key site in early Irish Christianity. St. Patrick in 433 lighted a fire on the hill site in order to challenge local Pagans to convert. One of his successful converts later built a monastery on the site. Today, the remains of the monastery and of the 1512 Slane friary, which was in use until 1723, are worth a look. The views from the hilltop site are quite stunning. Two other monastic properties are worth seeking out. North of one of the hardest to learn to pronounce Irish towns, Drogheda (DRA-huh-duh), is the **Old Mellifont Abbey** off N51 and R168. On the banks of River Mattock, the abbey was the first Cistercian house in Ireland (1157). Mostly ruins, the Gatehouse and 14C Chapter House are the most complete. Also a major ruin is **Monasterboice,** 8 miles north of Drogheda by N1. This 6C monastery contains half of a round tower, but what attracts the most attention is the fine 9C high cross with wonderful carvings.

To us the second most impressive sight in Ireland, the first is the Book of Kells at Trinity College, is **Newgrange.** Follow signs off N51 east of Slane village to the *Bru na Boinne* Visitor Centre, with interesting displays, a nice bookshop, and pleasant coffee shop. You reach the graves of Newgrange and Knowth via a shuttle bus from the visitor centre. Newgrange, 3000 BC, is the best example of a passage grave in western Europe. The grave is 85 feet in diameter and 37 feet tall, and occupies 1.25 acres. It is a magnificent cairn encircled by 97 kerb stones. On the guided tour you actually get to go into the passage lined with standing stones which leads to a corbelled chamber a third of the way into the structure. A roof box opening at the front allows light to reach the depth of the inner chamber for 17 minutes on the day of the winter solstice (December 21). We visited Newgrange twice and plan to go again, it's that fascinating. Another tomb can be visited at Knowth (2500-2000 BC), but much of it is under excavation, as is a third tomb at Dowth. In high season you must book your tour days ahead, and off season you may still have to wait an hour for your tour. Plan at least two hours to visit Newgrange.

About 25 miles northwest of Dublin by R154 is the village of Trim. On our first day in Ireland in 2002, we drove out from our B&B in Swords just to get a feel for driving on Irish roads. Eventually we wandered into Trim, stopped at a fish and chip shop, and took our dinner over to the grounds of **Trim Castle.** Opened to visitors in 2000, the Medieval stronghold (1172) is the largest Anglo-Norman castle in Ireland. Trim Castle may be recognizable as the castle used in the Scottish movie "Braveheart." Across the river from the castle by bridge is the stone arch called Sheep Gate and a fragment of the town wall.

Our last touring suggestion for this book is the capital city of **Dublin.** Neither Anne nor I are fans of big city's, but we both love Dublin. It doesn't mean we spend a lot of time in the city, but on each trip we try to plan a day or two for just wandering around. We plan to stay out of town (Swords, Skerries, Greystones) and then take the DART (Dublin Area Rapid Transit) in for the day. Once we stayed at an airport hotel and took the bus to town. It makes a much more pleasant visit than trying to drive in the metropolis. Excellent tour guides exist for Dublin and you should plan to get one, but we would be remiss if we didn't give you a list of our favorite spots in town. These are the spots we've gone to an enjoyed or go back to, and most are within walking distance of the downtown train station. The top in our list is Trinity College to see the **Book of Kells** and the Library's Long Room. The college is a vibrant city campus, busy with students and tourists. During the season the lines to view a page of the famous illuminated text may be quite long and the number of visitors is limited. Plan ahead or show up early. Even off-season there could be a wait, but in May and September we've never waited more than a few minutes. Next is **Christ Church Cathedral** a few blocks from the college. The 12C cathedral has some wonderful carvings and windows, but be sure to take a trip down to the crypt to see the church's spectacular treasures. **St. Stephen's Green** (a park) is always an interesting place to visit to people watch. Don't miss the statue of Molly Malone and her pushcart near the Grafton Street entrance to the park. **Grafton Street** is the main shopping street in Dublin and is always busy. We try to stop at **Bewley's** for coffee and a sweet as we wander Grafton Street. **Temple Bar** is a lively street near the River Liffy filled with pubs and restaurants; touristy but fun. Temple Bar in Temple Bar is a good spot to hear traditional music in the afternoon. Cross the river via the 1816 **Ha' penny Bridge,** named for the toll that had to be paid to cross the bridge up until the early 20C. On O'Connell Street, the **General Post Office** is the spot to visit to see a piece of history from the 1916 Irish Rising. Dublin also has excellent galleries and museums, such as the Dublin **Writer's Museum** and the **National Gallery.** Accessible from the Hop-on-Hop-off buses are sites such as the **Jameson Distillery,** the **Guinness Brewery** (with the best view of Dublin from its upper floor), the **Old Gaol** (a rather long tour), and **St. Patrick's Cathedral.** This is only a starter list of what to see and do in Dublin. Don't miss an opportunity to spend some time off the golf course and in the city.

## Chapter Eight:
## B&Bs in Ireland

Milestone House B&B, Dingle

As we looked out toward the rich farmland of the east coast, the afternoon sun streamed into our room in our first B&B in Ireland. We booked Hollywood B&B near the tiny village of Ballyboghil because it was close to the Dublin airport, and because of the enticing picture and description in *Bed and Breakfast Ireland: Town and Country Homes or Farm House,* a yearly book available from Failte Ireland (the national tourist board). After a short nap to rid our travel-addled brains of some of the cobwebs of travel, we were ready to discover Ireland.

We could have chosen to lodge at standard or luxury hotels, but chose instead to stay in Bed and Breakfasts and small guest houses for several reasons. A major reason for staying in B&Bs in Ireland is the shear number available. More than 3500 Bed and Breakfasts and farmhouse B&Bs are spread over the landscape. The traveler can find a B&B in almost any area of the country you are likely to visit. Bed and Breakfast stays also offer amenities that hotels, even the poshest, don't, such as intimate guest lounges and home-style meals. Costs in B&Bs are as much as 50 percent of a hotel stay. Finally, and most importantly, B&Bs and small guest houses are homes. People willing to share their homes with strangers tend to be friendly, helpful, gregarious, and caring. When Anne got sick in Galway (either because the mead she had at Dunguaire Medieval Banquet the night before didn't agree with her, or perhaps that one glass would have been enough), Marie and Tom at Bayberry House couldn't have been more concerned if we'd been family. Several of our B&B hosts started out as just hosts and are now personal friends. Oh, they still charge us to stay—that's business—but they treat us as friends rather than clients.

## HOW TO FIND A B&B

Several methods for finding Bed and Breakfasts in Ireland are available to the traveler, and we've used them all. One year we booked only our first lodging (Hollywood B&B) and our last (a Dublin airport hotel because of an early flight). For all our lodging for the rest of the trip, we either called ahead to a B&B in our next location by using the Failte Ireland book or another guide book, asked our hosts to call ahead for us, or stopped in a Tourist Information Office and had them book for us (for a small fee). Only in one instance did we just stop at a B&B because of their sign, and that turned out to be a good find (Chestnut Lawn in Sligo). All of these systems work and have their own advantages and disadvantages:

**Using a Guide Book.** Rick Steves, Fodor, Lonely Planet, and others (including this guide) will give you information about B&Bs in specific locations. Other guide books will recommend places with minimal descriptions.

**Host Recommendation.** We discovered on our first trip in 2001 that many B&Bs belong to what amounts to a network of B&Bs. If you like the B&B you are staying in, it is likely that you would like one they recommend. The downside to this system is that a given host may not have a recommendation in the area to which you're traveling. And of course, if you don't like the B&B you're in, the system doesn't work. Also, there is little opportunity to see details ahead of your visit.

**Use Tourist Information Office.** Stopping in at an information office is a great way to book a stay in a new area, but it takes extra time that you could be spending on the golf course.

This brings me to the method we now use on all our trips: we book ahead via the internet. If you are like me and like to have everything arranged, the kind of person willing to trade a little spontaneity for peace of mind, the internet is your godsend. Many of the lodgings in the Bed and Breakfast Ireland guide list a web address. Regional and local tourist web sites will give links to local B&Bs, guest houses, and hotels. The advantage of using the web to find lodging is that, in a way, you've already met your hosts when you look at their web site. Much can be learned from an establishment's web page besides the basics of facilities, amenities, price, and location. We find a strong correlation between the quality of the web site and the quality of the lodgings. I particularly look for sites which provide extras, such as links to information about local attractions, golf courses, and eateries. The following is a beginning list of sites we've used to find good lodgings:

www.ireland.com
**www.discoverireland.com**
**www.ireland-bnb.com**
**www.townandcountry.ie**
**www.irishbnb.com**
**www.visitwicklow.ie**
**www.cork-guide.ie**

No system is foolproof. We've managed to find inadequate lodging in Scotland, Wales, and Ireland by several methods. For the most part, though, we've been pleased with the Bed and Breakfasts we've stayed in Ireland.

## *WHAT MAKES A GOOD B&B*

Obviously, whether you like a B&B is a personal decision. No guide or personal recommendation can guarantee that you will enjoy your stay at O'Flaherty's Guest House. We've had several friends stay at Irish B&Bs we've recommended and they loved their stay as much as did we. We've also recommended one of our favorites stays in Scotland to two lady friends and had them come back and say the accommodations were okay, but the hosts were cold and aloof. To us they are the most caring and giving people in the world, but we are a couple and golfers. Maybe that makes the difference. Whether from a guide book (including this one) or personal recommendation, remember that the evaluations are subjective. Take them as advice, not guarantees.

Now, to a list of what to us makes a quality Bed and Breakfast:

**Location.** Whether in town, out in the country, or on the beach, is the location where you want to be. The White Cottages in Skerries set along the bay with crashing waves only feet below, or Seapoint House B&B sited on a finger of Clew Bay, are just two examples of B&Bs we've found that we would return to just for their locations.

**Cleanliness.** You can forgive a dust bunny or two, but you have a right to expect a high level of cleanliness.

**Fair Price.** In resort locations you can expect to pay higher prices (€80-90 for a double at current prices), but other areas should be more reasonable (€60-70). Many establishments will give discounts for longer stays.

**Information about the Facility.** A good B&B will have easy access (through web, brochure, or advertisement) to information about the facilities.

**Quality Breakfast.** The Irish pride themselves on the great breakfasts at their B&Bs. Expect to be fed quality fare. It wasn't very positive to pick up an orange out of the breakfast basket at a highly touted B&B and see that the bottom was completely gray with mold. Obviously, they hadn't checked the basket in a couple of days. The better B&Bs will have either several choices for breakfast or some unusual items that can be ordered. Pancakes for breakfast was a special treat at Bayberry House in Galway, especially after a couple of weeks of traditional breakfast items.

**Personality.** The high quality B&B will have hosts who are friendly and outgoing personalities, and always make you feel welcome. Expect, too, to find that many of the lodgings themselves have personalities of their own. The 4000 year old 14 foot tall standing stone in front of Milestone House in Dingle certainly makes it unique.

**The Extras.** The best of the B&Bs have all of the above qualities and more besides. For example, in Dingle Barbara Carroll at Milestone House has booked us dinner reservations ahead of our arrival because she knew it was going to be a busy evening in town. At Claddagh House in Ballina, when rain arrived early
Agnes McElvanna brought in and dried clothes we left on her line to dry. The little extra things can make a B&B stay very special.

## PAYING

When paying for your Bed and Breakfast stay you have several options, all at the discretion of the B&B. All will accept cash, and for many that is all they will accept. Some, in our experience less than half, will accept payment by credit card. When paying by credit card don't be surprised to have a B&B add a small surcharge to cover the cost of using credit cards (usually three to five percent). A few who accept credit cards will give a small discount if you use cash.

A method of payment unique to Ireland is a system of vouchers. From the Tourist Board or agents dealing with self-guided tours, you can purchase vouchers good for specific dates in specific accommodations (hotel, small guest house, B&B, ensuite or not) for a set price per night. Most of the B&Bs listed in the Failte B&B and Farmhouse guides will accept these vouchers. We've used the vouchers on two of our early trips, but would not again. They were convenient, just tear out that day's voucher and hand it over to your hosts. Vouchers have their problems, though. Since they come at one price and cover a range of accommodations, we found that more times than not we had paid a higher price for our stay than we needed to. Freddie Jones in Sligo and Tom Cotter in Galway educated us about the cost to the B&B. The B&B receives less than the full amount of what the traveler pays for the voucher, but most lodgings used to subscribe to the system to keep in good standing with the tourist bureau who send lodgers to them. If you are offered such a system, we'd suggest you refuse it. Instead, our recommendation is to use credit cards when you can and cash the rest of the time.

One other note about paying for lodging is the matter of tipping. Many travelers will not even think about leaving a tip at a B&B, yet would never fail to leave a gratuity at a restaurant. We believe, unless there is a reason not to, in leaving a gratuity of about 10 percent. We have found that often our hosts will thank us for the thought, but refuse to take the tip. Others will accept the offer with great thanks.

## WHAT HOSTS ARE FOR

Bed and Breakfast hosts are, well, hosts. They share their home and run the B&B. Any good host will do much more, especially if asked. We've had hosts book golf or restaurant reservations. Almost all will have recommendations for local attractions, pubs, eateries, laundry, etc. Many times our B&B hosts have done us a great service by giving us directions for the best route for our travels, or a short-cut we wouldn't know about. We generally have a small bag of food, veggies and cheese, for snacks and lunches, and we've always been able to put them in the kitchen refrigerator. In the morning, Anne takes her small insulated bag down to breakfast as a reminder to pick up our stored items. The important point is to ask. Most B&B hosts are great resources, willing to help.

## BE A GOOD GUEST

In one golfers' hotel in Dornoch, Scotland, we got a room next to a group of Americans on a golf tour. They came in late, drunk, loud, and when we knocked on the wall they got louder. After several 2 AM complaints to the management, they finally got the group semi-quiet. That's a problem we've never had in a B&B. Guests are most often respectful when in someone's home. Some reminders, though, about how to be a good guest in a Bed and Breakfast might be worthwhile:

- Treat your room as if it's someone's home—it is.
- Be quiet and considerate of your hosts and other guests.
- Be aware of and follow prescribed timelines. From talking to many B&B owners in Ireland, Scotland, and Wales, we find one of their biggest frustrations is the guest who comes for breakfast at 9:15 when notices tell them breakfast is served from 8:00 until 9:00.
- Check early on details such as breakfast times, visa or cash, eating in rooms, etc.

## B&BS IN THE SOUTHEAST:

In each of the following sections of this chapter, we detail specific B&Bs or Guest Houses in which we've stayed. We've tried to make sure the information we provide is current, but the B&B business, like the restaurant business, is always in flux.

### ARCHWAYS, THE B&B, Rosslare, Co. Wexford
On Rosslare Road near the harbour.
(053) 915 8111   www.thearchways.ie  €95
Recognized as Ireland's Best B&B in 2013 by one source, Archways is a modern comfortable six room B&B on 1.5 landscaped acres.  Known particularly for its homemade sausage, breakfast offerings are large.  Check with them about dinners as well.

### AUBURN GUEST HOUSE, Cork, Co. Cork
On Wellington Road, it's one of the closest to downtown. Refer to map on website.
(021) 450 8555   www.auburnguesthouse.com
Rooms are nice and the staff is efficient.  Best feature is the location so close to downtown.

### THE BLUE HORIZON B&B, Kinsale, Co. Cork
On Laherne Hill at Garrettstown Beach near the Old Head area.
(021) 477 8217   www.thebluehorizon.com  €80
This cozy retreat is a family run B&B and pub with great views. Mary and Jimmy McCarthy are wonderful hosts and the pub is popular with locals as well as tourists.

### DOONEEN HOUSE B&B, Kinsale, Co. Cork
On Bandon Road (R600) only minutes from town.
(021) 477 2024   www.ireland-bnb.com
Eileen O'Connell is a welcoming hostess and Dooneen House has pleasant bedrooms and a comfortable guest lounge.

## DUNROMIN B&B, Kilkenny, Co. Kilkenny

On a main road out of town (N10, the Dublin road) on the east side. Within easy walking distance of the main town shopping area and the castle.

(056) 776 1387  www.dunrominkilkenny.com  €60

Dunromin is a lovely older home with cozy rooms and a convenient guest lounge. Besides the great breakfast that Val serves, the main attraction is Tom and Val. Tom, a member at Kilkenny Golf Club, and Val are well informed about local sites and touring throughout Ireland. Both are very helpful. One morning on our second stay, Tom gathered Anne and I and the other guests (two lady teachers from Australia) into the parlor. One of the gals sat at the piano and Tom played his button box and played the bodhran/drum (with a special foot pedal he invented). Val had pulled out some sheet music, and we all sang good old Irish ballads. It was homey and comfortable.

## FERNROYD HOUSE, Cork, Co. Cork

At 4 O'Donovan Rossa Road about a mile west of downtown Cork off Western Road (N22).

(021) 427 1460  www.fernroydhouse.com  €60

Fernroyd is a beautiful house in a nice neighborhood. The rooms are very comfortable. On our last stay we had what was almost a mini-suite with extra large shower. The location is within walking distance of downtown shopping, restaurants, and cathedrals. Be warned, though, not to do what I did. After walking 18 holes at Cork GC, we returned to Fernroyd and I walked all through town and back. Then we both walked back in the evening to dinner. By the time we got back to Fernroyd my feet were killing me. I had to take a buggy (something I hate to do) for golf the next day. Don't overdo the walking. Avril and Tom are great, informative hosts. Ten golf courses are within 20 minutes drive from Fernroyd House.

## LA CASA B&B, Kilpedder, Greystones, Co. Wicklow

In Kilpedder, a suburb of Greystones, off the main coastal road, about 10 minutes by car from the closest DART (Dublin Area Rapid Transit) station in Bray.

(012) 819 703  homepage.eircom.net/~lacasabb
A pleasant home with nice rooms. Mary Doyle is an excellent hostess. She arranged golf for us, when we couldn't find a course open, looked up DART schedules, and handled noisy guests well.

## PINEFOREST HOUSE, Blaney, Co. Cork
Less than a mile from town on Elm Court, tucked into the trees.
(021) 438 5979  www.pineforestbb.com  €60
Pineforest House is a very pleasant B&B with typical bedrooms and a dining area which overlooks the garden. Breakfast menu offered more choices than some others, and a few unusual items. Janette is quick with good advice about the local area. On the day we left Pineforest House I left a rain coat in the closet. We got almost to Macroom before I noticed the coat was missing. Back we went, missing our tee time at Macroom GC (we finally played the course a different year). When we got to the door, Janet was there with the coat.

## ROSEDENE B&B, Portlaoise, Co. Laois
On a side street (Mountrath Rad) off the Limerick road (N7) on west side of town.
(057) 862 2345  www.ireland-bnb.com  €66
Pleasant rooms and friendly hosts (Lily Saunders). Good location for getting to town or continuing travels.

## ST ANTHONY'S GUESTHOUSE, Dungarvan, Co. Waterford
On Clonea Road, Abbeyside, about 10 minutes walk from Dungarvan town.
(058) 44 749  st-anthonys-guests.com
Pleasant rooms and Kay and Tom are gracious hosts.

## THORNBROOK HOUSE, Cashel, Co. Tipperary
On Dualla Road (R691) a little north of town.
(062) 62 388  www.thornbrookhouse.com

A well landscaped home with comfortable room. Mary Kennedy is a pleasant hostess and provides a good breakfast. About a ten minute walk to the Rock of Cashel.

## B&BS IN THE SOUTHWEST:

### ABBEY COURT B&B, Kenmare, Co. Kerry
On R569 less than a mile from downtown, down a long drive by an old abbey.
(064) 42 735  www.abbeycourtkenmare.com  €70
Abbey Court provides great accommodations with large bedrooms and lovely lounge sitting rooms with views of forest and river. Friendly, helpful hosts provide one of the best breakfasts we've had. Within walking distance of town.

### DOIRE LIATH BANTRY B&B, Newtown, Bantry, Co. Cork
On N71 just north of Bantry.
(027) 50223  www.bantrybedandbreakfasts.com  €70
Traditional Irish home only 10 minutes walk from town. Sean and Therese provide and extensive breakfast menu. The B&B is only a mile from Bantry Bay GC and has nice views of Seekin Mountain from the garden.

### NORTHWOOD HOUSE, Killarney, Co. Kerry
5 Muckross View, Killarney, off the ring Road south of town, about 15 minutes walk to town.
(064) 37 181  www.narthwoodhouse.com  €60
Very comfortable well equipped and decorated rooms in a good location. Provided a hearty breakfast. Josephine was very helpful and gave us good advice about driving the Ring of Kerry. She was the first one to tell us to ignore the tour books and drive the same way as the buses in order to avoid nose to nose confrontations with large buses.

### RATHMORE HOUSE, Killarney, Co. Kerry
On Rock Road (N22, the main Dublin road) one block northwest of downtown towards Tralee.
(064) 32 829  www.rathmorehousekly.com  €76

Clean older rooms and furnishings have almost a hotel feel. The location, though, is just about perfect and Pat and Mary Carmody make wonderful hosts; very knowledgeable about the local attractions. They also provide a good breakfast.

### THE GARDENS B&B, Killarney, Co. Kerry
On Countess Road in the middle of town.
(064) 663 1147   www.thegardensbnb.com   €80
Good location on a quiet street close to town.   The Gardens provides a nice breakfast and good value.

### MILESTONE HOUSE, Dingle (*An Daingean* on new road signs), Co. Kerry
On the main road through Dingle (R559) about 1 km out of town just after crossing the bridge.
(066) 915 1831   www.milestonedingle.com   €80
Milestone House has modern, large, well appointed bedrooms and a great lounge which turns into a greeting and meeting place. The breakfasts are great with fresh fruit salad daily and the specialty of the house, Michael's Brown Soda Bread, the best in Ireland. As wonderful as the house is, it is Barbara and Michael Carroll (both golfers) who make Milestone a destination B&B. On our first visit, Barbara met us at the door and asked if we liked Irish music. When we said yes, she arranged tickets to an Irish concert that night and made dinner reservations for us at Ashe's Pub. The next day, as we headed out to play golf at *Ceann Sibeal* GC, Michael sent us off with a loaf of his soda bread to go with our cheese. Milestone House gets its name from *Gallen na Cille Brice* (meaning "milestone"), a 14-foot-tall 4000-year-old, early Bronze Age, standing stone in front of the house.

### RUSSELL'S B&B, Dingle, Co. Kerry
About half way up The Mall (one of Dingle's main streets, aka Spa Road or R559) from the first roundabout as you enter town.
(066) 915 1747   www.russellsdingle.com

Russell's is excellently located near all the action in town. Mary Russell is a wonderful hostess, friendly and helpful. She also provides a delicious breakfast including fresh fish.

### TEACH AN PHIOBAIRE GUEST HOUSE (House of the Piper), Tralee, Co. Kerry

A couple of miles north of town on the main road to Listowel and the Shannon River ferry (N69).

(066) 712 2424

www.homepage.iercom.net/~teachanphiobaire

The House of the Piper is a great B&B with large bedrooms and a very nice guest lounge. The breakfast is good and Michael and Tricia Dooley are top notch hosts. Michael is a world renowned Irish bagpipe (uilleann pipe) maker and a golfer. Tricia was super accommodating when we needed to have breakfast early to make a tee time. Michael, a true Irishman, tells some interesting golf stories. Once he was invited by a friend to play in a tournament at Waterville GC. Never one to turn away from a little competition, Michael met his friend at the club. Quickly the friend pulled Michael aside and told him the tournament was for Catholic priests and that they were entered as Father Murphy and Father Dooley. Never was Michael more thankful for the Irish gift of gab than when they won the tournament and had to give winner's speeches as Father Murphy and Father Dooley. Another story Michael told us was about the time a limo pulled up beside him as he was walking in town. A back window rolled down and the occupant asked if Michael knew the way to Tralee Golf Club. Michael said he did and started to say, "Aren't you...," but thought, no, of course he is. At that point Tiger Woods invited Michael to get in and direct the driver to the club. Michael rode with Tiger and Mark O'Meara out to Tralee, and then was driven back to town in the limo. Great tales!

### TREBOR HOUSE B&B, Limerick, Co. Limerick

On the main road into town from Ennis (N18) about a mile from downtown (walkable).

(061) 454 632   www.privatestays.com   €65

Good location on a main road, yet close enough to town to walk. The rooms, including the guest lounge, are comfortable. Joan and Jim are friendly and helpful tour guides and hosts.

## B&BS IN THE WEST:

### ARDAN HOUSE B&B, Ennis, Co. Clare
At 3 Dromard, Lahinch Road (N85) on the west edge of town; it is the center house in a small development.
(065) 682 9794   www.ireland-bnb.net
Ella and Mike are very friendly and accommodating hosts. Rooms are new, large, and nicely decorated. Ardan House has a pleasant guest lounge and internet available.

### ASGARD GUESTHOUSE, Galway City, Co. Galway
Three minutes walk from town center on College Road, just off N6/N18.
(091) 566 855   www.galway.net/pages/asgard
Asgard Guesthouse is a friendly, family run B&B with comfortable rooms.  Home baked breakfast items.

### ATLANTIC VIEW B&B, Clifden, Co. Galway
A mile north of town on N59.
(095) 21 291   www.atlnticviewclifden.com
A friendly B&B with great sunset views from the front. Bedrooms are pleasant and the breakfast room had a nice view.  Our hostess, Margaret, was both friendly and helpful.

### BAYBERRY HOUSE, Galway City, Co. Galway
On the west side of town off Taylor's Hill Road about two miles up from the coast   road.  Bayberry is actually on a road (Bishop O'Donnell Road) off Taylor's Hill, turn into the street at a roundabout.
(091) 525 171 or 525 212   www.bayberryhouse.com
Tom is very friendly and interesting to visit with. We've spent several evenings sitting in the living room (open to guests) solving the world's problems [And from world conditions you can tell how successful we were.]. Bayberry has lovely, classy

rooms including the breakfast room next to the living room. Marie's breakfasts are special. Fresh fruit salad is always available and she will make special items, such as pancakes. On our first stay (we've stayed several times) Marie asked if we liked Black Pudding (blood pudding). We said, "Not really." Marie told us that maybe we just needed to be served the "good stuff." The next morning she had some special Black Pudding for us to try. I found I did like it, but it's still not a favorite for Anne. On one of our visits we told Marie we were going out to Connemara. She warned us that lots of loose sheep would be on the roads, and then said, "I don't want you to bring back a leg of lamb."

## CHURCHFIELD HOUSE, Doolin, Co. Clare
On R479 about a mile from the harbour, across from two great music pubs.
(065) 707 4209   www.doolinaccommodations.com
Renovated in 2003, Churchfield is a superior B&B because of the house, the location, and particularly Maeve Fitzgerald, the hostess (everyone's favorite aunt or grandmother). The bedrooms are pleasant and the upstairs guest lounge is wonderful. Maeve tells great stories, knows everyone in the area (she could tell us the musical background of a young player we'd heard the night before), and serves homemade scones and rhubarb/ginger jam at every breakfast. We have friends who would stay at Churchfield just for more of that jam.

## MULCARR HOUSE, Lahinch, Co. Clare
On Ennistymon Road (N67) about a mile east of town, across the road from Lahinch castle course.
(065) 708 1123   www.enchantingireland.com
Great location where you can walk to town or to the Lahinch golf courses. Comfortable bedrooms and a bright breakfast room. The breakfast was good, but I don't remember the details because we had such a good conversation with other guests.

### ADARE HOUSE, Westport, Co. Mayo
About a half mile from downtown and about the same from the harbour on Quay Road.
(098) 26 102   www.adarehouse.net
Older rooms, but neat and clean and well appointed. Friendly, helpful hosts who serve a good breakfast. Very knowledgeable about local happenings.

### THE ARCHES COUNTRY HOUSE, Donegal, Co. Donegal
About five miles from Donegal Town off N15 on Lake Road, about a mile and a half from the main highway.
(074) 972 2029   www.archescountryhse.com
Arches has a beautiful setting overlooking Lough Eske. The bedrooms are huge and have great views. The relaxing atmosphere makes you want to sit around and take in the scenery. Noreen serves a great breakfast, and pays attention to individual needs. One year she made us a special reservation at Pier 1 in town. She told them it was our anniversary, even though it wasn't. When we arrived at the restaurant, we were seated at a specially prepared candlelit table with the best view in the house.

### CHESTNUT LAWN B&B, Sligo, Co. Sligo
On Strandhill road (R292) 3 km from downtown Sligo.
(071) 916 2781   www.chestnutlawn.com
Friendly hosts, after all, they're Joneses. Freddie will talk your arm off. On one of our stays, we sat on the patio and visited with Freddie and an Australian couple for two hours until we all got too cold. The rooms are comfortable, one has a nice cupola for sitting and reading or writing. The Joneses provide a good breakfast.

## DOVEDALE B&B, Westport, Co. Mayo

About 3/4 mile from downtown area (long walk) on the west end of town off N59 towards Newport.

(098) 25 154  www.dovedale-ireland.com

Pleasant rooms and typical breakfast.  Hosts were not very helpful—couldn't tell us about golf in the area even though they belong to Westport GC, and had no recommendations for meals.

## ISLAND VIEW HOUSE, Ballyshannon Road, Tullaghcullon (near Donegal), Co. Donegal

One mile south of Donegal Town on R267 off N15.

(074) 972 2411  www.islandviewbedandbreakfast.co.uk

Good spacious rooms, well stocked.  Serves a nice breakfast. Friendly hosts.  May be a little too far for most to walk to town.

## MOUNTAIN INN, Coolaney (near Sligo), Co. Sligo

Ten miles out of Sligo at the far end of the village of Coolaney. Follow signs.

(071) 916 7225  www.mountaininnireland.com

The Mountain Inn is rustic, clean, and comfortable, but don't expect five star accommodations. The rooms are pleasant and well stocked with enough room to spread out drying golf gear. One of the advantages of The Mountain Inn is having a small, quiet pub on premises. We spent two evenings in front of the coal fire in the pub visiting with locals about world events, golf courses, sheep, and how to make a great hot toddy. The Lipsetts are great hosts, cooks, and barkeeps. Bar meals are available for guests.

## ROSEWOOD COUNTRY HOUSE, Adara, Co. Donegal

Just before town on N56 from Donegal to Killybegs.

(074) 954 1168  www.privatestays.com

Both the bedrooms and guest lounge are large and nicely appointed. Typically good breakfast with the addition of fresh baked muffins and homemade jams. We liked that breakfast was served at a large family table because it promotes conversation more than individual tables.

### SEAPOINT HOUSE FARM B&B, Westport, Co. Mayo

About 6 miles west of Westport off N59. Take a minor road toward the bay following signs (about 3 miles) until the road dead ends at Seapoint House.

(098) 41 254  www.seapointhouse.com

Seapoint House is a lovely home with a spectacular location beside Clew Bay and its islands, though it is slightly inconvenient to town. The bedrooms are as nice as the setting, and we didn't mind at all that there was no TV in the bedroom. The guest lounge downstairs with large TV is big and comfortable. The O'Malleys are interesting, knowledgeable, and gave us some great recommendations. When you stay, walk along the bay and cross over to one of the islands for a wonderful sunset.

### *B&BS IN NORTHERN IRELAND:*

### CAIRN BAY LODGE, Bangor, Co. Down BT20 5HS

Off B21 on Seacliff Road (the Mourne coastal route) near Bangor GC (haven't played there yet).

(028) 914 67636  www.cairnbaylodge.com  £80

The house is more than a hundred years old, but has only been a B&B for the last 15 years.  It that time it has garnered numerous awards especially for its great breakfasts with fun choices.   Both a beauty spa and the Starfish Cafe are connected to the B&B.

### ROSE PARK HOUSE B&B, Derry, Co. Londonderry BT48 0HL

On Rosemount Ave off Craggen Road or B507.

(028) 7128 5962  www.roseparkhouse.com  £60

This 19th century home has won numerous awards and is known for its incredibly friendly hosts—Thomas is most helpful.  Within an easy walk of some fine pubs, the B&B is only 15 minutes from the middle of town.

## VALLEY VIEW COUNTRY HOUSE, Bushmills, Co. Antrim, Northern Ireland

About four miles from town; one mile on B17 to Ballyclough Road, then three miles to the farm. Post code is BT57 8TU.
(028) 2047 1608   www.valleyviewbushmills.com
Very comfortable bedrooms and sitting room or guest lounge. Valerie is a dear; friendly and helpful. She serves a great breakfast, as well, with fresh baked goodies. Valley View is a quiet location from which to explore the whole of the north coast, from Londonderry and the courses on the Inishower Peninsula to Cushendall on the east.


## *B&BS ON THE EAST COAST:*


## CELTIC LODGE GUESTHOUSE, Dublin, Co. Dublin

81-82 Talbot Street in the heart of the city, minutes from Connally Train Station and the bus station.
(018) 788 810   www.celticlodge.ie
Celtic Lodge feels more like a B&B than a big city hotel, but the rooms are just nice hotel rooms. The Celtic Pub next door is accessible from the hotel.


## HOLLYWOOD B&B, Hollywood, Ballyboghill, Swords, Co. Dublin

The house is six miles northeast of Swords on R129 between Ballyboghill and Naul, across from Hollywood Lakes GC.
(018) 433 359   www.bedandbreakfastireland.net
Hollywood B&B is a pleasant place to stay near Dublin, the airport, attractions such as Newgrange, and lots of golf. Rooms are big enough and well supplied. Hosts are personable and helpful, though we knew we were in Ireland when we asked the road number we would take to Newgrange. Mr. Farrell said, "Number? Our roads don't have numbers. You just go down the road to the red barn on the left, take the next right, and turn left at the big white farmhouse. Straight ahead."

## MARLINSTOWN COURT B&B, Mullingar, Co. Westmeath

Beside the Marlinstown Roundabout (northeast end of town) on the N52 Mulligan bypass.

(044) 934 0053  www.marlinstowncourt.com

Marlinstown Court has nice big rooms and wonderfully accommodating hosts. We had not booked our Mullingar stay here, but when we got to the B&B we had booked, we discovered the husband had died a few days earlier. That B&B, of course, was not open, but they sent us down the road to Marlinstown Court. Not only did they put us up, but made arrangements for our complete stay. We were sorry we couldn't stay where we planned, but were more than delighted to find an outstanding B&B at Marlinstown Court. The breakfast was very good, as well.

## NUREBEG HOUSE B&B, Carrickmacross, Co. Monaghan

On the Old Ardee Road about 2 miles south of Carrickmacross on the right.

(042) 966 1044  www,nrebeghouse.com

Catriona Grimes is a very friendly, helpful hostess. The bedroom was comfortable on a stormy night. We were fascinated watching from our bedroom tons of bunnies in the field in back of the house.

## THE WHITE COTTAGES, Skerries, Co. Dublin

On the north edge of town on the beach road (Balbriggan Road, R127). The Cottages are the last residence on the beach side on your way out of town.

(018) 492 231  www.thewhitecottages.com

We've stayed several times and find it hard to think about staying anywhere else when we're in the Dublin area. The B&B is within an easy walk of town and the harbour area. In fact, one of our great delights in Skerries is walking along the beach from White Cottages to our favorite restaurant, Stoop Your Head. White Cottages is, also, within walking distance (though it's a long walk) of the DART station and downtown Dublin is less than an hour away. As enticing as Dublin is, we find it hard to leave the accommodations at White Cottages.

The bedrooms are wonderful with lots of extras. We've stayed twice in the Crow's Nest, a skylighted upstairs room. Below is the guest lounge which has a small kitchen and nook for writing which looks out onto the ocean. Breakfast is one of the best we've had in Ireland and is served in the lounge. Carol comes in and prepares breakfast in the small open kitchen next to the lounge. It's fun to be able to talk to our host as she works. The parking is tight, but everything else is outrageously perfect.

# Chapter Nine:
# The Best of Ireland

Tralee GC, Co. Kerry

## A GREAT DAY IN IRELAND

Our last breakfast at Rathmore House B&B in Killarney was just as good as our first—large portions, well prepared. Pat, our host, had time to visit with us this morning. It's always a treat to get to talk with our Bed and Breakfast hosts about local attractions or issues of the day. The international perspective is quite enlightening. Having packed the car, we said our good-byes to Pat and Mary and headed for our golf for the day at Dooks Golf Club.

The route from Killarney to Dooks GC passes right by Killarney Golf and Fishing Club where we had played

Mahoney's Point course the day before. We stopped in at the pro shop to meet head pro, Tony Coveny, a member of the Senior European Tour, who hadn't been in yesterday. Tony gave us a more personal history of the Killarney courses and some insights of life on tour. We broke off our visit sooner than we wanted in order to make our 10:00 tee time.

The drive from Killarney to Dooks took longer than I anticipated for a couple of reasons. First, it always seems to take longer to get where you're going in Ireland—small roads, great scenery, farm implements on the roads. Second, we had to negotiate through an accident scene. A motorcyclist had collided with a car just minutes before we arrived. The Guardia were directing traffic around what we found later was a fatal accident. The accident reminded us that as foreigners (even though driving in the British Isles seems so natural now), we need to always drive cautiously, especially when the motorcyclists in Ireland and the United Kingdom tend to drive fast and wild. We did arrive at Dooks GC in a timely fashion, and after greeting Declan, the golf manager, made it to the first tee ten minutes ahead of our time. An American tour group (several fourballs) were waiting impatiently for us to tee off. As we teed up, they were loud, obnoxious, and made a couple of snide comments about having to follow a woman. I think that paying big money for a tour where every detail is arranged for you, leads some to act as if they own the course. Luckily, we both hit fine drives and none of the groups ever came close to catching us. We did see some of the Americans again as we helped them find the correct tee on one of the newly redesigned holes. Their attitude changed a little after we helped them and they found out we were writing about the course. One even ordered a copy of our Scotland book. The golf at Dooks was outstanding. A lovely course on a lovely day, and without wind. When the wind's up, Dooks can play wildly tough.

After our round we browsed the new golf shop (I browsed, Anne bought) and had a Guinness in the lovely lounge which we'd seen under construction last year. From Dooks we drove back through Kiloglin to pick up our route to one of our favorite Irish towns, Dingle. The drive on R561 along Castlemaine Harbour is spectacular in the sun, with grand vistas of the harbour, Inch Beach, and across Dingle Bay to the Kerry Peninsula. Anne and I stopped a couple of times for photos before the road turns a little inland near Anascaul.

Arriving at Dingle starving, our first stop in town was to grab a small bite of lunch at a tearoom, followed by a Guinness ice cream cone. Okay, we tried it, and it isn't a do-again flavor. Hunger slacked, we wandered from shop to shop, enjoying the pleasant day, watching locals and tourists, not shopping for anything in particular. We did visit a small deli next to the Old Smokehouse Restaurant for some flavorful Irish cheese we could have for lunches on the courses. By now it was 4 PM and time to check-in at our Dingle lodgings.

Milestone House B&B is about a mile west of town on the main tourist route around the Dingle Peninsula (R559). It's hard to miss Milestone House because right in front is a 14-foot-tall 4,000-year-old standing stone (the milestone). Proprietor Barbara Carroll met us at the door with smiles and hugs—not everyone gets that reception, but this was our third visit—and an offer of tea and biscuits (cookies). In the guest lounge we visited with two young Americans from Los Angeles and Barbara until our friends, Scott and Jane, arrived. Several times we've arranged to meet friends at some point in a trip, and it has always worked out well. The six of us visited for a while as Barbara brought tea and biscuits for Scott and Jane. We decided to meet again in the lounge just before our dinner reservations in town. Scott and Jane headed to their room for a rest; they had driven in from Kilkenny. Anne went down to our room to do some futzing (a form of obsessive organizing). I walked down to the edge of Dingle Bay for photos.

The town was crowded with visitors taking advantage of a three-day holiday weekend, so we were thankful that Barbara had suggested making reservations ahead of our arrival for dinner at Out of the Blue, a fantastic seafood bistro across from Dingle Harbour. The four of us had to wait only a short while for our table in the cramped, busy restaurant. The wait was pleasant, but great smells were making us even more hungry. Scott and Jane were ending the second day of their trip and we were a week into ours with lots to share from all sides of our corner table. Our dinners were as fine as Anne and I had remembered from a previous visit; Anne had scallops and I had seafood chowder and mackerel salad. All our meals were so artistically presented that I took photos of each person and their plate. Other patrons must have thought we'd never seen high class dinners before.

By the time we finished our repast the evening pub crawl had begun. With more than a dozen interesting pubs in the small Dingle shopping area, the town is built for a pub crawl. We started by listening to a session at O'Flaherty's, then moved to John Benny's, and ended with a stop at Cronan's, one of three special pubs in town which are shops by day and pubs at night. For many, a pint or two at each pub is the order of the day, but for those of us light drinkers, a half Guinness can be nursed a long time. That's one of the lovely features of most Irish pubs, nobody pushes you to buy more drinks. A lively session at O'Flaherty's, poor seats at John Benny's, and crowds at Cronan's left us ready to return to Milestone House.

As we walked from the top of town down to the car at the harbour we made our plans for touring together tomorrow. Anne and I enjoy touring alone, but we also enjoy sharing our travels with good friends.

## STOP FOR A BITE OR A BREW

In the chapters we've mentioned more than sixty pubs, restaurants, bistros, and tearooms. We've also described countless golf course lounges or pubs. Most are good enough to recommend to our friends. Which ones would we say are the best in various aspects? After pouring over notes and cataloguing memories, we present this list of special recommendations:

### Best Seafood Restaurant
1. O'Grady's, Barna
2. Out of the Blue, Dingle
3. Stoop Your Head, Skerries

### Best Restaurant
1. Oscar's, Enniskillen
2. Blair's, near Blarney
3. The Old Smokehouse, Dingle
4. Rossini's, Cork

### Best Location
1. The Strand Pub, Strandhill
2. Quay Cottage, Westport
3. Out of the Blue, Dingle
4. Stoop Your Head, Skerries
5. Dom's Pier 1, Donegal City

### Best Pub Food
1. McDermott's, Doolin
2. Roadside Tavern, Lisdoonvarna
3. *Grainne Uaille,* Newport

### Most Historic Pub
1. Sean's, Athlone
2. Kyteler's, Kilkenny

### Best Music Pub
1. Matt Molloy's, Westport
2. 3 pubs in Doolin
3. Sheehan's, Killarney

### Best Golf Course Food
1. Glasson Golf and Country Club, Athlone
2. Strandhill GC, Strandhill
3. Rush GC, Rush
4. Tralee GC, Tralee

5. Murvaugh GC, Donegal

**Best Golf Course Pub**
1. Rosses Point, Sligo
2. Killarney Golf and Fishing Club, Killarney
3. *Ceann Sibeal* GC, Dingle

## *OUR TOP PICKS FOR GOLF*

In each chapter we've described the parkland and links courses, 9-hole and 18, which we've played in our trips researching this book. We've played the famous and the out-of-the-way, the expensive and the dirt cheap. We haven't played a single course we couldn't recommend for one reason or another. But which courses are the best? That would depend upon who's playing. I have an American-Irishman that I play with every weekend. He hates blind shots. I doubt that he'd like a course like Spanish Point or Cruit Island. We can't say what is best, only what we liked the best. In the categories of Parkland 18, Links 18, Parkland 9, and Links 9, Anne and I have each selected the courses we like the best. These are the courses we'd go back to first or plan a trip around. Remember, like everything else in this book, our choices are subjective. They're our lists. With that caveat, we present Our Top Picks.

## 18 Hole Parkland Courses

**5. Westport Golf Club, Westport.** The views are magnificent out to the bay and Croagh Patrick. The course offers a fair challenge and a good variety in the holes with water, elevation, trees, and bunkers to consider in shot making. The members are friendly and the clubhouse is inviting. It's a parkland gem amongst great links courses.

**4. Cork Golf Club (Little Island), Cork City.** This fantastic Alister MacKenzie design, a combination parkland with links-like quarry holes, rewards good shots and penalizes wayward shots, but always fairly. The course offers great variety in the challenges it throws at players—long carries, bunkers, elevation changes, water, vicious vegetation. It also hosts one of the most picturesque parkland holes I've encountered. The 15th is a blind shot beauty with cliffs and Irish cottage above the green.

**3. Mahoney's Point, Killarney Golf and Fishing Club, Killarney.** Not the sternest of the Killarney courses, Mahoney's Point is a great combination of beauty and challenge. With good variety in the holes, the views of mountains and lakes can't be beat. Fairways are wide and the course is forgiving without being a pushover. I love the drivable par 4 (15th) and the eighteenth is a stunning finishing par 3. After your round enjoy one of the finest golf course pubs in Ireland.

**2. Headfort Old Golf Course, Kells.** Less challenging than Headfort New, the Old course has a charm missing from its tougher and younger sibling. We can't say that Headfort Old is easy; it certainly got the best of me. But its a fair challenge—stay straight, play smart, and score well. The huge, mature trees give Old the feel of Augusta National (or at least, what I imagine Augusta must feel like). The beautiful clubhouse with a view over the 18th green is a fitting end to a round.

**1. Glasson Golf and Country Club, Glasson.** Was it that the weather was perfect or that the ball was flying well that day? Whatever the reasons, Glasson is an easy pick for me for my favorite Irish parkland course. Everything about the course is top class. The vistas from the high holes are spectacular. Glasson offers plenty of variety in its challenges, with lakes and ponds, elevation changes, doglegs, blind shots, and intimidating bunkers. The course and grounds are immaculately groomed and the clubhouse is world class. And if that's not enough to love about Glasson, the staff is the best in the world. We'd match the Glasson Golf and Country Club experience against any parkland course any place.

## 18 Hole Links Courses

**5. (tie) Narin and Portnoo Golf Club, Portnoo.** What a wonderful find! When we first played the course it still had electric fences around some of the greens to keep the cows off, but its rustic nature is only part of its charm. The views to the sea are outstanding and the course offers up a nice variety of challenges. The turn holes nine and ten are particularly memorable as you first hit down toward the sea and then blindly back up over the ninth green. A fun course.

**5. (tie) Enniscrone Golf Club, Enniscrone.** Anne would place this course higher on the list than do I. We both agree Enniscrone is a great course, but the twice we've played it has been in high wind and heavy rain. It's hard to judge the course when I've never seen it at its best. The dunes here are as dramatic as any course in the world and taller than most. The course has a nice variety of holes and challenging greens, but the 15th is my favorite—a long uphill hole with large swales and penal bunkers to negotiate.

**4. Dooks Golf Club, Glenbeigh.** This course has been recently renovated, yet retains a feel of the venerable course it is. With great views of Dingle Bay and Peninsula and the mountains of the Kerry Peninsula, Dooks is stunning in almost any condition. Challenges abound, such as fair blind shots and the ever-present wind. The layout is excellent as holes are oriented to give you all wind direction in a single round. Number one and 18 make a great start and finish, and, of course, you have to end up in the lovely new clubhouse with one of the best pro shops in Ireland.

**3. Connemara Golf Club, Ballyconneely.** Linksland unlike Enniscrone, Tralee, or Carne, but linksland all the same. Connemara plays in a rocky, high, flat land with small dunes and large rock outcroppings. On a good day the course sparkles. It plays wide and looks easy, but is definitely a championship challenge. The greens are one of the best features of the course—undulating and fast. Beside the wonderful big course is a challenging 9-hole course nearer the sea. Both courses have grand vistas of the sea and mountains of Connemara. The staff, from pro shop to grounds crew, is friendly and helpful.

**2. Tralee Golf Course, Tralee.** This course has it all; a world class clubhouse, the Arnold Palmer connection, unrivaled vistas, and massive dunes. Palmer said he built the front nine, but that God built the back nine. The course is tough any time, but in the 40 plus mph winds in which we played, the course is brutally tough. Yet, wind or no wind, the course is similar to most of Palmer's other courses, fair. The course may be groomed like a resort course, but the grooming only enhances the naturalness of the design. With many memorable holes, the 12th, a dramatic dune-to-dune par three with no bailout area, will stay with me always (especially since I made the green against the wind).

**1. Carne Golf Club, Belmullet.** This course, the last course designed by famed Irish architect Eddie Hackett, proves his design genius. The course is fun, no matter how you play. The dunes land is unbelievably dramatic as the course plays into and through some absolutely wild land. The challenges are as dramatic as the layout and the views, and the greens are magnificent. Each hole seems to get better than the last until you reach the 18th, one of the strongest finishing holes we've ever played. Anne and I have no disagreement about our most favorite course in Ireland, Carne Golf Club.

**9-hole Parkland Course**

**4. Lismore Golf Club, Lismore.** Take away a weak first and ninth hole and the remaining seven would make a great short course. Two through eight have nice variety and can play tough, but fair. The clubhouse is newly remodeled and very nice.

**3. Bushfoot Golf Club, Bushmills, Northern Ireland.** This course is a combination links and parkland design with nice variety in the holes and some sweet views to the sea. Slight changes in elevation are used to make the course more interesting, and it doesn't hurt its charm that a steam train cuts through the course. A different green at 3/12 for those playing 18 is a nice touch, as is the 9-hole price.

**2. Parknasilla Golf Club, near Sneem.** Is it a 9-, 12-, or 18-hole course? We include it in the 9-hole list mostly because we don't have a 12-hole list. The options of playing different lengths of course is one of the nice features of Parknasilla. Another of its qualities are the great sea lough views and dramatic forest land. Blind shots will create plenty of challenge, and the 12th hole is a nice finish.

**1. Swinford Golf Club, Swinford.** Very interesting and demanding holes provide enough challenge to raise Swinford to the top of our list of short parkland courses. Challenges includes creek crossings, mature trees, elevation changes, doglegs, blind shots, crossing holes, and tricky greens. Like Bushfoot, Swinford has a second green at 8/17 for those playing a full round. The community support we saw for junior golf also helped endear the course to us.

**9-hole Links Courses**

**5. Castlegregory Golf and Fishing Club, Castlegregory.** A nice course with holes unique from each other. First two are more parkland, but then the rest play in dunes along the bay. The course offers great views some nice risk/reward challenges. We applaud the club's attitude in their decision not to sell out to Greg Norman Developments.

**4. Spanish Point Golf Club, near Milltown.** Presenting great views of Mal Bay, Spanish Point is a challenging course; difficult, but fair. You really have to think about your shots on this course, especially the blind ones. We've always met friendly folks here.

**3. Connemara Isles Golf Club, Connemara Peninsula.** Out in the middle of a beautiful nowhere is the rustic (yet relatively new) Connemara Isles course. Tough holes characterize the course with a ton of challenges and three sea crossings. The thatch-roofed clubhouse is a plus.

**2. Rush Golf Club, Rush.** Isolated, yet very near the Dublin metropolitan area, Rush offers the feel of out-of-the-way Ireland. The course has tough holes which will challenge the best golfers, yet is never unfair (unless the wind blows hard). The views from the course and clubhouse, which offers the best food in town, are brilliant.

**1. Cruit Island Golf Club, near the Donegal airport which is near Dunglow.** Some would call this the Best 9-hole Course in the World (rivaled only by Durness GC in Scotland), and not be far from right. Cruit Island GC has it all: unique holes, plenty of risk/reward, magnificent views, an isolated location (which would be a great drive even if it weren't for golf), and a pleasant clubhouse. You would be hard pressed to find a more enjoyable nine holes of golf anywhere.

### THE BEST OF THE ATTRACTIONS

With plenty to see and do on the Emerald Isle, how do you select what to visit? You could make the choices we have, to return again and again to Ireland. Or you can prioritize and revel in the choices you make. The following would be our picks for the Must See attractions in various categories:

**Ancient Ireland**
1. Newgrange, Co. Meath
2. Ciede Fields, Co. Mayo
3. Carrowmore Megalithic Cemetery, Co. Sligo

**Religious**
1. Clonmacnoise, Co. Roscommon
2. Kells Round Tower and High Crosses, Co. Meath
3. Rock of Cashel, Co. Tipperary

**Cultural**
1. Book of Kells, Trinity College, Dublin
2. Kilkenny Castle, Co. Kilkenny
3. Muckross House, Co. Killarney

**Geological**
1. Giant's Causeway, Co. Antrim, Northern Ireland
2. The Burren and Cliffs of Moher, Co. Clare
3. The Rings of Kerry and Dingle

## *AND NOW, THE BEST OF THE BEST*

The Best of the Best in Ireland is easy to select. It's not a golf course, though you will find it on all the golf courses. It's not a restaurant or even the oldest pub, but you will find it in restaurants and pubs. It's not a B&B, but definitely Ireland's Best are in the B&Bs. The Best of the Best in Ireland is the Irish Spirit exhibited by its people.

If you have no other reason to visit Ireland, visit to meet Padraig O'Toole at Auchnanure Castle, Barbara and Michael Carroll in the Milestone House, Mazz O'Flaherty in Dingle, Tom and Val Rothwell in Kilkenny, Freddy Jones in Sligo. We love the Irish people we meet in the restaurants and pubs, in the B&Bs, and on the golf courses. As a people the Irish are witty, playful, well educated, loquacious, gregarious, and engaging. They are at the same time caring and care free. They alone would be sufficient reason to plan a trip to lovely Ireland. Oh, and the golf ain't bad either!

## *ENJOY IRELAND! SLAINTE!*

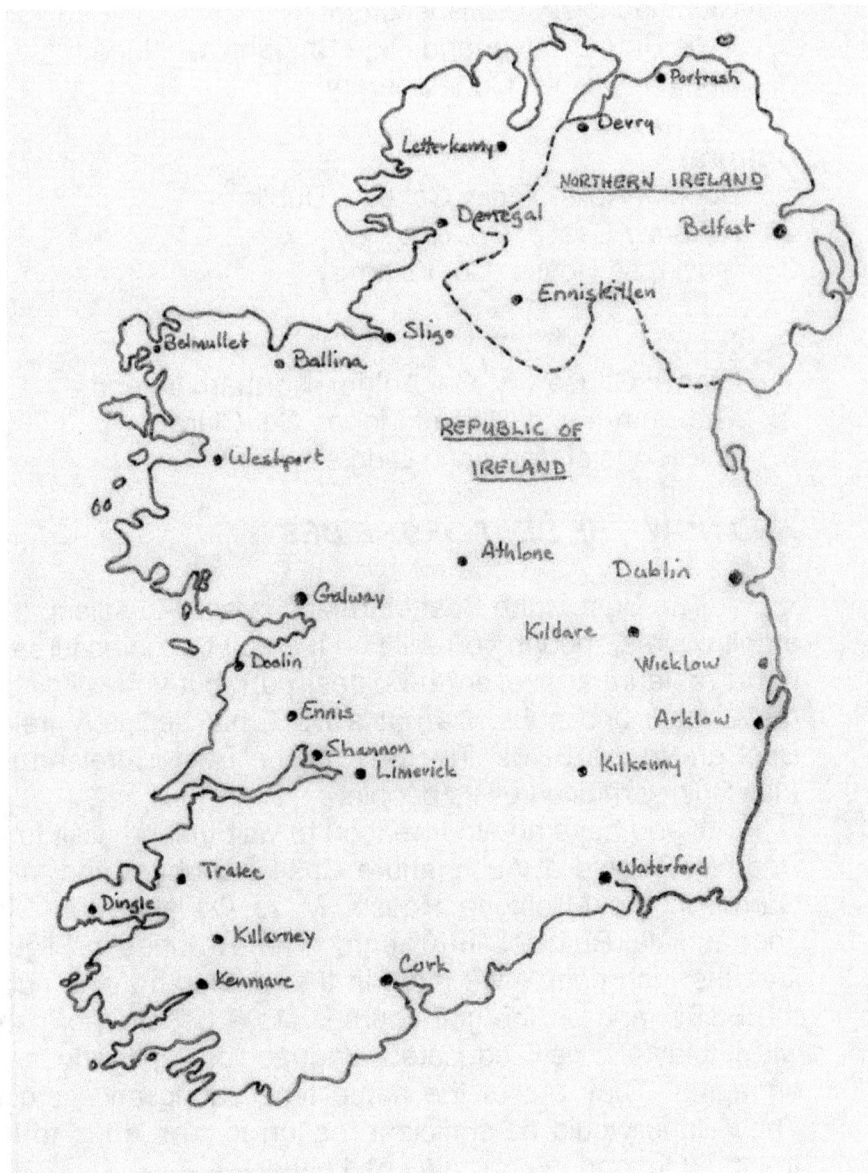

# INDEX OF COURSES

281